OUDS

A CENTENARY HISTORY OF THE
OXFORD UNIVERSITY DRAMATIC SOCIETY
1885–1985

OUDS

A CENTENARY HISTORY OF THE
OXFORD UNIVERSITY DRAMATIC SOCIETY
1885–1985

<hr />

Humphrey Carpenter

With a Prologue by
ROBERT ROBINSON

<hr />

Oxford   New York
OXFORD UNIVERSITY PRESS
1985

Oxford University Press, Walton Street, Oxford OX2 6DP

London New York Toronto
Delhi Bombay Calcutta Madras Karachi
Kuala Lumpur Singapore Hong Kong Tokyo
Nairobi Dar es Salaam Cape Town
Melbourne Auckland

and associated companies in
Beirut Berlin Ibadan Mexico City Nicosia

Oxford is a trade mark of Oxford University Press

British Library Cataloguing in Publication Data
Carpenter, Humphrey
OUDS.
1. Oxford University Dramatic Society—History
I. Title
792.'0222'06042574 PN2596.09209
ISBN 0–19–212241–X

Library of Congress Cataloging in Publication Data
Carpenter, Humphrey.
OUDS: a centenary history of the Oxford University
Dramatic Society, 1885–1985.
Includes index.
1. Oxford University Dramatic Society. I. Title.
II. Title: O.U.D.S.
PN3191.G7078 1985 792'.07'1142574 84–20559
ISBN 0–19–212241–X (U.S.)

Set by Wyvern Typesetting Ltd.
Printed in Great Britain by
Butler and Tanner Ltd.
London and Frome

Preface

In 1983 Tessa Ross, then President of the Oxford University Dramatic Society, decided along with her Committee that the Society's forthcoming centenary should be celebrated with a book. The Oxford University Press expressed itself keen to publish the history of OUDS, and I was asked to write it. So it was that I found myself in a rather impertinent position. Impertinent, because as an undergraduate at Oxford I had observed OUDS and its goings-on from a respectful distance, as a humble musician in the orchestra pit of the Playhouse, or as an even humbler scene-shifter backstage. The occupants of the stage itself seemed from that viewpoint to be giants or demigods; indeed one sometimes had the impression that they saw themselves in that light too. It seemed strange, but fun, as the Society's official historian, to find myself privy to at least some of their secrets, and those of earlier and later OUDS performers.

I conducted much of my research in near darkness, for the best place to gather information was quite clearly at the very heart of the Bodleian Library at Oxford—the bookstack itself, where tattered volumes of theatrical newspaper-clippings and old theatre programmes, lovingly assembled by long-deceased OUDSians, now nestle alongside the rather forbidding rows of *Isis*, *Cherwell*, the *Oxford Magazine*, and other journals whose critics regularly pronounced in Olympian fashion upon the achievements and failures of successive OUDS generations. At first I envisaged a short book, but there proved to be many stories worth telling—and even now I have had to leave out a good deal. Nevertheless I have tried to stand back from the chronicle of productions good and bad, and to ask what motives really lay behind such frenetic theatrical activity. The book is intended, therefore, as more than just a list of plays and their performers; it is a small attempt at social history.

I owe much to two previous chroniclers of OUDS: Alan Mackinnon, co-founder of the Society and author of *The Oxford Amateurs* (1910), which contains a very full record of the early years; and Michael Pimbury, whose *Short History of the OUDS* brings the story up to 1955, the year in which it was published. The present archivist of the Society, Jason Morrell, handed over to me all the OUDS records which are not

permanently in the Bodleian, and the longest-serving Senior Member of OUDS, Dr Merlin Thomas, kept a benevolent eye on the project, together with Tessa Ross who started it off. Many old members and friends of OUDS generously provided me with recollections. I must first thank Robert Robinson for his splendid prologue, and then, in alphabetical order, Lindsay Anderson, Christopher Ball, Peter Bayley, Anthony Besch, Michael Billington, Gyles Brandreth, Peter Brook, Michael Croft, Anthony Curtis, Peter Dews, Frank Dibb, the late Michael Elliott, Ronald Eyre, John Fernald, Patrick Garland, Sir John Gielgud, Alan Halliday, Christopher Hampton, Frank Hauser, Giles Havergal, Charles Hodgson, Richard Ingrams, P. J. Kavanagh, Sir Osbert Lancaster and his wife Anne Scott-James, Daphne Levens, Ken Loach, David Marks, Sheridan Morley, Sir Peter Parker, Sir Geoffrey Johnson Smith, Elizabeth Sweeting, Stephen Wall, Professor Glynne Wickham, David William, and Emlyn Williams. Unless otherwise stated, most quotations in the book are from previously unpublished recollections written specially for it by these people. The typescript was read and improved by Rona Treglown (who as Rona Bower was the 1969 OUDS Juliet), while Judith Luna and Ena Sheen at the Oxford University Press provided sympathetic editorial guidance.

It only remains for me to wish OUDS a happy hundredth birthday, and much prosperity during its second century.

HUMPHREY CARPENTER

Oxford, 1984

Contents

Illustrations

ix

Illustrations

Nevill Coghill directing in Worcester College garden
(Bodleian Library)

Patrick Garland as Coriolanus, 1959

Nevill Coghill, Richard Burton, and Caroline Bennitt rehearsing for *Dr Faustus*
(Billett Potter)

An Osbert Lancaster Pocket Cartoon at the time of *Dr Faustus*, 1966
(*Daily Express*)

Richard Heffer and Michael Wood in David William's modern-dress *Hamlet*, 1967

Diana Quick takes over the Presidency from David Marks, Hilary term 1968

Michael Gwilym and Rona Bower as Romeo and Juliet, 1969

Imogen Stubbs, Yvonne Cohen, and Jenny Waldman in Stephen Pickles's production of *The Three Sisters*, 1980

Patrick Harbinson's production of *Cyrano de Bergerac*, 1982

David Abraham in Lorca's *Blood Wedding*, 1983

Prologue

BY ROBERT ROBINSON

I REMEMBER it as always being dusk, with a breeze lifting the notices on the walls of someone else's college lodge, as you walked through the arch under the yellow light which had just been turned on, and went up an alien staircase with the fatuous expectation of a punter entering a casino. The actual audition would have very little to do with dramatic skill, since it was unlikely in the extreme that the aspiring undergraduate actually had any, or indeed if he displayed the faintest vestige of it, that his examiner (no less self-appointed than the candidate himself) would have recognized it. But what raised the hearts of both parties was the possibility that each would find the other's effrontery an endorsement of his own. It really couldn't have been otherwise, though the outcome of the encounter was seldom as symmetrical an exchange as took place when a man who had criticized my impure vowels ended by offering me the leading part in the play he was about to produce. Not until he led me to the door did I dimly fathom that one member of the walking-wounded had recognized another—'Don't worry about those vowers of yours,' he said, 'I'm sure they'll come along sprendidry.'

What joined us all was a common wish to shine, an acceptable motivation in the young, even though the desire would always outrun the performance. There is at this moment a lawyer on Highgate Hill whose desperate totterings, left and right (designed to indicate the effect of heavy seas on a vessel about to founder), drew a wondrous hilarity out of lines Shakespeare couldn't have dreamt had a laugh in them; a marine insurer not a million miles from the Kingston By-pass who to this day does not know that his unique stiff-legged walk threw fresh light on one of the Bard's tragic heroes, in that the audience found itself preoccupied with the question, did he or did he not have a broomstick up each trouser leg; and a lady of mature years, long a pillar of the WI in Sussex, who, draped in the usual sort of winding-sheet associated with sixteenth-century juvenile leads, was still able to hoist it up to her knicker-leg, withdraw a handkerchief (white samite, natch), and sneeze into it as the hero carefully impaled himself on a rubber sword.

We expected much of our audiences, we put them to the test. When some of us exhumed a dreadful play by John Ford and staged it in Wadham garden, I do believe we really thought they would rise to their feet and cheer simply because this was the first performance the piece had received in four hundred years. Wading through the fustian like Burke and Hare, we took well over three hours to reach the first interval, at which time it was clear that our own merciless solemnity had not been matched by the spectators, and chaps' own mothers and fathers who had come up specially were seen tip-toeing away into the murk, never to return. Towards one o'clock in the morning the curtain more or less came down, though by then the audience had been reduced to a few sports who afterwards frankly confessed they'd stayed on only to find out if Perkin Warbeck, the luckless hero (then clad in nothing but his stockings, and tied to a stake), could keep his face straight while his thighs underwent a severe tickling in the course of being clutched at by the kneeling heroine during the final twelve minutes of leaden apostrophe.

But there is nothing a determined narcissist will not endure. Shortly after my triumph as Perkin Warbeck, I was to be seen, naked save for a pair of shiny knickers, and covered in green scales, being poled across the Isis in a punt strewn with fairy-lights. Indefatigable attendance at auditions had secured for me the role of the River God, in a masque that had been written by a girl poet for the birthday of one of her chums. The entertainment was to be initiated by the vessel, with myself as its cargo, being shunted across the river to one of the college barges, on whose upper deck the audience was assembled. Things got off to a slowish start, for not only was the current running strongly but the oarsmen were drunk. Three times we bore down upon the barge and three times were swept past it. By the time the punt was sullenly twisting on its own axis in front of the barge, the audience lining the rails were crying with laughter, and though the poet's lines were well-turned I was fairly well-turned myself as I delivered them, since, the punt revolving in one direction, I was obliged to revolve in the other. It was at this point that the first penny landed at my feet, one of the oarsmen tipped over into the briny, and both the poet and her friend were in floods of tears.

Perhaps it was the ornate, not to say rococo, location of the audience on that occasion that made me feel the real play was taking place off-stage: the play that was disrupted did not disrupt the real play, of which

the one you auditioned for was simply an ingredient—and on the night in question a pretty minor ingredient at that, as later on, with my green scales swathed in a handy raincoat, a bottle of South African sherry at my lips, and viewing the various *tableaux vivants* which had developed, I was able to judge. But carrying the thought a little further, I doubt if anyone who was a member of that OUDS party which toured *The Alchemist* and *King Lear* round the campuses of the Middle West so long ago could feel, either then or now, that the plays had a tenth the fictional power of the event itself—a power which sometimes seemed to seed itself within the performances as they were taking place.

For instance, how strange it was to be playing two parts simultaneously, that of the Duke of Burgundy and that of a man who has stuck his crown together with elastoplast and feels the gum melting under the heat of his head. I have written about this event,[1] but even the act of writing it down has not exorcised my conviction that the relationship between Lear and Cordelia cannot compare in intensity with those moments lived through by a man whose toy crown is creeping millimetre by millimetre down his skull. In this brief space of time it seemed to me that the entire apparatus of this production of *King Lear* had been brought into being simply so that, a short while after the play began, a fifteen-second micro-drama could develop. Lear grabbed me by the shoulder, we waltzed into the wings, but not before the crown had spun round my neck like a well-thrown horse-shoe. It was as though the play of which mere *plays* were a simplified version had decided to sidle on stage for a moment, and show its strength.

And, perhaps naturally, it is fragments of this larger piece, this more comprehensive drama, which remain, while all the lines I ever merely learned are long gone and have left no trace behind them. What were the first words that Tybalt spoke? What was it Face began the proceedings with? Or Cassio, or Mephistopheles? Silence now, at any rate. But I still smell the dust hanging in the air of a deserted lecture-room, the syringa in a college garden where the words were spoken, footsteps, someone smiling; sights and sounds which were unremarkable but unforgotten, part of an entertainment in which there was no division into actor and audience, and for which no audition was required.

[1] See p. 172.

HAMLET. My lord, you played once i' the university, you say?
POLONIUS. That I did, my lord, and was accounted a good actor.

Hamlet, III. ii

I

Contentious Beginnings

THOUGH 1985 marks the centenary of the first performance of a play by the Oxford University Dramatic Society, acting had been going on in Oxford for at least four centuries before the OUDS was constituted. And for three of those centuries there was a bitter struggle between those who wanted plays and those who considered the theatre sinful, dangerous, and a downright waste of money.

The earliest known dramatic performance in Oxford was in 1486, in which year a Magdalen College account book notes a payment 'for the making of a tomb for Easter'. This probably refers to one of the dramatizations of the Gospel narrative which were often staged within church services at this time. Magdalen seems to have gone in for such things regularly, judging from further notes of payments for costumes and 'props' for use in the chapel during the early sixteenth century; and on at least one occasion a full miracle play seems to have been acted there—on St Mary Magdalen's day, 1506, so it would have been a representation of the life of that saint, after whom the college is named.[1]

In fact liturgical plays were presented in Oxford chapels and churches long before that time, though detailed records do not begin before the late fifteenth century. On the other hand F. S. Boas, in *University Drama in the Tudor Age* (1914), calls it 'remarkable that Oxford and Cambridge, whether the Universities or the towns, should hold such a small place in the records of English drama before the Tudor period', and observes that only 'the most meagre traces' can be

---

[1] Alan Mackinnon, a founder of OUDS and chronicler of undergraduate theatre, states in his book *The Oxford Amateurs* (1910), p. 2, that 'at the beginning of the twelfth century the miracle play of *St Catherine* was acted at Oxford'. Mackinnon gives no source for this statement, which seems dubious in view of the lack of evidence of any such thing found by the very thorough F. S. Boas, author of *University Drama in the Tudor Age* (1914) and other works on the subject. Mackinnon also states, again giving no authority, that 'some Balliol students are known to have mounted and acted a morality play in the reign of Henry VI'.

found there of Miracle plays; nor is there any single medieval Miracle or Morality play which can be connected specially with either place.

But though there is no collection of Oxford Mysteries to put alongside the great York or Chester cycles, it was not long before the University began to develop its own brand of drama, originating not in liturgical or religious practice but growing from the more riotous side of student life. At Merton College in 1485 (the year in which the college Register begins) it was the custom to elect a Rex Fabarum, alias 'King of Christmas' or 'King of Misrule', from among the undergraduates. Chosen in November, he led the Christmas merriments in college (students stayed in Oxford for Christmas in those days) and imposed 'very ridiculous' punishments for offences against his code of behaviour. He also had to provide some sort of dramatic entertainment. The same sort of custom could be found in Magdalen, Christ Church, and St John's during the sixteenth century and probably earlier. (Those not familiar with the University should realize that each college went its own way with its social life, just as happens today.) A variation at New College and All Souls was to choose a Boy Bishop from the choristers; he was dressed in a cope and mitre, had to read the service, and was led about with mock pomp. This was no casual piece of whimsy but an ancient custom of inverting authority; William of Wykeham actually provided for it in his foundation of New College. The Boy Bishop's term of office usually included some kind of dramatic entertainment.

By 1607 play-acting was a big part of this kind of celebration. In that year the students at St John's revived an old college ritual which had lapsed for some time: they elected a 'Christmas Prince' or 'Lord of the Revels' from among their number. He found himself in charge of what amounted to a full-scale drama festival.

The name of the person chosen was Thomas Tucker, and he certainly had to sing for his supper. His 'reign' began at the end of November and went on till Shrove Tuesday. He was given mock titles referring to the college and its lands—'Lord St John's, Duke of St Giles, Maister of the Manor of Waltham [Walton], Gouvenour of Gloster Greene'—and he was the principal actor in several of the plays that were the chief entertainment during his rule. The plays, in Latin and English, were specially written by members of the college. Some of them were heavy stuff full of classical allusions, but one of them dealt with the low life of Oxford, and featured a pub landlady and a noisy

drunk. The student who recorded these events (in a manuscript now in St John's library) described the first known appearance of Coarse Acting on an Oxford stage. The young man playing the drunk, he tells us, had 'much pleased and done very well' in rehearsals, but on the night he was 'so ambitious of his actions that he would needes make his part much longer than it was, and stood so long upon it all that he grew tedious'. On top of this, the scenery had a tendency to fall down, and at moments the whole thing seemed an embarrassing failure. Yet by the end of Thomas Tucker's reign these Jacobean undergraduates and graduates had certainly learnt something about stagecraft; the reporter observes that it was 'almost incredible' how well they had learnt to perform.

The medieval universities did not encourage students to read Latin or Greek plays, let alone any drama in their native language; but by the sixteenth century a rediscovery of classical drama had begun, and in Rome and other southern European universities there were performances of plays by Seneca, Plautus, Euripides, and Aristophanes. This movement reached Oxford around the middle of that century, and in 1554 we find the Dean and Chapter of Christ Church trying to set a limit on how much was spent each year on plays: 'For two Comedies 20s a piece and for two tragedies 40s a piece.' These plays were performed as part of the college's annual Lord of Misrule entertainment. Anthony Wood says that Christ Church presented four each year, 'a Comedy in Lattin & a Comedy in Greek and a Tragedie in Lattin and a Tragedy in Greek'. By this time Oxford students were also acting some of the comedies that had been written in Latin earlier in the sixteenth century by Dutch and German schoolmasters, in imitation of Roman comedies. Often translated into English, these plays gave comically realistic pictures of the life of the times. One of them, *Thersites*, performed during the 1540s, has a reference to the Oxford Proctors (the University's disciplinary officers) and to Broken Hays, a piece of waste-ground near Oxford Castle, where fugitives sometimes hid:

> The proctoure and his men I made to renne [run] their waies,
> And some wente to hide them in broken hays.

Oxford playwrights soon began to emerge. The first was Nicholas Grimald, born in 1519, who studied at Brasenose and then became a Fellow of Merton and a lecturer at Christ Church. His first published

play, *Christus Redivivus, Comedia Tragica* (1543), is livelier than its title might suggest; it dramatizes the events surrounding the Resurrection, and has a quartet of comic soldiers as well as stage directions for an earthquake and lightning. It was performed to an audience of University and townsfolk by members of Brasenose, and a number of other stage pieces by Grimald, including a play about John the Baptist, were produced in Oxford during this period.

Presumably Grimald's stuff went down well at Christ Church, for when that college found itself about to entertain Queen Elizabeth on a royal progress in 1566 it decided to do so largely by means of plays (Cambridge had done the same thing two years earlier). An elaborate stage was built in the hall with a canopied seat for the Queen on it, and a Latin comedy and tragedy were performed for her. She dozed through them, but woke up when a third piece began. This was *Palamon and Arcyte*, an English play based on Chaucer's *Knight's Tale* and written by Richard Edwardes, Student of Christ Church and Master of the Children of the Chapel Royal. Elizabeth made enthusiastic comments during the performance and afterwards commended Edwardes, but the occasion remained in people's minds more for what happened offstage than on. During the performance 'there was, by part of the stage which fell, three persons slain: namely, Walker, a Scholar of St Mary Hall; one Penrice, a Brewer; and John Gilbert, Cook of Corpus Christi College; beside five that were hurt: which disaster coming to the Queen's knowledge, she sent forthwith the Vice-chancellor and her Chirugeons to help them'. Though the deaths and injuries were not enough to stop the performance, the whole thing nearly came to a halt when the script called for a pack of hounds baying 'vppon ye trayne of a foxe'. The hounds were duly assembled in Tom Quad, outside the hall windows, and bayed on cue—with the result that the excited audience abandoned the play and rushed out to see what was happening.

It is striking that this 1566 performance was done under the auspices of the whole University: the actors were not all members of Christ Church and there was a general pooling of resources. The staging at this and subsequent Oxford performances before royalty was lavish: Holinshed describes a 1583 *Dido* at which 'the tempest . . . hailed small confects, rained rosewater, and snew an artificial kind of snow'; and when Charles I watched a play at Christ Church in 1636 there was scenery which moved without visible assistance, a chair which was

'seen to come gliding on to the stage', and 'the perfect resemblance of the billows of the sea rolling'. Trick effects like this caused a stir even among the spectators from court, and had an influence on theatrical practice outside Oxford. Not surprisingly, the account books at Christ Church record large sums disbursed for staging, scenery, and machines, and in the University archives there are elaborate lists of costumes, with such entries as

20 Tuckes & Tresses of hayre to hange loose of browne, black, fflexen or any coulors, for 20 nymphes.

1 longe black beard and hayre vncurled for a magitian.

10 goates beards and pols of shorte hayre of goates color for Satyres.

This was for a performance before James I in 1605.

The *Dido* play that had the rose-water rain and the artificial snow was by William Gager of Christ Church, who wrote a number of Latin dramas during the 1580s, and was the first Oxford playwright to have his work printed at the University Press. But by this time, if a man chose to write for the theatre he had to endure some sharp attacks, for strong objection to play-acting was now being raised by the Puritan faction. John Northbrooke's *Treatise, wherein . . . vain Playes or Enterludes . . . are reproved by the Authoritie of the Word of God* (1577) was a typical Puritan pamphlet attacking the theatre, and some Oxford men supported it. John Rainolds, President of Corpus Christi at the end of the sixteenth century, quarrelled in print with William Gager the Christ Church playwright on the subject of theatricals. Rainolds was not himself altogether innocent of the taint of the stage: he had been one of the company of actors who entertained Elizabeth in 1566, on which occasion he had taken a female role. The memory of this 'drag' performance upset him deeply; in 1599 he was declaring vociferously that the appearance of 'men in wemens raiment' was condemned by Scripture and by Calvin, of whom he was a follower. His battle with Gager formed the basis of his book *Th' Overthrow of Stage-Playes*, published that year. In it he attacked Sunday performances (sometimes given when royalty visited Oxford), and compared acting to such time-wasting activities as 'to rifle in ale-houses, or to carouse in taverns, or to steale deere or rob orchards'. Gager replied at length and equally passionately, declaring that theatricals could be beneficial both morally and educationally—though, typically for a university man of his time,

5

he had a poor opinion of professional actors, who were commonly regarded as little better than social outcasts.

These 'common Stage Players' who often visited Oxford during the late sixteenth century, Shakespeare undoubtedly among them, raised the hackles of authority not so much on moral or religious grounds as because they gave overcrowded public performances in tavern yards and other low places of entertainment, thereby helping the spread of plague. In 1575 the Privy Council charged the Vice-Chancellors of Oxford and Cambridge to forbid players to perform within five miles of either University, chiefly because of the danger of infection. At Oxford, Convocation passed statutes forbidding 'any Master Bachiler or Scholler above the age of eighteene to repaire or go to see any such thing under paine of imprisonment'—those under eighteen were to be dealt with at the discretion of the Proctors. No doubt the undergraduates cheerfully ignored this; certainly the players continued to visit Oxford, and the Vice-Chancellor began the extraordinary practice of bribing them to go away again. At the same period the city authorities welcomed touring companies, even patronized them officially, so that during the 1580s and 1590s there was the comic spectacle of Town handing over money to actors to encourage them to stay, while simultaneously Gown was paying out what F. S. Boas has called 'a sort of theatrical Danegelt' in the hope that they would cut their visit short. The first quarto of *Hamlet* (1603) declares that the play 'hath been diuerse times acted by his Highnesse seruants . . . in the two Vniversities of Cambridge and Oxford', but the performances by Shakespeare himself and the other members of the King's Company can never have had any official approval, and so presumably took place well outside the University precincts.

By 1600 academic hostility to the professional theatre was almost universal. At Cambridge in about 1602 the anonymous author of one of the *Parnassus* plays (a satirical trilogy) jeered at Marlowe, Jonson, and Kyd, whom he regarded as purveyors of trash, and branded actors as 'leaden spouts/That nought doe vent but what they do receiuve'. Nevertheless the universities themselves were a breeding-ground for many of the popular playwrights of the period. John Lyly was an undergraduate at Magdalen before he made his name with *Euphues* (1579), and afterwards lent costumes to his old college for plays there. George Peele, author of *The Old Wives' Tale*, was at Christ Church in the 1570s before becoming an actor and playwright, and in 1583 he

helped to organize a Christ Church theatrical entertainment for a European princeling. Robert Greene, dissolute playwright and pamphleteer, studied at Oxford after taking his Cambridge MA. Anthony Wood says the dramatist George Chapman had an Oxford education; Francis Beaumont was at Broadgates Hall (later Pembroke College); John Marston was at Brasenose and Philip Massinger at St Alban Hall. Indeed the universities became a byword as a source of precocious young writers. James Shirley's 1632 play *The Witty Fair One* includes a character who observes: 'What makes so many scholars then come from Oxford and Cambridge, like market-women, with dorsers full of lamentable tragedies, and ridiculous comedies, which they might here vent to the players, but they will take no money for them.'

If Oxford tended to be supercilious towards the host of successful London playwrights it had spawned, its own contributions to the drama could seldom be valued highly. F. S. Boas states drily that Tudor Oxford 'left nothing of first-rate interest' in the way of plays. Certainly there was nothing that matched up to *Gammer Gurton's Needle*, conceived at Cambridge in the 1560s. Boas points out that 'it can scarcely be a matter of chance that most of the tragedies . . . were performed at Oxford, and nearly all the comedies at Cambridge', but he gives no explanation for this. Perhaps Oxford had not yet discovered that drama could be fun. When James I came there in 1605 he was so bored with the Latin plays that it was only with difficulty that his attendants persuaded him not to walk out. He grumbled loudly, and eventually fell asleep. His queen and her ladies were upset during the performance of a Latin pastoral by the appearance of 'five or six men almost naked'—presumably the Satyrs whose goat-beards are recorded in the account books. Even that pillar of the University, Sir Thomas Bodley, had to admit that the plays 'were very clerkly penned, but not so well acted, and somewhat over-tedious'.

Actually things were often just as bad at Cambridge. In 1613 Prince Charles and the Elector Frederick went there and saw a so-called comedy which lasted for six hours; the Elector slept through most of it. Charles I came to Oxford a few years later and had to sit through the unspeakable *Technogamia, or the Marriage of the Arts*, which had already bored audiences at Christ Church. He 'endured it with great impatience'. Things went almost as badly when the King made his last Oxford visit before the Civil War. This time the first play he saw was

Passions Calmed, or the Floating Island, specially written by the Public Orator of the University, William Strode of Christ Church. Ingratiatingly designed to give comfort to Charles, it was a topical reflection on the folly of rebellion and the value of strong monarchy. But the court was dreadfully bored; Lord Carnarvon called it 'the worst that he ever saw, but one that he saw at Cambridge'. They were just as bored the next night when Archbishop Laud, the Chancellor of the University, presented a play at his own expense in his college, St John's. After supper the royal party took its seats yet again in Christ Church, for *The Royal Slave* by William Cartwright, one of the Proctors. No doubt by this time they feared the worst, but at last here was a play that pleased them—perhaps because the music was by Henry Lawes and the designs by no less than Inigo Jones. Queen Henrietta Maria was so delighted that she afterwards borrowed the costumes and had the piece performed at Hampton Court by the royal company—who (no doubt to the delight of Oxford) 'came short of the University actors'.

The Civil War virtually killed off English theatre, and stage performances were usually suppressed during it, though in January 1646 Charles I did watch a play while he was garrisoned at Oxford, 'to keep up his spirit instead of good successes from his soldiery'. The theatre remained under a ban during the Commonwealth, and it was not until 1657 that professional companies once again appeared in Oxford. From that time on it became the custom for troupes of London actors to make an appearance there at least every few years, usually in July at the time of the 'Act' (what later became known as Commemoration, the University's time of festivity at the conclusion of the Trinity or summer term). They performed in the yard of the King's Arms in Holywell, and in such non-University places as the Guild Hall and the New Tennis Court. Jonson's *Volpone* and *Epicoene* were among the pieces staged, in 1663 and 1673. Such things drove undergraduates into a state of great excitement. They 'pawn'd books, bedding, blankets' to buy tickets, which were very expensive. Consequently the University authorities soon began to complain, and the old Puritan objections reappeared. Directly after the Restoration in 1660 a comedy called *The Guardian* was acted in Oxford by a company of 'scholars' performing 'in the new Dancing School against St Michael's Church'; it included a burlesque of a typical Puritan. The Puritans responded by issuing a pamphlet attacking it, and recorded gloatingly that 'he that acted the old Puritan broke a vein, and vomited so much blood, that they thought he would

8

have died . . . Also a woman that joined with them in their play is also dead.'

The visits from the professional companies became more sporadic, with the University adopting an increasingly hostile attitude towards them. In 1680 the Vice-Chancellor received an application for permission to perform from the company of the Duke of Ormonde, who was then the Chancellor of the University. He replied discouragingly, observing of play-performances that 'severall young Gentlemen of good Estates & fortune are vndone by them, and the poorer sort of scholars spend that money on these Playes wch should support y^m for a considerable space of time in this place & when y^t small stock fails y^m they sell their books to procure more'.

No doubt the temptation for undergraduates to go to the theatre was increased by the fact that as many as ten different plays might be presented during the actors' Oxford season; the company put on shows twice daily, in the morning and afternoon, so as to pack in as many people as possible before the colleges shut their gates for the evening. This was attractive for the actors, for they got double pay for the twice-daily shows at a time of year (midsummer) when the theatre usually did poor business in London.

Of course the undergraduates did not visit the theatre only to see the plays. In July 1661 we find the first recorded instance of an Oxford theatrical love-affair. One Richard Walden who was studying at Queen's attended performance after performance by the visiting actors, having fallen for the charms of Mistress Anne Gibbs who was in the cast. He wrote a set of poems to her, and hung about what served as a stage door; but before the company had come to the end of its run he was summarily removed from Oxford to the bosom of his relatives, who looked unfavourably on the prospect of an actress in the family.

The actresses themselves seem to have relished this aspect of the Oxford visits. Colley Cibber, who came there several times with touring players, paints a rather sanctimonious picture of the whole business, recording that the company contributed fifty pounds from its takings towards the repair of the University Church, and declaring that Oxford had a more sophisticated taste than London—the 'flashy wit' that delighted the metropolis was, he says, only rated in Oxford 'at its bare intrinsic value', while Shakespeare and Jonson were regarded there as having 'a sort of classical authority'. But this was mere flattery, while the fifty pounds would undoubtedly have been extorted from the

9

actors rather than given voluntarily. A more realistic account of relations between the actors and their audience was given in 1713 when one of Cibber's contemporaries, the actress Miss Willis, delivered an epilogue at the close of the company's Oxford season. She spoke warmly of the stage-ladies' admiration for the physical charms of the undergraduates, particularly those who happened to have peerages, and she concluded:

> Wou'd I had never seen this Book-learn'd Town!
> Not that you less to me than all are kind:
> But when I go, I leave my Heart behind.
> Our *London* Beaus are easily withstood:
> But here, I find, I am but Flesh and Blood . . .
> Is it in OVID's Art you learn to Hide the hook,
> Whilst you surprize and take us by the Book?
> Must of my Hopes, some Dowdy be Partaker?
> Must I resign you to a vile Bed-maker? . . .
> Beyond our Hopes we've found a Welcome here,
> And wish (with some of you) it might be ev'ry Year.

But alas for Miss Willis and those others who, like early Gaiety Girls, hoped to catch themselves a peer by practising the *ars amatoria* in Peckwater Quadrangle or Magdalen Grove when official backs were turned: her epilogue was indeed a final speech, for no other visit by the players took place before a Licensing Act of 1737, designed to control theatres throughout England, led to the banning of any dramatic performance in Oxford University or within five miles of the city.[2] The curtain fell, and stayed down; and the eighteenth century is virtually a blank page in the history of Oxford theatre. Glynne Wickham, former OUDS member and now Emeritus Professor of Drama at Bristol University, writes:

The attack mounted on actors and acting in Shakespeare's time by the rising tide of Calvinist sympathizers which culminated in the closure of all play-houses in 1642 left its indelible imprint upon academic attitudes to drama which the re-establishment of two theatres in London following the Restoration of the Monarchy did little to change. The great era of university plays and masques, of school drama in Latin and English, of 'university wits' and

---

[2] The Act, which made a similar provision for Cambridge, also placed censorship of plays in the hands of the Lord Chamberlain, and controlled the use of theatres in London; elsewhere licensing of theatres was carried out by local magistrates.

playwright-director-dons had vanished, and was destined to be followed by a dark age lasting more than two centuries.[3]

Ironically, this was the period when Oxford University's standard of teaching fell to its lowest level yet, so that most undergraduates were left to idle away their days in drinking, card-games, and other occupations beside which even a Puritan would have considered the theatre worthwhile. Occasionally a faint flicker of theatrical activity arose in undergraduates' rooms, in the form of a charade or a burlesque for private performance. But in general the theatre remained not so much under a moral cloud as in a state of neglect.

The official ban on visiting players was removed during the 1790s, and in the last year of that decade a touring company gave performances of *The Rivals*, *Robinson Crusoe*, and other pieces at the Racket Court in 'St Aldgates'. Yet the University as a whole took little interest in drama for several decades after this. There is a legend, quite without foundation, that John Henry Newman wrote an opera during his undergraduate days in the 1820s, and that it was called *Jezebel, or the Scarlet Lady of Rome*. Rather more plausible is the story that one of his contemporaries, a certain Denison of Oriel (afterwards an archdeacon), tried to form a dramatic club without success. But it is not until the 1840s that anything really stirred.

The revival, when it came, started at Brasenose, a college then notable for its high spirits. In 1847 a group of undergraduates there decided to get up a play for performance, not in Oxford, where such things were still scarcely acceptable to the authorities, but at the Henley Regatta, which was attended by a large Oxford contingent. They chose a burlesque of *Macbeth* written by Frank Talfourd, a Christ Church undergraduate who was co-opted into the group; he was the son of the lawyer and well-known Victorian playwright Sir Thomas Talfourd, whose blank-verse tragedy *Ion* (1836) had been performed by Macready. Frank Talfourd himself played Lady Macbeth, and according to one of its members it was 'an extremely scratch company, hardly one of whom had ever made an essay at acting'. Among them was 'the hugest and rowdiest of Irish undergraduates', one Paddy Nicholson, who played one of Banquo's murderers. A professional prompter had been hired from Drury Lane in the hope of injecting

[3] 'A revolution in attitudes to the dramatic arts in British universities, 1880–1980', *Oxford Review of Education*, III, 2 (1977), p. 115.

some degree of theatrical discipline into the proceedings, and when this unfortunate person attempted to reprove Nicholson for making up his lines and departing from the script, he found himself threatened with 'a huge blunderbus ... with several barrels' with which the Irishman had armed himself for the part. Another performer, a 'wretch' playing the Gentlewoman, got drunk at the performance and swore he would not go on stage without a sword, so 'a dirk had to be assigned to the fair creature before the sleep-walking scene could be presented'. Macduff lost his helmet in the backstage mêlée, and went on attired in the 'well-known hard straw and broad blue ribbon of the Oxford eight', which of course won a round of applause.

Macbeth Travestie was such a success that the Brasenose group performed it again in London at the Talfourd family house, with Dickens in the audience. They took to calling themselves the Oxford Dramatic Amateurs, and even hired a London theatre and put on a show on Boat-Race night in 1849. More significantly, during 1848 they actually staged a performance in Oxford—the first public dramatic entertainment given there by undergraduates since the seventeenth century. This time the play was Talfourd's father's tragedy *Ion*, and it took place in Brasenose. The production was not a success; one of the principal actors deserted the company at the last minute to go to a college ball, and the Messenger so fluffed his lines that the corpse began to giggle. However, the 'ODA' kept going during the 1850s, putting on pieces like *Box and Cox* and a burlesque of *Hamlet*.

The character of a typical 'theatrical' undergraduate of this time is described in *The Adventures of Mr Verdant Green* (1853–7), a comic novel by 'Cuthbert Bede' (Edward Bradley) set chiefly at 'Brazenface' College, Oxford. Mr Foote, the specimen of this *genus* described by the author, is, however, not a member of that fictitious college but of St John's.

Mr Foote himself was a very striking example of the theatrical undergraduate. Possessing great powers of mimicry and facial expression, he was able to imitate any peculiarities which were to be observed either in Dons or Undergraduates, in Presidents or Scouts. He could sit down at his piano, and give you—after the manner of Theodore Hook, or John Parry—a burlesque opera; singing high up in his head for the prima donna, and going down to his boots for the *basso profundo* of the great Lablache. He could also draw corks, saw wood, do a bee in a handkerchief, and make monkeys, cats, dogs, a farm-yard, or a full band, with equal facility. He would also give you Mr Keeley, in

'Betsy Baker'; Mr Paul Bedford, as 'I believe you my bo-o-oy!'; Mr Buck-stone, as Cousin Joe, and 'Box and Cox'; or Mr Wright, as Paul Pry, or Mr Felix Fluffy. Besides the comedians, Mr Footelights would also give you the leading tragedians, and would favour you (through his nose) with the popular burlesque imitation of Mr Charles Kean, as *Hablet*. He would fling himself down on the carpet, and grovel there, as Hamlet does in the play-scene, and would exclaim, with frantic vehemence 'He poisons hib i' the garded, for his estate. His dabe's Godzago: the story is extadt, ad writted id very choice Italiad. You shall see adod, how the burderer gets the love of Godzago's wife.' Moreover, as his room possessed the singularity of a trap-door leading down into a wine-cellar, Mr 'Footelights' was thus enabled to leap down into the aperture, and carry on the personation of Hamlet in Ophelia's grave. As the theatrical trait in his character was productive of much amusement, and as he was also considered to be one of those hilarious fragments of masonry, popularly known as 'jolly bricks' Mr Foote's society was greatly cultivated; and Mr Verdant Green struck up a warm friendship with him.[4]

Fired by the success of the Brasenose amateurs, undergraduates at Balliol began a similar enterprise, and a company was formed which included Edmund Warre, future headmaster of Eton. The authorities were apparently very dubious, but at least one performance was put on in the college. It included *To Oblige Benson*, a farce by Tom Taylor, the future editor of *Punch*, who came to Oxford to see the performance. The programme for this occasion survives, and one notes that the male undergraduates who played all the women's parts did so under female pseudonyms. They also had themselves photographed in costume. Brandon Thomas's *Charley's Aunt* perhaps reflects this enthusiasm among mid-nineteenth-century undergraduates for disguising them-selves as the opposite sex.

Oxford was of course an almost entirely male community at the time, and there was at least a slight homosexual element in the fondness for 'drag' which characterized many of the college productions of the 1840s and 1850s. More than a whiff of scandal certainly hung about the Shooting Stars, a dramatic club founded at Oxford in 1866—the first to be based not on one college but to draw its members from the whole University. In June that year it mounted a comic production in the Masonic Hall in Oxford, and in November there was a Shooting Stars performance at the town's Victoria Theatre. Both performances were reviewed very favourably by *The Times*, and their success con-

[4] 'Cuthbert Bede', *The Adventures of Mr Verdant Green*, reprinted by Oxford University Press (1982).

tributed to the acting mania that gripped Oxford at this time. Alan Mackinnon's history of Oxford theatre records that 'there was talk of separate dramatic societies at Pembroke, at Christ Church, and perhaps half-a-dozen others'. A group was formed at St John's, and during 1866–8 it performed *The Rivals*, *She Stoops to Conquer*, and some ephemeral pieces, among them a burlesque *Iphigenia* at the Holywell Music Room. But then in the winter of 1869–70 there was (according to J. G. Adderley, another pioneer of Oxford drama) 'a great London scandal' in which some of the Shooting Stars were implicated, and like a meteor the club fell to earth, bringing (at least for the time being) the whole of Oxford drama with it. Apparently one of the members of the club was charged with 'obscenity', and the wearing of female costume played a part in the incident. The scandal retarded the development of Oxford theatre by many years: without this Shooting Stars disaster Oxford might have acquired an official dramatic society, tolerated by the University, during the late 1860s—the decade in which Cambridge undergraduates persuaded their dons to give official acceptance to their Amateur Dramatic Club (ADC), founded in 1855 by F. C. Burnand of Trinity, author of *Box and Cox*. As it was, Oxford had to wait another twenty years.

The authorities now told the undergraduates that theatricals were 'exercising a baneful effect, taking up too much time, and thereby diverting the student's mind into unprofitable channels'. The Vice-Chancellor issued a decree banning dramatic performances within the jurisdiction of the University. And that, for the time being, seemed to be that.

Not only could undergraduates take no part in theatricals themselves, they were very nearly starved of professional theatre too. Professional touring companies occasionally appeared in Oxford—the young Henry Irving played Hamlet, Iago, and Macduff in 1864 and 1865—but this was usually in the Long Vacation, when the University (which still had the right of refusing licences to public performers) would tolerate such things only because most students were out of residence. Then there was the Victoria, also known as the Theatre Royal, the building where the Shooting Stars had appeared during their brief heyday. But this theatre, in most people's opinion, was worse than nothing.

The Victoria, direct ancestor of the New Theatre (now the Apollo), had a colourful history. It was not Oxford's first permanent theatre—a

building was opened in 1833 by a Mr Barnett, and a decade later 'Batty's Circus Royal' was presenting equestrian acts in premises in St Giles'—but it remained deep in local memory long after it had disappeared. It developed from public performances given under the name 'Theatre Royal' in the Star Hotel, Cornmarket Street, during the 1850s. These moved to the Town Hall; then, during the 1860s, the promoters established the Victoria Theatre, a building that stood in George Street but was reached through a dark passageway opening out of Magdalen Street.

F. S. Boas describes the 'Vic' as 'a low-class music hall', but in fact it was a 'legitimate' theatre, if of a very low kind. At first it had a resident company led by an actor-manager named Clifford Cooper, together with his wife. They seem to have been a Crummles-like pair, presenting vast numbers of plays, chiefly melodramas and farces, though Shakespeare was staged quite often—*Richard III* being advertised as if it were *Maria Marten* ('See the Bloodthirsty King die on Bosworth Field!!!'). Their shows were licensed by the University and the city authorities, presumably on the grounds that no undergraduate would waste his time going to them, and there is a nice irony in the fact that 'Vic' theatre bills, frequently advertising the physical attractions of some London soubrette, bear the legend 'By permission of the Revd the Vice-Chancellor and the Right Worshipful the Mayor'.

Strangers were sometimes led by its name to suppose that the 'Victoria Theatre' offered high-quality drama. An American visitor wrote from Stratford-upon-Avon to Matthew Arnold, then Professor of Poetry at Oxford, that he was 'looking forward to seeing our great Shakespeare worthily acted in the theatre you scholars of Oxford have dedicated to your gracious Queen'. In fact such high-quality touring companies as did bring Shakespeare to Oxford usually avoided the 'Vic' and set up their scenery in what Alan Mackinnon calls 'the dreary Town Hall or the cheerless Corn Exchange'. The chief trouble with the 'Vic' was its audience. Sir Frank Benson, who while a New College undergraduate often visited it, recalls in his autobiography:

The play was only of secondary importance. The real excitement was that the pit had to take umbrellas to shield themselves from being pelted and spat on by the gods in the gallery. The umbrella was not only a shield but a weapon of offence when the pit rushed upstairs to retaliate. The front row of the stalls spent most of its time destroying the instruments of the orchestra or putting them hopelessly out of tune. The dress-circle would rush on to the stage, via

15

the boxes, dance with those prima donnas who were pretty, engage in pugilistic encounters with the officials and actors, or attempt to give impromptu performances of their own, until driven back to their places by volleys of stones, sticks, bricks, eggs, oranges, teacups and potatoes from pit and gallery. The only calm moment was when all undergraduate sections of the house united in a *sauve qui peut* from a raid by the Proctors and their bulldogs [University police]. Then windows, doors, rain-pipes, roofs and stage-ventilators were quickly broken in rapid and undignified flight.[5]

When Benson himself gave a performance of *Hamlet* to an audience of dons and their wives at the 'Vic' in 1883, a large dog was let loose on the stage and 'bets were being offered and taken' on the result of the conflict; Benson drove the creature, a well-known 'Vic' interloper, off the stage with his sword. Earlier in the evening there was a faction-fight when a local politician entered the theatre.

While the 'Vic' was flourishing with the tolerance of the University authorities, undergraduate theatricals could only carry on a clandestine and rather half-hearted existence. There were private performances at St Edmund Hall and Christ Church, but a participant recorded that 'it took some courage to brave the disapproval of certain sections of the University'. One such performance took place at the beginning of November 1871 at the house of Mrs Hatch, the wife of the Vice-Principal of St Mary Hall. Her daughter Ethel was one of the child-friends of C. L. Dodgson of Christ Church, 'Lewis Carroll', and she approached the author of *Alice* for a prologue, which he duly provided. It came down firmly on the side of the actors, defending them against the objections of the sterner element in University society.

> Dear friends, look kindly on our little show;
> Contrast us not with giants in the art,
> Nor say 'You should see Sothern in that part';
> Nor yet, unkindest cut of all in fact,
> Condemn the actors while you praise the act;
> Having by coming proved you find a charm in it,
> Don't go away and hint there may be harm in it.

Dodgson was present at the performance, and recorded in his diary that 'the acting, as a whole, was very good, specially Mrs Hatch herself'. (He supported theatricals in his own college too, recording on 5 December 1863 that he attended a performance in the rooms of

---

[5] Sir Frank Benson, *My Memoirs* (1930).

an undergraduate named Berners, and mentioning that the female impersonations were good.)

However, official disapproval continued. When F. S. Boas entered Balliol as a freshman in the autumn of 1881 he received a copy of the *Statuta Universitatis Oxoniensis* which, under the title *De ludis prohibitis* ('Of prohibited recreations'), included the rule that neither *funambuli* (rope-dancers), *histriones* (stage-players), nor *gladiatores* (prize-fighters) were to be permitted to perform within the University or its precincts, nor were *academici* (members of the University) to be present at such performances. If the *histriones, funambuli,* or *gladiatores* were to contravene this ban, they would be 'incarcerated', while such scholars as attended their shows would be punished 'at the discretion of the Vice-Chancellor and the Proctors'. Actors, as Boas observes, 'were still classed with rope-dancers and prize-fighters'; the theatre was indeed a *ludus prohibitus*. But already the revolution was taking place which would remove the University's ban, and remove it finally.

2

The Battling Philothespians

IN the autumn of 1879 the Hon. J. G. Adderley came up to Christ Church from Eton. The son of Lord Norton, he belonged to a family celebrated at its Warwickshire home for the excellence of its annual amateur theatrical week. On arriving at Oxford he was disgusted that nothing better was offered to the drama-minded undergraduate than the low performances at the 'Vic', where he observed that 'the occupants of the stalls never scrupled to pelt the performers with any nasty thing they chanced to have in their hands or their heads'. It seemed to him ridiculous that the University allowed its junior members to attend such spectacles, but would not let them 'run the risk of contamination by witnessing, or taking part in, a play of Shakespeare, Sheridan or Goldsmith'. James Adderley also noticed that 'most right-minded people in Oxford were getting heartily sick of this state of things'; and although he was only eighteen and a freshman he determined to do something about it. As he put it, 'some of us undergraduates at Christ Church thought we would try and start a society similar to the ADC at Cambridge'.

Adderley gathered together a group of like-minded friends, among them one Hubert Astley, an expert female impersonator. According to one contemporary, Astley was 'well known at the University for his extraordinary powers of falsetto singing'; Alan Mackinnon describes him as 'the best delineator of female *rôles* I have ever seen'. Another contemporary, Gilbert Coleridge, has written: 'Hubert D. Astley was our bewitching leading lady with his waist reduced to 22 inches at least, and his gentle falsetto voice. His curtsy on receipt of a bouquet was a masterpiece.' The group held its first meeting on 5 December 1879 in Christ Church, 'to draw up rules for a society of amateur actors'. About six people were present. It was initially decided that the group should be called 'The Meteor Dramatic Corps' (surely an oblique reference to the ill-fated Shooting Stars), that '1 or 2 performances should be given

every term', and that the group 'should be limited in numbers'. Adderley was elected 'President and Secretary', and he purchased a sturdy volume in which the society's minutes were to be kept, inscribing on the first page his belief—crucial to the society's existence—that the University statute prohibiting *histriones*, *gladiatores*, and *funambuli* was directed merely against professional players and not amateurs. The society's name was gold-stamped on the front cover. By this time 'Meteor Dramatic Corps' had been abandoned in favour of a title that would express a love of the drama in suitably classical terminology: 'The Philothespian Society'.[1]

The minute-book duly had minutes entered in it, but they were mostly concerned with procedural details and wrangles; the real work of the Philothespians, the putting on of plays, was conducted not by the Committee but by Adderley himself, who operated a benevolent dictatorship. An early rule drawn up by the Philothespians was that 'the President shall be subject to the Society not the Society to the President', but this was wishful thinking. When two of the members had to drop out of the first production the Committee decided that the whole thing should be postponed; Adderley, however, simply carried on as if nothing had happened, and the performance took place in his rooms at Christ Church on the evening of 4 March 1880.

The considerable stir caused by this small-scale effort shows how many people at Oxford wanted the University to countenance the performance of plays. The production was entirely unambitious, consisting merely of several comic pieces: an original farce about the wooing of a servant-girl, called *The Area Belle*, in which Hubert Astley had the chance to trip about in skirts; a short parody by Adderley of Henry Irving as Macbeth; and Burnand's *Box and Cox*, almost a *sine qua non* of amateur shows at that time and known by heart to many spectators. As a lot of time had been wasted by the Committee trying to postpone the production, the whole thing 'was all got up in 4 days'. However, the prompter, described in the programme as 'Sir H. F. Lambert, Bart.', only 'used his voice once'.

In those days even country-house charades were often adorned with footlights and professionally painted scenery, and Adderley recalled the 'consternation' which prevailed among the authorities as these objects were carried through the Christ Church gates.

---

[1] The minute-book of the Philothespians, along with those OUDS minute-books that survive, is now in the Bodleian Library.

The Battling Philothespians

The Censors [college disciplinary officers] were dismayed, but hardly knew how to stop it. Unable to prevent our acting, they resolved to starve us out. There is an ancient rule in Christ Church that not more than four supper rations are allowed to each person. I wanted supper for 40, and accordingly made a special application, which was indignantly refused. But in Christ Church, where regulations abound, means of evading them are also plentiful; and the supper rule can be beautifully evaded in this way—though only four suppers are allowed, you can have as many to lunch as you like. Who could then prevent our ordering 40 luncheons and keeping them in a cool place till midnight, after the play, when we could eat them and call them suppers?

And so the audience of forty undergraduates sat down to their midnight lunch, well pleased with the inauguration of Christ Church theatricals—for as yet the Philothespians were chiefly a one-college affair. According to Adderley, their triumph was repeated a few days later, when they were invited to Christ Church Deanery to perform their plays before one of Queen Victoria's younger sons, Prince Leopold, who had been an undergraduate in the college himself and was visiting the Dean and Mrs Liddell, parents of Lewis Carroll's Alice. Adderley claimed that this command performance was reported in the local papers, so that 'we awoke to find ourselves famous'. Actually there is no record of the event in the Philothespians' minute-book, which contains all their press-cuttings; on the other hand the performance in Adderley's own rooms was widely reported in Oxford, and a correspondence now began in the *Oxford & Cambridge Undergraudate's Journal* on the subject of legalizing drama at Oxford, most letters being firmly in support.

Emboldened by their success, the Philothespians decided to confront Authority at once, and so determine their position as regards the University statutes. Adderley was instructed by his Committee to approach the Vice-Chancellor, but his nerve seems to have failed him, and eventually a two-man deputation was sent in his stead. These two, Elliot Lees and J. W. Gilbart Smith, were told by the then Vice-Chancellor, the Revd Dr Evan Evans, Master of Pembroke: 'You may do as you like in your Colleges as far as I am concerned, but publicly I forbid you to act.' This was a blow, since they had vaguely hoped for what the minute-book calls 'the Vice's permission', and they wanted to be seen beyond the walls of Christ Church. But it occurred to them that 'your Colleges' might be interpreted to include undergraduate lodging-houses, so plans were made to perform in a big room at 26

Cornmarket Street, where Gilbart Smith happened to have digs. Meanwhile the *Undergraduate's Journal* reported 'breathless interest' in the affair, and Shrimpton's of Broad Street published a cartoon by Elliot Lees showing the Vice-Chancellor peering approvingly at a sexy female performer on the stage of the 'Vic', but displaying outrage at 'a real play!!!'

The Cornmarket performances took place on 31 May and 1 June 1880, and were attended by an audience of about a hundred and forty. The programme was another typical amateur theatrical pot-pourri: a farce called *Ici on Parle Français*, the screen scene from *The School for Scandal*, and the burlesque *Villikins and his Dinah*. The tradition of having a baronet as prompter was maintained with Sir George Sitwell in the role, the future patriarch of the literary family being then a Christ Church undergraduate. The performers included Alan Mackinnon, a Trinity undergraduate who had just joined the Philothespians, for the society was no longer confined to Christ Church.

They were of course sailing close to the wind, and afterwards they heard that the Proctors had come to the entrance of the building during the performance, 'but on hearing that certain distinguished academic ladies were present, thought it best not to interfere, and accordingly retired'. Chief among those ladies was Mrs Liddell of Christ Church, who was in the audience with Alice and her other daughters. The Dean's wife was a match for anyone, including the Dean, and no Proctor was going to interfere while *she* was present.

The performance received favourable reviews in the local papers, and at this and other early Philothespian productions there was praise for the incidental music, which was provided by 'Herr Slapoffski'. This gentleman, frequently to be seen leading the band at the 'Vic', was a Pole whose real name was never remembered but who was said to have gained his sobriquet soon after arriving at Oxford when he was asked if he could play all the latest tunes; he exclaimed 'Oh yes, sare; slap off!' He provided entertainment at the Bullingdon Club dinners, where he and his band endured the members' drunken antics; his bill invariably included the item 'To bursting drum by Bullingdon gents, £5. 5s. 0d.'[2]

'The wonder to us,' declared one Oxford journal after the Cornmarket performance, 'is that the University Authorities should continue to withhold their countenance to a body of gentlemen who are

---

[2] Slapoffski's name may not have been a pseudonym. Kelly's *Directory* for Oxford in 1883 records: 'Slapoffski, Adolph, music warehouse, 9 Turl Street.'

capable of yielding so much pleasure and legitimate amusement.' Fired by this public encouragement, Adderley wrote to the Vice-Chancellor asking him to reconsider his decision—'begging him to patronize the society and give his serious attention to the subject of dramatic performances in Oxford'. He received no reply.

Adderley was now quite angry about the matter, and he and Elliot Lees went to Pembroke to try and catch the Vice-Chancellor off guard in his lodgings. The visit was not a success. 'The illustrious authority', records the Philothespian minute-book, 'emphatically refused his patronage or sanction to the Philothespian Society & deliberately declining to give any reasons for his answer (or his negligence in answering), and refusing to argue the question on the plea of want of time (really from want of arguments) he brought the interview to an abrupt conclusion by ringing the bell and bowing the Philothespians out of the room.' Quelled a little by this, the group mounted no productions during the remaining months of 1880. Moreover many of them had to do some academic work; the minute-book records that during the winter of 1880-1 'the members of the society were chiefly occupied in trying to pass Moderations. They were eminently success-ful in—being ploughed.'

Meanwhile the credit for persuading the University to countenance theatricals seemed in danger of being snatched from the Philothespians by another group, led by a New College undergraduate, Frank Benson, and including a young don at the same college, W. L. Courtney. These people decided to get up a performance of Aeschylus' *Agamemnon* in the original Greek, this being the first serious attempt to do such a thing in England. They saw their opportunity with the opening of the new hall at Balliol College, whose master, the celebrated Dr Benjamin Jowett, agreed to let them stage the performance there on 3 June 1880. It was done in an austere style, with a plain stage-design by Burne-Jones and the chorus chanting its words in a monotone. Benson played Clytemnestra—thereby discovering his vocation for the stage—and Courtney was the watchman. Jowett approved the whole thing energetically, and Robert Browning was among his guests at the performance. This *Agamemnon* received wide praise, but later the opinion prevailed that the acting had not been of a really high standard. Certainly the production was not successful when it was performed in London before an audience that included George Eliot, while Ben-son's *Romeo and Juliet*, staged in London a year later with himself as

Romeo, was a dismal failure. The Philothespians looked on these ventures with suspicion, and felt that the whole thing had been done to give Frank Benson an entrée to the theatrical profession. He certainly achieved that, becoming an actor-manager in a matter of months after leaving Oxford, before the Philothespians had even managed to mount their own first Shakespearian production. Oxford theatre had already become a matter of intense rivalry, of jockeying for position in relation to the acting profession.

The Philothespians' own next move was not really of a theatrical nature. In February 1881 they began to rent club-rooms at Miss Bennett's lodging-house in St Aldate's. These were sometimes used for entertainments—there was one in the summer of 1881, when a programme of songs and monologues was performed before an audience including the Warden of Keble College and his wife—but the rooms were really more for social purposes, and with their inauguration the Philothespians began to function as a dining and social club as well as a theatre group. The effects of this were soon to become apparent.

James Adderley was still prominent in Philothespian affairs, but much of the work was now being done by Alan Mackinnon, whom Adderley called 'a prince among stage managers, one of the few people I have ever met who could really manage amateurs without losing his temper'. Mackinnon began to organize auditions for new members, and also to get Philothespians together in the vacations to perform outside Oxford, often in aid of some charity or other. These performances were of a varying standard, and usually took place after minimum rehearsal. A Folkestone show in 1883 under Mackinnon's direction earned some biting comments from the local paper: 'A great deal of what went on upon the stage was wholly inaudible beyond the first two rows of stalls, and we were inclined to think that this was by no means the least pleasing part of the performance. Had it not been for the energetic articulation of the prompter we should not have had the faintest idea of the progress of the play.' Someone, presumably Mackinnon, has written in pained self-justification alongside this cutting in the minute-book that 'the plays were *all* got up in *one* day'.

It was of course less risky to perform outside Oxford than within it. In the Hilary Term of 1881 the Philothespians gave another 'private' theatrical round the corner from Christ Church, this time at a hall in Pembroke Street, and repeated the production (a couple of one-acters)

at the Corn Exchange, Aylesbury. Unfortunately the performance had to be at the unsociable hour of four o'clock in the afternoon, so that the actors could be back in time for college curfew—'like so many Cinderellas', said Mackinnon—and in consequence while the county gentry filled the front rows of the stalls, most of the remaining seats were empty. The Oxford performances of this show were better attended: the eminent philologist Professor Max-Müller was among the audience, though this time the influential Mrs Liddell was not present, 'owing to a personal request from the Vice-Chancellor'.

Dr Evan Evans seems not to have known what to do about these pestilential actors. When the Philothespians approached him yet again, in Trinity Term 1881, this time asking for permission to perform in the Holywell Music Room during Commemoration, he surprised them by consenting, 'and even signified his intention of being present . . . [as] he wished to gather some personal experience of our doings'. The Vice-Chancellor appears to have been persuaded by the argument that 'Commem' was technically in the vacation. But his consent was given on one condition, a dreadful one: that they should '*never do it again!*'

The Philothespians reluctantly agreed, realizing no doubt that since Dr Evans's wishes had been flouted more than once already, they could probably evade him again. All the same there was poignancy in the singing, during the burlesque *The Belle of the Barley Mow*, of the words 'We'll never play here no more, boys!', and the audience 'departed in the belief that they had witnessed the last effort of the popular Society'. This occasion marked an advance in the Philothespians' ambitions, for besides the burlesque the performance included *The Clandestine Marriage* by Colman and Garrick, a piece of more substance than they had hitherto attempted. Unfortunately the (male) undergraduate playing Miss Stirling 'carried on far too animated a conversation with the prompter, even for amateur theatricals'.

The Holywell performance was not of course the last. The Philothespians were back on the boards next term, in December 1881, when they staged more burlesques at a 'private' performance in Pembroke Street ('A little more rehearsing would have made it better,' records the minute-book). The following February saw the start of a pleasant tradition, the giving of an annual performance at the Corn Exchange, Bicester, during the week of the Bicester Hunt Ball. The show was given under the 'Distinguished Patronage' of various local gentry, and according to the newspapers was attended by 'crowded and

fashionable audiences', including the Hunt itself, 'all turned out in pink, forming a gay picture in the stalls'. There was even a special train to convey audience and performers to and from Oxford; the Proctors got wind of this, and waited on the platform for its return, which was long after the hour that college gates were closed. But the London & North Western Railway took a sympathetic view, and the train was halted a few yards up the line to disgorge its undergraduate passengers before arriving innocently at the station.

When 'Commem' came round again, in the summer of 1882, the Philothespians 'yearned for another show'. Fortunately the new Senior Proctor was a known supporter of the Society, the theologian Henry Scott Holland, then teaching at Christ Church. He had been to at least one of their productions, and Adderley put the whole matter before him, suggesting that 'if we gave our performance in a rather more private manner' the Vice-Chancellor might not object. Scott Holland 'threw himself heart and soul into the matter' and saw the Vice-Chancellor, whom he discovered to be good-natured in the business but also unwilling to give open sanction to acting. Dr Evans 'said he would rather not be applied to; if the performance was really going to be private he would say nothing, but if the matter was directly brought under his notice he must say "no"'. Or, as the Philothespians' minute-book puts it, 'the Proctor gave the President to understand that provided all sale of tickets and sending of circulars was done privately . . . Dr Evans would *wink*'. The problem was how to interpret 'privately': circulars were sent out, describing the performance as private but also stating that tickets, price five shillings each, could be purchased from Adderley at Christ Church. A copy came to the notice of a don ill-disposed towards acting, and he sent it to the Vice-Chancellor, who on receipt 'declared that the performance was illegal' and warned the Philothespians that 'extreme penalties would ensue on prominent members unless all money that had been received were returned and no more taken'.

So the money was returned, and the performance, again in Holywell, given free of charge ('though acknowledgement is due to many of our patrons for kind subscriptions'). The minute-book records that 'the President [Adderley] visited the Vice Chancellor after the performance was over and received from the reverend gentleman a short lecture during which he winked as was generally expected. Then a general shaking of hands took place and probably shedding of tears. *Tableau*.

Curtain.' Adderley's recollections of the occasion, written six years later, were rather more dramatic. According to him, Evans was not satisfied by the return of the money, and sent for Scott Holland and told him: 'I shall have to send somebody down.' On the morning of the performance (says Adderley) he himself was summoned to call on the Vice-Chancellor in five days' time; not being able to face the delay, he went to Pembroke at once, was admitted to Evans's presence, and told him: 'I cannot wait till next Thursday: I hear you are going to send me down: I want to know if this is true before I go and act. I shall not act if you are going to send me down.' Evans answered: 'How do you know I am going to do anything of the kind? . . . I decline to answer, sir; you must come on Thursday; I cannot speak to you.' Adderley therefore had to leave the room 'with a heavy heart' and proceed to Holywell to play Madame Phillipeau in *A Husband to Order* by J. Maddison Morton and Amanthis in *Little Toddlekins* by Charles Mathews. 'I spent a very miserable five days . . . but . . . thanks almost entirely to the Senior Proctor, Dr Evans was persuaded to look kindly on the matter. It was his last day of office when he sent for me. "I am glad", he said, "not to have to do anything disagreeable, as this is my last day of office; I shall not trouble you any more after to-day. Goodbye,"—and he shook hands.'

This did indeed mark the end of the Philothespians' conflict with authority, but a split now began to develop in their own ranks. Adderley, due to take his final Schools in the coming academic year, resigned the presidency. Mackinnon observes that he had already 'ceased to exercise a rigid supervision over the election of members', so that 'men of very inferior stamp . . . managed to creep into the Club'. In short, the Philothespians were going to the bad. The decadence was not sexual, as it had been with the Shooting Stars—the frequent assumption of female clothes seems to have had no effect on their private lives. But the existence of club-rooms, and also the Society's close connection with Christ Church and its rich and titled Old Etonians, meant that the Philothespians were fast becoming just one more 'set' in which to eat, drink, and gamble.

The 'non-acting' element among them managed to elect a puppet President to succeed Adderley, Gerald Gurney from New Inn Hall. Adderley, observing this with regret, remarked that the society 'had not made as much progress as it ought in 3 years. It was still comparatively unknown and did not contain all or half the really good actors in

Oxford.' The old order had broken up: Astley the female impersonator had left Oxford, and Mackinnon was giving up the stage (at least temporarily) for academic work, along with Gilbert Coleridge of Trinity, another stalwart. Yet during this time of crisis the Philothespians acquired a member who, more than any other, gave them the quality of theatrical performances necessary to their survival, or rather to their rebirth as the OUDS.

Arthur Bourchier had already decided while at Eton that he was going to be a professional actor. He came up to Christ Church at Michaelmas 1882 and at once made a take-over bid for the ailing Philothespians, getting himself on to the Committee, persuading the Society to drop all performance of burlesques and concentrate on more substantial plays, and generally convincing them that they had 'commenced a new era'. By the end of his first term at Oxford he had displaced Gurney as President, and was starring in Lord Lytton's comedy *Money* at the Holywell Music Room. Under his presidency the minute-book ceases to be a neatly written record (by Adderley) of Committee meetings, and becomes instead a wild, melodramatic scrawl. Adderley, when all was said and done, was a rather gentlemanly figure who happened to have a taste for amateur acting (he eventually became a clergyman with socialist sympathies, working largely in slum parishes). Bourchier lived only for the theatre.

The Vice-Chancellor was now none other than Jowett, to whose term of office the Philothespians had eagerly looked forward, since he had given encouragement to the Balliol *Agamemnon*. 'The Jowler' was indeed far more liberal to them than poor harassed Dr Evans had been, but he did not quite let them off the hook. When Adderley went to see him a few months after he had taken office, in order to clarify the Philothespians' position, he was received 'with the greatest courtesy', and Jowett even invited the entire Committee to come and see him the next day. They assembled, and were told that the University would now allow them to perform publicly—but on two conditions: they must act only Shakespeare, and the female parts must be taken by lady amateurs.

These new rules were the best possible thing that could have happened to the Philothespians. Despite Bourchier's resolve that there should be no more burlesques, it would have been difficult to wean members entirely from the Box-and-Coxerie which had dominated their diet since their foundation, and which gave them an air of

country-house theatricals. Shakespeare presented the challenge the society needed in order to mature. As to the women's parts, Jowett's rule was no doubt made partly because of a fear of the moral consequences of transvestism; but here too the old habit of men portraying women was holding back the Philothespians and giving their productions the air of a charade. Hubert Astley may have played milkmaids to a tee, but few of his contemporaries could do the job properly. A typical exponent seems to have been one Freddy Glyn, later Lord Wolverton, a 'heavy' rowing man who was somehow persuaded to take the part of Georgina Vesey in *Money*. Mackinnon recalls that he 'greatly objected to shaving his moustache, and at the entreaty of the Committee finally consented to compromise the matter by having it gummed over with gold-beater's skin, which was always proving refractory, and qualifying the fair "Georgina" to enter the ranks with the "bearded lady"'. Moreover Arthur Bourchier, who was playing 'Georgina's father, spoke in a much higher pitch than Freddy Glyn, so that 'Georgina' brought the house down on the first night with the line 'How about the ear-rings you promised me, dear papa?' delivered in *basso profundo* at a volume more suited to the towpath than the stage.

Jowett's decree, then, was really entirely benevolent, a rock on which serious drama at Oxford could at last be founded. However, opposition from senior members of the University did not melt away. It would continue to rumble in the background of Oxford theatricals for many decades, and as late as the 1950s an elderly don was said to have remarked of the foundation of the University dramatic society seventy years earlier, 'It was Jowett's greatest mistake.'

At the beginning of the term following Jowett's decree, Michaelmas 1883, the Philothespians began to rehearse *The Merchant of Venice*, this having been chosen to give Bourchier the chance of playing Shylock, and also because the supply of actresses was adequate for it.[3] For a time, indeed, there appeared to be a surplus of ladies, and a good deal of amusement was caused in the press by the announcement that there would be two Portias, Mrs W. L Courtney and Miss Ethel Arnold. The rumour that they would actually rival each other on stage proved false; Mrs Courtney, wife of the New College don who had helped Frank Benson stage the *Agamemnon*, had only agreed to play Portia provided

[3] Frank Benson was due to perform *The Merchant* as part of his company's Shakespearian season in Oxford, shortly before the Philothespian performance. He generously withdrew the play from his repertoire, and the Philothespians responded by entertaining him to dinner at the end of his week in Oxford, and toasting him with speeches.

that she did not have to appear every night during the play's week-long run, so she alternated with Miss Arnold. Her husband, now a supporter of the Philothespians, was cast as Bassanio, and Alan Mackinnon played Gratiano. 'Herr Slapoffski' was no longer required in the musical department, this now being in the hands of a talented Oriel undergraduate named Lionel Monckton, later the composer of *The Arcadians*. He wrote and conducted an original score for *The Merchant of Venice*.

Not everyone expected the best. 'The attempt seems too vaultingly ambitious', remarked the *Daily News*. 'Probably the essay will be most leniently judged if regarded as only a practical kind of way of studying Shakespeare.' But no such condescension was necessary. The production opened at Oxford Town Hall on Tuesday 4 December 1883, and began with a prologue spoken by James Adderley (who had now taken his degree, but was maintaining a close interest in the Philothespians) and written by Frederic Weatherley, an Oxford 'coach' who later became a successful writer of song-lyrics—his greatest success was 'Roses of Picardy'. In the prologue, Adderley impersonated an old Doctor of Divinity returning to the University; he is shocked to discover that acting is going on, but agrees to put it to the test. Then came *The Merchant* itself, in which Bourchier naturally carried away most of the honours, his Shylock being generally commended for not simply mimicking Irving. Even the sceptical *Daily News* allowed that he was in 'the front rank of amateurs', and greater praise came from Clement Scott in the *Daily Telegraph*: 'Seldom has an amateur performance gone off from first to last with such smoothness . . . The Shylock of Mr Bourchier is really remarkable for its moderation and its thoughtfulness.'

Jowett was in the audience at least once during the week's run; but there was one reminder of the old state of affairs when one of the Proctors, egged on by an officious 'Bulldog', attempted to apprehend an actor who was passing from a bicycle-shop which served as dressing room to the Town Hall stage door, on the grounds that he was not wearing a cap and gown as all undergraduates were required to do after dark. 'Your name and college, sir?' enquired the Proctor. The actor, W. Bromley-Davenport of Balliol, answered 'Launcelot Gobbo, Number One, High Street, Venice.'

A short tour followed the Oxford run of *The Merchant*, the Philothespians performing for one night or matinée at the Memorial

Theatre, Stratford-upon-Avon (opened in 1879 but as yet without a resident company), at Leamington Spa, at Charterhouse School, and at the Vaudeville Theatre in London, where a veteran Shakespearian actor sitting in the stalls took Bourchier's carefully planned dramatic pauses for 'dries', and 'could not resist officiating as prompter'. Meanwhile a cartoon circulated in Oxford depicting the trial scene, with Shylock as the embodiment of 'prejudice' (against undergraduate theatricals) and Portia ('Common Sense') defending 'Philothespian' (who has the face of Bourchier) against him; the Duke, sitting in judgement, has the features of Jowett.

In fact the Philothespians nearly fell foul of Jowett not long after their Shakespearian triumph, for they performed an adaptation of Anstey's *Vice Versa* at Bicester for the Hunt Week with a professional actress in the cast, which Jowett said was not permitted by the rules he had made for the society. They also gave an entertainment at Oxford Town Hall in May 1884 in aid of the local fire brigade, and this proved to be the last performance under the Philothespian name.

At Michaelmas 1883, while *The Merchant of Venice* was in rehearsal, the Society had moved into new club-rooms in Canterbury House, King Edward Street. The new premises had better facilities for members wishing to dine, and club colours were introduced—a blazer adorned with a ribbon of pink and old gold, and a sash to be worn at club dinners. The Philothespian had become just another Oxford dining club, like the Bullingdon or Vincent's, and its non-acting members could be seen all too frequently lounging about the streets in their club colours, or spending the day playing baccarat in the club-rooms. Bourchier, only in his second year, was inclined to tolerate this as long as it did not interfere with his own ambitions as an actor, but Adderley and Mackinnon, though they had both technically 'gone down' from Oxford, realized that everything they had laboured to build might soon be destroyed. Oxford had no need of more dining clubs, they argued, and it was apparent that the University authorities were already looking unfavourably on the Philothespians for their 'club' activities, not least because the bills at King Edward Street often went unpaid, and the debts were mounting. The revival of drama at Oxford might be snuffed out again if it were not quickly dissociated from the 'Philothespian Club', as the Society had now become.

Mackinnon, prime mover in the plan for secession, visited Bourchier and Adderley in the vacation to get their support. On 12 October 1884

he wrote to Adderley: 'I hear there is not the least chance of the Club being allowed to live beyond the year . . . How are we to patch up an impecunious Club without a sufficient number of members to pay off their debts?' He also composed an address to the Philothespians, which was read to members by Bourchier, at the club-rooms: 'You have done all that a Club *can* do in Oxford by setting the drama on a worthy pedestal, now *rivet* that work by handing it over to the Varsity itself.' Mackinnon's intention was to establish a dramatic society quite separate from the Philothespians, which would not be brought down in their ruin. His hope was that 'free from club and class jealousies, the Drama may rest for ever in the arms of the *Oxford University Dramatic Society*, mindful of her earlier traditions under the tutelage of the good old Philothespians!'

3

'A Third-Rate Histrionic Company'

THE creation of the new Oxford University Dramatic Society went smoothly enough, and during the Michaelmas Term of 1884 a Provisional Committee was constituted on what Mackinnon called 'popular lines'. By this he meant that the new 'OUDS' was intended to appease everyone: representatives of all the popular factions in the University were included in it. The Philothespians had nearly killed off drama in Oxford because they had turned into a drinking and dining club, but *ex officio* on the first OUDS Committee were the Presidents of the two leading clubs of that sort, the Bullingdon and Vincent's. Indeed the then President of Vincent's, A. G. Grant Asher of Brasenose, was chosen as first President of the OUDS, though he seems to have had absolutely no interest in the theatre. The President of the Oxford Union (the undergraduate debating society) and the captains of all the leading University sports clubs were included too. James Adderley wrote of this: 'Nothing of the kind [a drama club] succeeds at the university unless it is backed up by the "bloods" and the "blues", so we put on our first committee the presidents of all the crack clubs.'

However, the organization of plays was left in the hands of Bourchier as 'Acting Manager' and Mackinnon as 'Stage Manager', and it soon became apparent that this first Committee was merely a public relations exercise, and would take no active part in the running of the Society. It seems to have disintegrated soon after its formation, leaving only a Secretary and (now and then) a Treasurer. Even the office of President went into abeyance fairly quickly, and the Secretary was the chief officer of the OUDS for most of the first eighteen years of its existence.[1] No minute-books seem to have been kept in the early years.

What mattered, of course, was not formal organization but the

---

[1] The abbreviation 'OUDS' was at first pronounced to rhyme with 'moods' rather than 'clouds'. Nigel Playfair, a member during the 1890s, wrote: 'I do not know when the "Owds" first began to be spoken of, and I succumb to that pronunciation with considerable distaste.' Until about 1945 it was common to speak of 'the OUDS'; the usual form nowadays is merely 'OUDS'.

energies of the small handful of individuals who got up the productions and marshalled the casts. In the years between the formation of the OUDS and the First World War these were rarely undergraduates. W. L. Courtney, the New College tutor who had given the Philothespians his support, was the first 'Senior Member' of the OUDS (a don sitting on the Committee in an advisory role) with the title of Auditor but in fact exercising his influence in all kinds of ways during the 1880s and early 1890s. Arthur Bourchier continued to play leading roles and helped to organize productions for several years after he had taken his degree. Above all, Alan Mackinnon, who had technically left the University some time ago, kept the Society going during its first decade. 'Stage Manager' was the term then used for what is now described as 'Producer' or 'Director', and in Mackinnon's case that is what it meant: he produced virtually every OUDS play up to 1895.

Despite his huge contribution to the OUDS, and the fact that he wrote the history of the Society's first twenty-five years, Mackinnon remains an oddly shadowy figure. He played leading parts in many of the productions, and seems to have been quite a passable performer, while as 'Stage Manager' he was clearly a good organizer, if rather uninspired. He had a private income and was able to spend much of his time organizing and acting in country-house theatricals; he also managed two well-known amateur societies of the period, the Canterbury Old Stagers and the Windsor Strollers. The first of these gave an opportunity for former OUDS actors to tread the boards again once a year, during Canterbury Cricket Week, and the second had strong Oxford connections too. However, Mackinnon eventually had to give up his OUDS involvement because of 'my political work as a private secretary', so the amateur stage was not quite his only occupation.

Given the intention of Mackinnon, Adderley, and Bourchier that the OUDS should break with the Philothespian dining-club ways, it seems odd that one of the first actions of the new Society in 1884 was to take club-rooms, in the High Street; Mackinnon says that they were all 'proud' of the rooms when they first moved in. But at this early stage in the new Society's history the 'clubbable' element played only a small part in its life, and attention was quickly turned to the choice of play for the first production—the performance 'with which the Society should commence its career and justify its existence'.

The policy in these early days, which was of course limited by

Jowett's rule that the Society should perform only Shakespeare, was to choose plays that did not usually receive productions upon the professional stage. There were many of these. The contemporary professional theatre was ruled entirely by actor-managers who had no interest in anything that did not give them starring roles, and preferably big parts for their wives too. In consequence most of the history plays, with their spreading of the honours among as many as three or four chief actors, remained unperformed. When Frank Benson and his company took over the Memorial Theatre at Stratford in 1886, he intended to perform all Shakespeare's plays, but as the years passed he frequently rejected the less familiar works, 'sometimes because he knew they would be unprofitable to tour, more often because they did not contain suitable leading roles for himself and his wife'.[2] The original OUDS considered that it had something of a mission to get these plays on to the boards. It made a fairly thorough job of it, but unfortunately operated its own star system, so that leading parts were repeatedly given to the same people, with little attention to what a modern director would call 'company work'.

The first choice was *Henry IV, Part 1*, which Mackinnon claimed had 'not been performed for half-a-century'. Indeed its last appearance was probably around 1815, in a version by John Philip Kemble. However, there were many people in Oxford who knew it well. When Mackinnon went to Jowett to tell him of the choice, he mentioned that the lithe and definitely not rotund Gilbert Coleridge had been cast as Falstaff. Jowett snapped out: '"Am I not vilely fallen away?"' And on Mackinnon's observing that a Mistress Quickly had not yet been chosen, Jowett 'dryly remarked that there were plenty to be found in Oxford'.

Lady St Leonards agreed to take on the part of Quickly. She and Lady Edward Spencer Churchill, who was also in the cast, were the first of several titled ladies from the environs of Oxford who acted with the OUDS. This was partly a consequence of the continuing Christ Church and aristocratic element in the Society, and also because amateur theatricals were carried on energetically in the houses of the rich and titled, thereby providing a supply of blue-blooded ladies who were at least competent to take minor Shakespearian parts—they were none of them called on to provide a Desdemona or a Lady Macbeth, or even a Goneril. Not surprisingly, they were rather reserved about the

---

[2] Sally Beauman, *The Royal Shakespeare Company* (OUP, 1982), p. 32.

business of acting with the OUDS young men. Gilbert Coleridge recalled, of Lady St Leonards as Quickly: 'To her, as Falstaff, I had to make boisterous love, and she half-resented my chucking her under the chin, but to sit on my knee was not to be thought of, so the arm of my chair had to be provided as a harder substitute for my padded legs.' W. L. Courtney was given the job of bowdlerizing texts where necessary, to spare the blushes of the lady performers and the North Oxford audiences.

Bourchier was cast as Hotspur, Edward Harington of Christ Church (later a county court judge) played the King, and Ernest Holman Clark of New College doubled as Glendower and First Carrier; he was to share with Bourchier the honour of being the first OUDS members to go on the professional stage. Mackinnon himself played Hal as well as 'stage managing'. In keeping with the fashion of the time, he produced the play in heavily realistic style, despite the limitations of the Town Hall where the production again took place. He engaged between thirty and forty 'supers' to provide armies for the battle scenes, recruiting them from University athletes; the Captain of Cricket was cast as Bardolph. As to scenery, he devised 'a setting of rural scenes, some scattered bushes, and a fair-sized hillock'. None of this gave trouble, but Gilbert Coleridge as Falstaff was 'much disturbed as to the composition of his false stomach'. On the first night Mackinnon told him he did not look fat enough, whereupon Coleridge stuffed the first pile of clothes he could find in the dressing-room up the front of his tunic; this proved to be a dress-suit belonging to Bourchier, who was not pleased. Coleridge also found the solid padding too hot, so a 'substructure of wicker' was devised for later performances; this had the disadvantage of creaking when he moved, and it also 'developed a tiresome kink when he fell headlong in the Battle of Shrewsbury'.

The opening night, 9 May 1885, was a Saturday towards the beginning of the summer term. The proceedings began with a prologue written by George Curzon, an All Souls fellow who belonged to the OUDS, spoken by Cosmo Gordon Lang, then a Balliol undergraduate and President of the Union. He was dressed as a Doctor of Divinity, presumably because Adderley had been so garbed when delivering the prologue to *The Merchant of Venice* a year and a half earlier; Mackinnon (in *The Oxford Amateurs*) suggested that it was also a premonition of Lang's future clerical eminence—he eventually became Archbishop of Canterbury. The prologue celebrated the final

stage in the treaty-making between the University authorities and the Drama:

> O, gentle audience, Don and Undergraduate,
> Less gentle might be if o'er long I bade you wait.
> The Curtain's rising—at this shrine of Science
> We meet to join in nuptial alliance
> *Oxford*, a bachelor *praeclaro nomine*,
> And the famed Grecian maiden called Melpomene . . .³
> This time at least, Sirs, let it be no fable!
> But bid the Bride as now the curtain rises
> Loud welcome to a home beside the Isis.

The audience so addressed included the Bishop of Oxford, the Deans of Westminster and Christ Church, and Jowett himself, who was afterwards enthusiastic about the fruits of his tolerance. Gilbert Coleridge breakfasted with him a day or two later, and after the usual chilly beginning (the Jowler was no conversationalist) dared to ask for 'criticism and hints'. He was given some very practical pieces of advice: 'One was that, when a comedian soliloquizes, he should look at his audience and take them into his confidence, and not look at the boards or scenery; select someone at the back of the audience, preferably a fat man, and play at him till he laughs.' Coleridge followed the advice, and found that it worked. Had Jowett missed a vocation to the music hall?

Clement Scott of the *Daily Telegraph*, the then reigning British dramatic critic, wrote enthusiastically of the production, and it received good notices in all the London papers—for these were the days when almost any event in Oxford attracted the widest coverage from Fleet Street. The standard of reviewing was not high; to a modern reader most drama notices of the 1880s and 1890s are bland and uninformative, conveying little more than who played what, and contenting themselves with rather empty-sounding compliments to most of the performers. But the newly founded *Oxford Magazine* (edited and written by dons for a predominantly donnish readership) was generally more perceptive. On this occasion its anonymous reviewer spoke of *Henry IV* as 'the greatest of historical comedies . . . so hard to act because there are two worlds in it in ironic alternation'. He observed that Mackinnon's Hal 'moved in both worlds well, but much the best in the Boar's Head world . . . Seeing there was (we believe) little stage tradition for Mr Coleridge to work on, his Falstaff was most remark-

---

³ The Muse of Tragedy.

able . . . Mr Bourchier . . . showed . . . that he has gone on and not back since his Shylock, and that Hotspur came very natural [*sic*] to him.'

But the review to which one turns with the greatest interest was by Oscar Wilde. He had gone down from Magdalen six years earlier, and though he had scarcely begun his brilliant literary career he was already widely known, and caricatured, as the figurehead of English aestheticism. After the performance he attended an OUDS Club Dinner and made a speech. (The *Oxford Magazine* reported that the meal was 'at the expense of each member privately. The fate of the last Dramatic Club was a wholesome warning'—a reference to the winding-up of the Philothespians, which was now taking place.) Wilde wrote to Frank Benson's brother describing the OUDS production as 'charming', and on 23 May his notice of it appeared in the *Dramatic Review*. Wilde himself was rather proud of the piece, remarking that it would turn everyone at Oxford to pillars of salt. It is here quoted in full:

HENRY THE FOURTH AT OXFORD

I HAVE been told that the ambition of every Dramatic Club is to act *Henry IV*. I am not surprised. The spirit of comedy is as fervent in this play as is the spirit of chivalry; it is an heroic pageant as well as an heroic poem, and like most of Shakespeare's historical dramas it contains an extraordinary number of thoroughly good acting parts, each of which is absolutely individual in character, and each of which contributes to the evolution of the plot.

Rumour from time to time has brought us tidings of a proposed production by the banks of the Cam, but it seems that at the last moment *Box and Cox* has always had to be substituted in the bills. To Oxford belongs the honour of having been the first to present on the stage this noble play, and the production which I saw last week was in every way worthy of that lovely town, that mother of sweetness and of light. For in spite of the roaring of the young lions at the Union, and the screaming of the rabbits in the home of the vivisector, in spite of Keble College, and the tramways, and the sporting prints, Oxford still remains the most beautiful thing in England, and nowhere else are life and art so exquisitely blended, so perfectly made one. Indeed in most other towns art has often to present herself in the form of a reaction against the sordid ugliness of ignoble lives, but at Oxford she comes to us as an exquisite flower born of the beauty of life, and expressive of life's joy. She finds her home by the Isis as once she did by the Ilyssus; the Magdalen walks and the Magdalen cloisters are as dear to her as were ever the silver olives of Colonos and the golden gateway of the house of Pallas: she covers with fan-like tracery the vaulted entrance to Christ Church Hall, and looks out from the windows of Merton; her feet have stirred the Cumnor cowslips, and she gathers fritillaries in the

37

river-fields. To her the clamour of the schools and the dullness of the lecture-room are a weariness and a vexation of spirit; she seeks not to define virtue, and cares little for the categories; she smiles on the swift athlete whose plastic grace has pleased her, and rejoices in the young Barbarians at their games; she watches the rowers from the reedy bank and gives measured music to the pulse of their oars; she gives myrtle to her lovers, and laurel to her poets, and rue to those who talk wisely in the street; she makes the earth lovely to all who dream with Keats; she opens high heaven to all who soar with Shelley; and turning away her head from pedant, proctor, and Philistine she has welcomed to her shrine a band of youthful actors, knowing that they have sought with much ardour for the stern secret of Melpomene, and caught with much gladness the sweet laughter of Thalia. And to me this ardour and this gladness were the two most fascinating qualities of the Oxford performance, as indeed they are qualities which are necessary to any fine dramatic production. For without a quick and imaginative observation of life the most beautiful play becomes dull in presentation, and what is not conceived with delight by the actor can give no delight at all to others.

I know that there are many who consider that Shakespeare is more for the study than for the stage. With this view I do not for a moment agree. Shakespeare wrote his plays to be acted, and we have no right to alter the form which he himself selected for the full expression of his work. Indeed many of the beauties of that work can only be adequately conveyed to us through the actor's art. As I sat in the Town Hall of Oxford the other night, the majesty of the mighty lines of the play seemed to me to gain new music from the clear young voices that uttered them, and the ideal grandeur of the heroism to be made more real to the spectators by the chivalrous bearing, the noble gestures and the fine passion of its exponents. Even the dresses had their dramatic value. Their archaeological accuracy gave us, immediately on the rise of the curtain, a perfect picture of the time. As the knights and nobles moved across the stage in the flowing robes of peace and in the burnished steel of battle, we needed no dreary chorus to tell us in what age or land the play's action was passing, for the fifteenth century in all the dignity and grace of its apparel was living actually before us, and the delicate harmonies of colour struck from the first a dominant note of beauty which added to the intellectual realism of archaeology the sensuous charm of art.

As for the individual actors, Mr Mackinnon's Prince Hal was a most gay and graceful performance, lit here and there with charming touches of princely dignity and of noble feeling. Mr Coleridge's Falstaff was full of delightful humour, though perhaps at times he did not take us sufficiently into his confidence. An audience looks at a tragedian, but a comedian looks at his audience. However, he gave much pleasure to everyone, and Mr Bourchier's Hotspur was really most remarkable. Mr Bourchier has a fine stage presence,

a beautiful voice, and produces his effects by a method as dramatically impressive as it is artistically right. Once or twice he seemed to me to spoil his last line by walking through it. The part of Harry Percy is one full of climaxes which must not be let slip. But still there was always a freedom and spirit in his style which was very pleasing, and his delivery of the colloquial passages I thought excellent, notably of that in the first act,

> 'What d'ye call the place?
> A plague upon 't—it is in Gloucestershire;—
> T'was where the madcap duke his uncle kept;
> His uncle York;'

lines by the way in which Kemble made a great effect. Mr. Bourchier has the opportunity of a fine career on the English stage, and I hope he will take advantage of it. Among the minor parts, if there be any minor parts in this play, Glendower, Mortimer and Sir Richard Vernon, were capitally acted, Worcester was a performance of some subtlety, Mrs Woods was a charming Lady Percy, and Lady Edward Spencer Churchill, as Mortimer's wife, made us all believe that we understood Welsh. Her dialogue and her song were most pleasing bits of artistic realism which fully accounted for the Celtic chair at Oxford.

But though I have mentioned particular actors, the real value of the whole representation was to be found in its absolute unity, in its delicate sense of proportion, and in that breadth of effect which is only to be got by the most careful elaboration of detail. I have rarely seen a production better stage-managed. Indeed I hope that the University will take some official notice of this delightful work of art. Why should not degrees be granted for good acting? Are they not given to those who misunderstand Plato and who mistranslate Aristotle? And should the artist be passed over? No. To Prince Hal, Hotspur, and Falstaff, D.C.L.'s should be gracefully offered. I feel sure they would be gracefully accepted. To the rest of the company the crimson or the sheep-skin hood might be assigned *honoris causa*, to the eternal confusion of the Philistine, and the rage of the industrious and the dull. Thus would Oxford confer honour on herself, and the artist be placed in his proper position. However, whether or not convocation recognises the claims of culture, I hope that the Oxford Dramatic Society will produce every summer for us some noble play like *Henry IV*. For in plays of this kind, plays which deal with bygone times, there is always this peculiar charm, that they combine in one exquisite presentation the passions that are living with the picturesqueness that is dead. And when we have the modern spirit given to us in an antique form, the very remoteness of that form can be made a method of increased realism. This was Shakespeare's own attitude towards the ancient world, this is the attitude we in this century should adopt towards his plays, and with a feeling akin to this it

39

seemed to me that these brilliant young Oxonians were working. If it was so, their aim is the right one. For while we look to the dramatist to give romance to realism, we ask of the actor to give realism to romance.

OSCAR WILDE

Wilde was a little carried away by the novelty of the occasion. Reading between the lines of the many reviews the production earned, it is evident that most of the actors, with the exception of Bourchier, were no more than passable. But clearly *Henry IV* gave the OUDS a most successful send-off by the standards of contemporary amateur performances.

For the time being, the momentum of this first production was easily sustained. Continuing objections to the deplorable goings on at the 'Vic' had led a number of people to confer about the possibility of building a new theatre in the centre of Oxford, which could be used by both University and city. W. L. Courtney was prominent among those connected with the scheme, and he obtained the support of Jowett as Vice-Chancellor, introducing a 'deputation of citizens' to him in October 1884 to discuss the subject. Two months later Courtney was among those who signed a public letter appealing for subscriptions for a new theatre 'on a site lying between New-Inn-Hall Street and George Street'. The total cost would be about £13,000, and a limited liability company was to raise the money by public shares. The scheme went ahead with a local man named Drinkwater as architect, though the theatre was in fact built on the north side of George Street on a site adjacent to the 'Vic', just to the west of Victoria Court. (The 'Vic' stood on part of the land now occupied by Debenham's department store.) Meanwhile the 'Vic' itself was closed down on the grounds that it was a fire-risk. So, at least, goes the official story, but Oxford legend has a more colourful version. According to an OUDS member who joined a few years later, Dr H. E. Counsell, a two-act play was being performed at the 'Vic' one evening:

At the end of the first act there was an affecting scene in which the hero was saying goodbye to the heroine. He declared that he was going away to India for perhaps twenty years but swore to return in the end and make her his bride. He was wearing a pair of absurdly large check trousers and on his final protestation there came a shout from the undergraduates, 'Yes, but not in those trousers! Don't you dare to come back in those trousers.' But, in the second act twenty years later, he appeared in the same trousers and was greeted by another shout from the undergraduates, 'We told you not to come

40

back in those trousers. Take them off, take them off at once. If you don't, we will.' The actor tried to continue with the scene, but the undergraduates stormed the stage and the miserable man escaped by the stage door to be pursued all the way down Cornmarket Street.[4]

This episode is said to have caused the curtain to come down at the 'Vic' for the last time.

The new theatre was built in only four months. When opened, it officially had the title of the Theatre Royal, the name that had been used by the 'Vic'—which suggests that there was some continuity between the management of the two establishments. However, it was generally known, and advertised itself, as the New Theatre, a name which it and its successor retained for nearly a hundred years.[5] Its original manager, one of the promoters of the scheme, was named Lucas, but by the early 1900s it and the Oxford Theatre Company, its proprietors, were under the management of C. C. Dorrill. Members of the Dorrill family continued to manage the theatre, eventually as its proprietors, until the early 1970s.

The original New Theatre was a modest-sized building, much smaller than that which replaced it on the same site in 1933 (the present Apollo Theatre). It held about nine hundred people and was on the usual late-Victorian pattern, with stalls, dress circle, upper circle, and gallery. Judging from such few photographs as survive, it was an average specimen of theatre architecture of the period. The proscenium was twenty-four feet square and the stage, 'replete with all modern contrivances and machinery', had a depth of thirty-three feet from the footlights to the back wall. For the OUDS it was a perfect home.

The Society and its supporters had in fact driven melodrama and music hall out of the centre of Oxford. The functions of the 'Vic' were taken over by an establishment on the other side of Magdalen Bridge, near the bottom of the Cowley Road, known at various times as the Empire Theatre or the East Oxford Theatre. (The site is now occupied by the Basil Blackwell publishing business.) Surviving programmes from it, which advertise 'Bicycles carefully stored during the perform-ance at a nominal charge of 2*d*. each', record that during the early 1900s patrons could enjoy such works of dramatic art as *The Anarchist*

[4] H. E. Counsell, *Thirty-Seven the Broad* (1943).
[5] A place of entertainment known as the New Theatre had operated in Oxford during the 1830s.

Terror, a play of the Penny Dreadful school, with scenes entitled 'The Crypt under the Monastery' and 'The Electrocution Chair: The Terror Tortured and finally Killed by the Monster of his own Creation'.

Meanwhile at the New Theatre the OUDS settled in happily, choosing *Twelfth Night* for the opening of the theatre on 13 February 1886. The press was there in force, and the critic of the *Star* fully realized the significance of the occasion. After speaking admiringly of the theatre's 'bright blue and terra-cotta decorations, its ample stall space, its absence of private boxes, and its handsome plush act-drop', he went on to reflect that 'the *Funambuli et Histriones* have triumphed; and the New Theatre is something more than a roomy brick-and-mortar building—it is a temple erected to the Goddess of Victories'.

Jowett, who had made the victory possible, was among the first to take his seat in the stalls that opening night, and 'was greeted with tremendous cheers'. In the performance that followed, Holman Clark was Malvolio and Bourchier played Feste. He and W. L. Courtney supervised the production as Mackinnon was unable to 'stage-manage' on this occasion—though he was among the 'supers' during at least one performance, together with James Adderley. Coningsby Disraeli of New College, nephew of Benjamin, played Second Officer and First Lord. Oscar Wilde was again among the reviewers; by this time the novelty of seeing Shakespeare acted by 'young Barbarians' seems to have worn off a little.

On Saturday last the new theatre at Oxford was opened by the University Dramatic Society. The play selected was Shakespeare's delightful comedy of *Twelfth Night*, a play eminently suitable for performance by a club, as it contains so many good acting parts. Shakespeare's tragedies may be made for a single star, but his comedies are made for a galaxy of constellations. In the first he deals with the pathos of the individual, in the second he gives us a picture of life. The Oxford undergraduates, then, are to be congratulated on the selection of the play, and the result fully justified their choice. Mr Bourchier as Feste the clown was easy, graceful, and joyous, as fanciful as his dress and as funny as his bauble. The beautiful songs which Shakespeare has assigned to this character were rendered by him as charmingly as they were dramatically. To act singing is quite as great an art as to sing. Mr Lechmere Stuart was a delightful Sir Andrew, and gave much pleasure to the audience. One may hate the villains of Shakespeare, but one cannot help loving his fools. Mr Macpherson was perhaps hardly equal to such an immortal part as that of Sir Toby Belch, though there was much that was clever in his performance.

Mr Lindsay threw·new and unexpected lights on the character of Fabian, and Mr Clark's Malvolio was a most remarkable piece of acting. What a difficult part Malvolio is! Shakespeare undoubtedly meant us to laugh all through at the pompous steward, and to join in the practical joke upon him, and yet how impossible not to feel a good deal of sympathy for him! Perhaps in this century we are too altruistic to be really artistic. Hazlitt says somewhere that poetical justice is done him in the uneasiness which Olivia suffers on account of her mistaken attachment to Cesario, as her insensibility to the violence of the Duke's passion is atoned for by the discovery of Viola's concealed love of him; but it is difficult not to feel that Malvolio's treatment is unnecessarily harsh. Mr Clark, however, gave a very clever rendering, full of subtle touches. If I ventured on a bit of advice, which I feel most reluctant to do, it would be to the effect that while one should always study the method of a great artist, one should never imitate his manner. The manner of an artist is essentially individual, the method of an artist is absolutely universal. The first is personality, which no one should copy; the second is perfection, which all should aim at. Miss Arnold was a most sprightly Maria, and Miss Farmer a dignified Olivia; but as Viola Mrs Bewicke was hardly successful. Her manner was too boisterous, and her method too modern. Where there is violence there is no Viola, where there is no illusion there is no Illyria, where there is no style there is no Shakespeare. Mr Higgins looked the part of Sebastian to perfection, and some of the minor characters were excellently played by Mr Adderley, Mr King-Harman, Mr Coningsby Disraeli, and Lord Albert Osborne. On the whole, the performance reflected much credit on the Dramatic Society; indeed, its excellence was such that I am led to hope that the University will some day have a theatre of its own, and that proficiency in scene-painting will be regarded as a necessary qualification for the Slade Professorship. On the stage, literature returns to life, and archaeology becomes art. A fine theatre is a temple where all the muses may meet, a second Parnassus, and the dramatic spirit, though she has long tarried at Cambridge, seems to be now migrating to Oxford.

> 'Thebes did her green unknowing youth engage,
> She chooses Athens in her riper age.'

The New Theatre was only just ready in time for the performance. The paint was not quite dry in the upper parts of the house, and one member of the audience was discovered still leaning against the wall some time after the play had ended. When asked by a curious onlooker whether he intended to 'stick the show once more', he 'replied with some asperity that he was already stuck'.

A new dramatic society, a new theatre: the victories had indeed been won, and Jowett set his seal on the matter a few months later, during

Trinity Term 1886, when he invited Henry Irving to lecture in Oxford, putting up the celebrated actor himself at the Master's Lodgings in Balliol, and introducing Irving to the lecture audience by remarking that he had contributed much to the understanding and appreciation of Shakespeare. The event would have been unthinkable only a decade earlier, and a cartoon, circulated at the time of the lecture, depicted Jowett as the Clown from the Harlequinade jumping over the back of the Policeman (who had the features of the Senior Proctor) with Frank Benson as Harlequin and W. L. Courtney as Pantaloon.

The victory was complete, but ironically the OUDS nearly collapsed as soon as it was won. 'There was nothing to keep it alive between the annual shows,' writes Claud Nugent, a member at this time, 'and consequently members did not care to pay subscriptions.' The High Street club-rooms failed to hold the Society together, and after a brief period they were handed over to the newly founded Gridiron Club, a wining-and-dining undergraduate body on the model of Vincent's and the Bullingdon. Fresh members did not join the OUDS as the old ones went down, and only a year after *Twelfth Night* the Society had become 'almost extinct'.

A rescue operation was mounted by a triumvirate of Mackinnon, Courtney, and Bourchier, who decided that something attention-catching must be chosen for the next production. No Greek play had been performed in Oxford since the 1880 *Agamemnon*, and it seemed to them that to stage another 'would be an admirable move, both for the sake of pleasing many of the authorities . . . and for the sake of the pecuniary advantage'—in other words, it would be cheaper to stage than a heavily realistic Shakespearian production. As there were no OUDS funds after the expensive *Twelfth Night*, Courtney himself generously put up the money; Mackinnon of course was to 'stage-manage'. Official permission to break the 'nothing but Shakespeare' rule was obtained.

Mackinnon's production of the *Alcestis* of Euripides played at the New Theatre during Eights Week of 1887. Mackinnon himself was Apollo, Bourchier was Death, and the future novelist A. E. W. Mason (best known for *The Four Feathers*), then a Trinity undergraduate, was a boisterous Heracles. Unlike the Benson *Agamemnon* in Balliol, the production made almost no attempt to copy classical Greek theatrical tradition, and looked much like a late Victorian melodrama. Bourchier, wreathed in filmy drapes and resembling Irving in one of his more

sinister roles, made his entrance through a trapdoor, enveloped in a cloud of steam. The machinery to produce this effect was not easily controlled, so that he had to face a nightly scalding from the steam-jets, while Mackinnon, who had arranged to be let down on flying wires, was almost strangled. Alcestis herself was played by the celebrated Greek scholar Jane Harrison, who had recently been lecturing in Oxford on Greek sculpture. She was fluent enough in the language of the play, but a hopeless actress; one reviewer called her 'by turns hysterical and stony'. For some reason she refused to be carried off the stage on a bier; perhaps the prospect of being carted around by the 'heavies' from the University Boat Club, who as usual took the walk-on parts, seemed indecorous to her. Mackinnon had to double as her corpse.

The production verged on the ridiculous, but it was a great popular success. The newspapers reported that in the weeks leading up to the first night copies of the *Alcestis* could even be seen in punts on the Cherwell, and at the end of the performance there was (according to the *Era*) 'a roar of applause'; moreover 'the booking is quite phenomenal'. There were, however, one or two critics who were more honest about their feelings: F. C. Burnand (author of the ubiquitous *Box and Cox* and founder of the Cambridge ADC) wrote in *Punch* that he had followed the *Alcestis* 'at a more respectful distance than I should an Opera in German', while the reviewer in *Truth* described Mackinnon's production as 'hopelessly disrespectful and inadequate', remarked that his Apollo was like a character from *opéra bouffe*, and alleged that on the first night 'the death scene produced audible merriment'.

Yet at the end of the run there was a surplus of two hundred pounds (Courtney having received his money back), and the OUDS was saved. The Committee was re-formed, and Mackinnon remained in Oxford for several weeks after the *Alcestis* in order to devise some means by which the Society might keep alive between annual productions. He decided that 'a system of smoking concerts' with 'little pieces and sketches' was the answer, and he also arranged for a proper succession of Secretaries to run the OUDS; he decreed that the holder of this office 'should always be an undergraduate'. So the OUDS 'Smokers' began, and proved a great success; at one time, around 1889, they were held every fortnight in the Clarendon Assembly Rooms in Corn-market, and each member was permitted to bring two guests. According to Claud Nugent, then Secretary, this led to recruitment of new

members in large numbers. A leading figure at the Smokers in the late eighties was Paul Rubens of New College, who performed his own comic songs at the piano, and later became a contributor of lyrics and music to West End operettas. He also wrote music for Cambridge Footlights shows between 1897 and 1907 (one of his brothers was at Cambridge), thus providing the first link between the OUDS and the celebrated Cambridge club, which was founded a year before the OUDS was constituted.

The OUDS was back on its feet again, but it still leant heavily on Mackinnon when the annual New Theatre production came round, and he continued to 'stage-manage' for another eight years. The choice of play seems to have been chiefly his, and the productions were ploddingly realistic. In 1888 he staged *The Merry Wives of Windsor*; in 1889 came *Julius Caesar* (Stewart Dawson, an Oxford graduate and old Shooting Star who now worked at the Haymarket in London, was the nominal 'stage-manager', but he worked from Mackinnon's plans); and *King John*, *The Two Gentlemen of Verona*, *The Tempest*, and *The Merchant of Venice* (again) followed in 1891, 1893, 1894, and 1895 respectively. There was some originality in the choice of plays, the policy of choosing rarely performed works still predominating, but nothing to surprise audiences in the performances themselves. Scenery was invariably heavyweight; for *The Merry Wives* Mackinnon had a Windsor Forest set 'with three cascades of real water, shrubs, etc., and the stage broken up into rocky plateaux of different elevations, with Herne's oak overshadowing the whole'. For *Julius Caesar* he commissioned designs from the fashionable and vapid painter Lawrence Alma-Tadema, and the result was a group of gigantic column-bases which dwarfed the actors. At other times the back-drops, front-cloths, and all the other appurtenances without which no play could then be performed were left in the hands of the New Theatre's own scene painter, or were bought from scenic artists in London; there was no question of undergraduates contributing to the design of the productions. Music was usually plentiful; for the *Alcestis* Mackinnon commissioned a score from C. H. Lloyd, the organist of Christ Church, while on other occasions Lionel Monckton came down to Oxford to conduct incidental pieces between the acts. At *King John* 'the great feature of the performance was Lady Radnor's band of ladies, who played all the incidental music' (the Countess of Radnor, an indefatigable amateur of the arts, had organized an all-female string

band). Sometimes all this was too much for the critics; one reviewer complained of bits of mangled Haydn and Beethoven filling the scene-change after the murder of Julius Caesar, and there was a huge roar of laughter in *King John* when Mackinnon, playing the Bastard, entered after Lady Radnor's female fiddlers had trilled away for several minutes and declaimed the line: 'Mad world! Mad kings! Mad composition!'

On two occasions during the later part of Mackinnon's regime the OUDS departed again from its diet of Shakespeare. In 1889, at a time when there was some revival of interest in Marlowe's plays, Mackinnon and Courtney thought it would be worth attempting *The Jew of Malta*, and permission was obtained from the Vice-Chancellor—though Courtney went through Marlowe's text revising it 'in such a manner as not to offend the moral sensibilities of an Oxford public'. But this emasculated *Jew* never saw the stage, for a few months later Robert Browning died, and Mackinnon decided that the OUDS should put on one of his plays. He chose *Strafford*, a heavyweight historical piece which had been commissioned by Macready in 1837 and performed then with notable lack of success—and never again. Mackinnon staged it in February 1890, and the performance was unmemorable. The other non-Shakespearian play in this period was the *Frogs* of Aristophanes, performed in 1892, and this was at least a success with the groundlings, Mackinnon throwing authenticity to the winds and staging it as a piece of broad comedy; the *Oxford Magazine* remarked that 'it might almost have been Gilbert and Sullivan', and reported that the rowing scene on the Styx had 'all the manner of the coach and the freshman out "tubbing"'.

The *Frogs* played to packed houses, but most OUDS productions at this period were rather sparsely attended, at least at the beginning of the week's run; it was the custom among undergraduates not to buy tickets until reports on the first night had been circulated. Perhaps Mackinnon would have had fuller houses if he had been more adventurous in casting; in fact he was ultra-cautious, giving the major parts to the same people year after year, often taking an important role himself, and filling up the minor parts with Christ Church athletes who had no serious interest in acting. There was little chance for a freshman to get a plum part on the strength of an audition, and so quickly make a name for himself; instead, the Society was in the hands of a small clique, few of whom were even undergraduates. For example John

Galsworthy, who was at New College from 1886, appeared as a 'super' in *The Merry Wives of Windsor*, but does not seem to have had his interest in the theatre kindled in any way by the OUDS; he took no further part in their productions, and it was not until many years later that he began to write plays. The only new name of any note to appear during the 1880s and 1890s did so not really on the strength of his own talent but because of his father's reputation.

Henry Brodribb Irving, elder of the two sons of Henry Irving, came up to New College to read Modern History at Michaelmas 1888, and at first made a poor impression. He chose to sport a white bowler or 'billycock' hat, which would have been tolerated in the case of an established eccentric but seemed to be a piece of 'side' or showing-off in a freshman. 'He and his hat became victims first of passive ridicule and then of physical assault,' writes his son Laurence Irving, observing that the hat was 'perched above a pair of penetrating eyes and a grave judicial countenance that intimated six months without the option of a fine'. Harry Irving (as he was then known) was not at all on close terms with his father, from whom his mother had separated soon after his birth, bringing up Harry and his brother Laurence in rigid independence from the great actor. But Harry could not help looking like the man who had taken the English stage by storm, and he had inherited a passion for acting. He soon joined the OUDS, and was hoping for a good part in *Julius Caesar*. He got Decius Brutus, little more than a walk-on, which disappointed him bitterly; but as usual the big parts were going to the old-stagers—A. H. E. Grahame, the then Secretary, was to be Caesar; W. J. Morris, a Jesus College MA and an old Philothespian, was cast as Mark Antony; Holman Clark came back to Oxford to undertake Cassius; while Arthur Bourchier inevitably was Brutus.

In fact Irving need not have fretted. On the first night he got a round of applause on his entrance (at which he was visibly taken aback), and the critics, who by now were all too used to Bourchier and his friends, eagerly turned their attention to the newcomer. Decius Brutus got almost more column-inches in the London papers than Caesar, Brutus, and Mark Antony together. Moreover an envoy from Lily Langtry visited Harry Irving backstage, offering him Orlando in her forthcoming *As You Like It* at the St James's Theatre. Irving declined, being 'increasingly absorbed in his work'. He seems to have been advised by W. L. Courtney, his mentor at New College, to keep away

from the professional stage at least until he had taken his degree. Ironically Courtney himself was soon lured away from Oxford to the *Daily Telegraph*, as literary editor—'almost the first defection of the Oxford don to Fleet Street', observes Laurence Irving, Harry's son. Courtney subsequently had a successful career as a critic and publisher.

This seems to have been the second instance of talent-spotting among the OUDS; a year earlier Beerbohm Tree had come down to watch *The Merry Wives of Windsor* 'with a view to testing the piece for future representation' (the play was then rarely performed), and he 'offered an engagement on the spot' to E. F. Nugent, who was playing Slender. No theatrical career materialized for Nugent, but clearly Harry Irving would continue to attract a lot of attention, so after *Julius Caesar* he was quickly upgraded by the OUDS and given the title roles in *Strafford* and *King John*. He undertook them conscientiously, and seems to have been an adequate Strafford, though as King John (according to his son) he 'lacked the technique to realize the subtle characterization he attempted'. In fact by the time of *King John* the novelty of his presence in the OUDS had worn off for the critics, and it had to be admitted that as yet his acting was simply a pale carbon-copy of his father's. The Henry Irving style, indeed, dominated the OUDS during these years; one reviewer was amused by this in *Julius Caesar*, and wrote: 'Whether it is that Irvingism is infectious or that Mr Irving is wilfully imitated at Oxford, the comic idea suggests itself at the crisis of the play that an Irving was being killed by a dozen other Irvings.'

Harry Irving left Oxford in the summer of 1891 and worked briefly and unsuccessfully in the professional theatre before turning to the law; he read for the Bar, and it was not until he had completed this that, in 1894, he joined Ben Greet's company and, as 'H. B. Irving', began to make a name for himself as an actor. It was in the Greet company that he met another ex-OUDS performer, Dorothea Baird, who became his wife. She had played Iris in the OUDS *Tempest* in 1894; at that time she was an assistant matron at Lynam's preparatory school in Oxford (later the Dragon School), and her success in a number of Oxford amateur theatrical performances led her to become a professional actress. She was the original Trilby in du Maurier's play in 1896, opposite Beerbohm Tree as Svengali, and this made her a national figure for a few years. She was also the first Mrs Darling in *Peter Pan* at the Duke of York's in 1904.

By the mid-1890s most of the OUDS 'star' actors who had earned attention in the productions during the first decade had gone. Arthur Bourchier went on the professional stage in September 1889, appearing with Lily Langtry as Jaques in the *As You Like It* for which Irving had been offered Orlando. By 1900 he was actor-manager in residence at the Garrick in London, and he later took over the Strand Theatre. Sir John Gielgud remembers seeing him during his own boyhood, 'acting in several undistinguished plays. I even managed as a young actor to get to see him personally about a part he was casting (which I failed to get) and was chiefly struck by the luxurious flat, which he also used as an office, at the top of the Strand Theatre.' Gielgud describes Bourchier's acting style as 'coarse'. Another of the original OUDS stars, Holman Clark, began a successful professional career with Ben Greet in 1891. With them and Harry Irving gone, there was no one outstanding.

Nigel Playfair came up to University College and soon joined the OUDS, appearing with Paul Rubens as the Mad Hatter and the March Hare in *Alice in Wonderland* in Worcester College gardens in June 1895—apparently the first OUDS open-air show. Playfair himself organized the production, and engaged Rosina Filippi as producer, but was told by the Vice-Chancellor that since it had not been officially permitted no money could be taken. The problem was solved by charging nothing for admission, but a fee for *going out*—'most suitable to a production of *Alice*', observed Playfair. C. L. Dodgson, Lewis Carroll himself, came to rehearsals though 'all we ever saw of him was a shy face peeping out from behind a tree and smiling'. But Playfair, who as an actor-manager in the 1920s was to achieve so much at the Lyric, Hammersmith, made no outstanding contribution to undergraduate theatre. Other familiar names may be glimpsed in the programmes of OUDS shows at this time: a parody of *Julius Caesar*, performed after the OUDS production of it in 1889 and entitled *Julius See-sawcer, or a Storm in a Tea-cup*, was written by Arthur Waugh of New College, father of Evelyn and Alec; and R. N. Dundas, later to become a famously (or notoriously) eccentric Christ Church tutor, was Nym in the 1888 *Merry Wives*. But there were no great discoveries of new talent, no remarkable achievements.

The undergraduate magazine *Isis* remarked sourly of *The Two Gentlemen of Verona* in 1893: 'The acting fell considerably below the just standard . . . No ill-timed laudations on the part of a charitably

disposed daily press should deceive the society as to the merit of its attempt.' Similarly the next year, 'The Tempest is raging with forcible feebleness,' complained the Pall Mall Gazette. 'What has Oxford done that it should have eight successive amateur performances of a Shakespearian play inflicted on it?' Sometimes the poor quality of the production was due to misfortune. In February 1890 no fewer than four different people had to undertake the part of Charles I in Strafford. A flu epidemic was raging, and it disposed of the actor officially cast for the part, who collapsed after the third performance. A day or two later the understudy was stricken, so Mackinnon took over the role, but he too was taken ill before the end of the run, so yet another Charles had to be found. But even at more fortunate times something seemed to be wrong with the composition of the OUDS. Its early links with Christ Church had not been severed, and Mackinnon habitually cast many of the smaller parts from that college, still giving them to beefy under-graduates who were scarcely at home on a stage. 'Is it not rather a pity that the OUDS does not draw its recruits from rather a wider range?' asked the Oxford Magazine in February 1889, when Julius Caesar had a cast in which thirteen of the thirty male actors came from Christ Church. 'Everybody knows of capable actors in the 'Varsity who never take part in its performances; and it is hardly possible that a single college, even though that college be the House, can produce a sufficient crop of histrionic talent to monopolize at least half the cast.'

Not surprisingly the Christ Church hearties did not altogether behave themselves on stage. On the last night of Henry IV, Part 1 in 1885 they were 'enterprising enough to rig up an American bar in one of the tents, from which the popping of corks somewhat distracted the principal players'. In King John the curtain went up one night to disclose a group of bishops firing at each other with peashooters. In the audience there was always a fair sprinkling of hearties who had come to laugh at their friends on stage, and they did this constantly, shouting 'ribald encouragement'. C. B. Fry the cricketer (then at Wadham) played the Prince of Morocco in The Merchant of Venice in 1890, and afterwards recalled how he had 'distinguished myself by the style and emphasis with which I remarked "Oh, Hell—what have we here?" On the second night a considerable company of my friends turned up to hear me do this, and they got ready to cheer and laugh, but I was aware of their intentions, and began the speech without the "Oh, Hell", and

scored.' (But according to another member of the cast he did not omit the 'Oh, Hell', and roared it all the louder.) Similarly in *The Two Gentlemen of Verona* (1893) the Honourable Oliver Borthwick as Second Outlaw had to declaim lines about being banished 'For practising to steal away a lady', whereupon 'a voice in the pit called out, "For shame, Oliver!"'

The general standard of behaviour among undergraduate performers and audiences alike was in fact low; Laurence Irving records that when not on the stage many of the actors 'lounged and chattered in the gangways of the auditorium and, between the acts, usurped vacant seats and seemed affronted when these were claimed by their rightful owners'. Of course any mishap on the stage provoked great merriment, and mishaps there were in plenty. In *King John* the entire British and French armies were trapped on stage owing to the accidental removal of a drawbridge, and Harry Irving and W. H. Goschen, who was playing the King of France, 'while both were in chain armour, became in an inexplicable manner fettered to one another by the links of the chain. The apparent brotherly affection had to be maintained through the stormy quarrel scene, and they left the stage like Siamese twins.' Occasionally there were deliberate pranks: in *The Merry Wives* Lady Abingdon, who was playing Anne Page, smuggled into the theatre a chair in her family's possession which 'when sat on promptly enclosed the occupant as in a vice, the only escape being through the pressure of a secret spring'. It was set on the stage, and Bourchier, who was playing Falstaff, unwittingly sat on it. The result was 'imprisonment of Falstaff, terrible language, and ringing down of the curtain in the middle of the scene to extricate him from his sorry plight'—a story that would seem too good to be true were it not for the puzzled reports in several of the newspapers that, 'owing to some mistake, the curtain fell in the middle of a scene, and Falstaff's execrations at this mishap could be heard in the remotest parts of the house'.

The tendency to treat OUDS productions as a laughing matter came, of course, to the notice of those who were still opposed to the performance of drama by undergraduates. Indeed it was possible to attack the OUDS simply on the grounds that it was not good enough; and this is what happened.

In February 1891, during the run of *King John* at the New Theatre, a letter appeared in the *Oxford Magazine*. Rather unusually for those days, the writer did not hide behind a pseudonym but identified himself

as Arthur Chandler, the then Vice-Principal of Brasenose (later Bishop of Bloemfontein).

SIR,—Until recently, intellectual study was regarded as at any rate a minor and optional object of an Academical career. But its survival in even this modest condition is now coming to be looked upon as an anachronism and an anomaly. The Oxford University Dramatic Society is absorbing the scanty hours which had not already been occupied by athletic exercises and philanthropic and literary societies. The University is being transformed into a third-rate histrionic company, in which the pass-man figures as a 'super,' and the honour-man aims at qualifying hereafter as a lesser light of a provincial stage. No objection on the ground of principle can of course be entertained, for principles have long ago been cast to the winds; and the OUDS owed its existence to the patronage of the Senior Proctor and Vice-Chancellor of the day. But, looking at results, we may be justified in asking whether the game is worth the candle. As to the merit of the acting I cannot speak from personal observation, as I have never attended any of the plays and never propose to do so. But I have no hesitation in declaring, both on *a priori* and *a posteriori* grounds, that it is inferior. *A priori*, it may be asserted that the performances *cannot* be good; the time at the disposal of the actor is too short, and their inexperience too great, to admit of a genuine success. And, *a posteriori*, I am informed by trustworthy authorities (by people, that is, who are neither actors nor the female relatives of actors) that in matter of fact they *are not* good, in the sense in which men ordinarily count goodness. Considered as amateur theatricals they are no doubt creditable; but is the great sacrifice of time and expenditure of trouble justified in order to win the qualified admiration which Dr Johnson accorded to the dancing bear?

Your obedient servant,
ARTHUR CHANDLER.

In the same issue of the *Oxford Magazine*, apparently quite without collusion, was printed a letter from someone who, unlike Chandler, had been to OUDS productions; he, too, felt that there was matter for complaint.

DEAR SIR,—I was present at the first performance of *King John* by the Dramatic Society, and I should like to enter a protest through your columns against the behaviour of a section of the audience. We are all worshippers of 'form' at Oxford; yet I can hardly conceive a more disgraceful exhibition of bad taste than what occurred on Wednesday night. During a considerable part of the performance, several men giggled in a perfectly childish manner. There were doubtless many causes of genuine amusement, in the various contretemps, which unfortunately interrupted the smoothness of the play. But there

was no reason why during those passages, which were intended to be tragic, senseless laughter should be indulged in to the annoyance of the performers as much as to the rest of the audience. This want of courtesy was especially noticeable in the scene in which Constance deplores her son's fate, in the famous dialogue between Arthur and Hubert, and at the commencement of the closing scene. The laughter was most noticeable in the dress-circle, and its effect was nauseous. Granted that the performance was not up to the level of a Lyceum production, it was an excellent piece of work for an amateur society. To criticise is easy; appreciation is a finer trait. The explosions of laughter which were heard were idiotic; and taking into consideration the fact that several ladies had been kind enough to pake part in the performance, the behaviour of a certain section of the audience was (to state it in the strongest terms) ungentlemanly.

I hear also that there has been little improvement in this respect since the first performance. There are every night some persons—chiefly 'Varsity men—among the audience who persist in mimicking, hissing, and laughing at the efforts of the performers. If these persons are unable to appreciate Shakespeare, or are unwilling to allow any merit to an amateur society, that is no reason why they should annoy the performers and the rest of the spectators by their want of 'form,' and thus bring discredit upon the taste of an Oxford audience.

Yours, &c.,
ERIC.

Surprisingly, the OUDS put up no defence against Chandler. The next issue of the *Oxford Magazine* contained a letter from Harry Irving, but he was concerned only to justify his transposition of certain of the King's lines, which had been criticized by the magazine's reviewer. The only reply to Chandler's blistering attack came from 'H.G.M.', an undergraduate reading Political Economy, who complained that 'the University is being transformed into a third-rate Economic Society', and continued: 'As to the merit of the Lectures I cannot speak from personal observation, as I have never attended any of them and never propose doing so. But . . . *a priori* it may be asserted that they cannot be good . . . and *a posteriori* I am informed by trustworthy authorities . . . that they are *not* good.'

A week later, in the *Oxford Magazine* for 15 February, the issue was taken up again seriously, by a writer who, though sharing some of Chandler's prejudices, was all too well informed about the real state of affairs within the OUDS.

SIR,—Surely 'imitation is the sincerest flattery.' Your correspondent

'H.G.M.' has evidently yet to learn that the employment of the 'tu quoque' argument makes it on *a priori* grounds at least probable that his case cannot be supported by serious evidence, and, after all, the connection between the Political Economy lectures and the OUDS is not quite so obvious as the professedly 'third-rate Economist' would have us suppose.

Until a more adequate defence is produced than that offered last week, the case against the OUDS, so well and clearly put by Mr Chandler, will go by default. I have long felt very strongly on the same point. Like Mr Chandler, I have never yet heard from a non-interested person any praise of the OUDS performances, and the approval of the competent and critical public would, in my opinion, have to be strong indeed to justify their continuance. The verdict of the press too (though I admit this is questionable evidence on either side) is 'comic,' 'dull,' 'rather below the level of ordinary Amateur Theatricals,' &c., and it is a matter of common opinion that most School plays would beat it out of the field.

The reason is not far to seek. With one exception (and that a non-resident graduate pressed into the service), those of the actors of my acquaintance, and they were no small number, were men whom I should have unhesitatingly selected as most likely to make themselves ridiculous rather than serious exponents of the dramatic art. The fact is, I firmly believe there is talent in Oxford capable of producing a first-rate performance, but the majority of good men hold back, for they find other things more important to occupy their time—and in my opinion rightly. Whether our line be μουσική or γυμναστική, or a healthy combination of both, for either kind of παιδεία Oxford offers unique advantages, and the Dramatic Art can in most cases be taken up afterwards. Unlike Plato, I believe the Stage to be an excellent institution both on grounds of κάθαρσις and ἀνάπαυσις, but until the OUDS cease to make us ridiculous in the eyes of the world, I would exclude the Drama 'from this State.' The argument that the Pass-man has time for this sort of thing, even if the Honour-man has not, will not much affect the case, so long as his histrionic ability 'lies under a bushel.'

Surely the reaction against the notion that the function of a University was purely scholastic has reached its climax, when not only healthy bodily exercises, which have their place in the regular development of life, but every distraction which may occupy the 'short intervals' still left for 'reading' is steadily encouraged.

I believe, Sir, with Mr Chandler, that this protest is not too soon.

Yours obediently,

Καιρός.

These criticisms must surely have bitten deep, and it is surprising to see no letter of justification or defence from Mackinnon, Courtney, or

others who had supported the OUDS faithfully since its foundation. The reply to this second attack, when it came, was from a Cambridge man, a London barrister named Raikes, who declared that he had 'carried away a very high opinion of the capabilities of the OUDS' after watching *King John*, and suggested that if the acting was really bad, 'it will in due course cease to attract an audience'. Καιϱός' duly responded in the next issue, reasserting 'that the OUDS, to justify its encroachment on valuable time, must meet with a largely preponderating balance of favourable opinion', and that 'so far from this, it is treated as a huge joke and provokes ridicule alike from friends and outsiders'.

And there the correspondence comes to an end, leaving one with the impression that there were few in Oxford in 1891 who could declare that the OUDS had as yet entirely justified its existence. Its performances were not altogether third-rate, but there was far too much of the second-rate about them.

4

Alf, Doggins, and Others

THE original OUDS club-rooms had been given up soon after the formation of the Society. In 1896, a decade later, the OUDS was sufficiently flourishing socially to feel the need for its own premises again. Philip Comyns Carr, the Secretary of the time (there was still no President), undertook the matter autocratically, finding rooms over a shoe shop in George Street opposite the New Theatre. 'Phil Carr was an enthusiast,' writes Nigel Playfair in his autobiography, 'and also had some of the attributes of a Chancellor of the Exchequer, for he took a lease of premises in George Street, furnished them with considerable luxury, and left future generations of undergraduates to deal with the sordid question of payment.' In fact the OUDS club-rooms, like so many undergraduate institutions of their day, survived largely on the perennial credit extended by patient Oxford tradesmen to the University.

The club-rooms brought the usual problems, and such minute-books as survive record instances of drunken 'rags', when members would bring inebriated friends and smash up the furniture. Perhaps more seriously, the revival of the 'club' aspect of the OUDS increased the social exclusiveness of its character. It was necessary to be 'put up' for election before an undergraduate could become a member, and this entailed being known to at least one or two of the smart set who dominated the Society. Once in, the OUDS member was the privileged inhabitant of a world which had more about it of Pall Mall than George Street. There was a dining-room, which soon acquired the reputation (according to *Isis*) of 'the most patronized cuisine in Oxford'. Indeed the *cognoscenti* could make interesting comparisons between the Oxford clubs: Vincent's, the Gridiron, the Bullingdon, and the OUDS. Compton Mackenzie, who while an undergraduate in the early 1900s belonged to all of them, does just this in his novel *Sinister Street* (1913); his hero Michael Fane judges Vincent's to be too

much devoted to 'muscular supremacy', calls the Grid 'normal', and the Bullingdon 'delightful', but seems uncertain about the precise nature and function of the OUDS.

The OUDS was at the opposite pole from Vincent's and if it did not offend by its reactionary encouragement of a supreme but discredited spirit, it offended even more by fostering a premature worldliness. For an Oxford club to take in *The Stage* and *The Era* was merely an exotic heresy. On the walls of its very ugly room the pictures of actors that in Garrick Street would have possessed a romantic dignity produced an effect of strain, a proclamation of mountebank-worship that differed only in degree from the photographs of actresses on the mantelpiece of a second-rate room in a second-rate college. The frequenters of the OUDS were always very definitely Oxford undergraduates, but they lacked the serenity of Oxford, and seemed already to have planted a foot in London. The big modern room over the big cheap shop was a restless place, and its pretentiousness and modernity were tinged with Thespianism. Scarcely ever did the Academic Muse enter the OUDS, Michael thought. She must greatly dislike Thespianism with all that it connoted of mildewed statuary in an English garden. Yet it would be possible to transmute the OUDS, he dreamed. It had the advantage of a limited membership. It might easily become a grove where Apollo and Athene could converse without quarrelling. Therefore he could continue to frequent its halls.

If, as Mackenzie suggests, the OUDS in the years before the First World War was largely devoted to getting its members into the professional theatre, it appears to have gone about it with a striking inefficiency. Even given that this was a poor, uncertain era for the English stage in general, with the old actor-manager traditions lingering painfully in the wake of the Victorian age and giving way only unwillingly to the reign of the producer, things were notably bad at Oxford. A few OUDS members entered the profession—Frank Stevens of Keble, who became an actor and pageant organizer as 'Frank Lascelles', and Charles Croker-King of Lincoln, later a successful film actor. One or two others made names in theatrical management, drama teaching, or production. But many young men who came up to Oxford with ambitions for the stage must have had their interest dulled by the shabby, ill-rehearsed productions that typified the Society from the 1890s almost until the First World War.

Part of the trouble was, of course, the University's insistence that Shakespeare be the main item in the OUDS diet, varied occasionally

with a Greek play but nothing else. There were attempts to get the rule waived, but they met with little success. In 1897 Philip Comyns Carr decided he wanted to mark the Diamond Jubilee by producing a double bill, Milton's masque *Comus* and the *Knights* of Aristophanes (in Greek). The *Knights* was judged acceptable, but there were plenty of pedants in the audience to point out the mistakes in pronunciation: one donnish reviewer gleefully declared that there were precisely one hundred and thirty-one errors. Permission to perform *Comus* was refused altogether, presumably because the masque deals with the attempts of a pagan godling to lure a lady out of her chastity. *The Taming of the Shrew* had to be substituted, performed on alternate nights with the Aristophanes; Carr himself doubled as Petruchio and producer, and the results were unmemorable. The *Oxford Magazine*, though usually far more conservative than the undergraduate *Isis*, was moved on this occasion to mock the Vice-Chancellor's ban on *Comus*, printing this dramatic fragment in the issue for 17 February 1897.

COMUS AND COMEDY: A MASK.

Dramatis Personae:—

W. SHAKESPEARE.   J. MILTON.   ARISTOPHANES.

Shakespeare. Knowest thou, Master Aristophanes, that thou art become a moral man and virtuous in thine old age?

Aristoph. Say not so, William, if thou lovest me.

S. But thou art: the thing is past contention. Hast not heard what has befallen thy loose comedies in the University of Oxon?

A. May I be expurgated, if I can tell.

S. They are adjudg'd by the Vice-Chancellor, the Doctors, and the Proctors, to be a proper exercise for the instruction and pastime of youth: marry, thou art translated: wert thou but alive, I trow they would make of thee a Bampton lecturer. These grave and reverend signiors have decreed that Master Milton the Puritan his mask of *Comus* is like moral philosophy, unfit to be heard by young men: and they have put thy play of *The Knights* in its place.

Enter MILTON, *agitated.*

Milton. These be strange matters, my masters, that I hear of in Oxon. What advantage is it to be a man over it is to be a boy at school, if serious and elaborat writings must not be utter'd without the cursory eyes of a temporizing and extemporizing Vice-Chancellor? if I must carry all my expence of Palladian oyl to the hasty view of an unleisur'd Licenser? and then not be licens'd when all is done, but be posthabited to mummeries of Cleons, and Falstaffs, and Petruchios, and pagan mysteries and conceits?

S. We have been deceived in thee, John. Methought thou wert a man of virtuous discourse, that tended to edification: yet now (for I must abide in the judgement of the learned) thou art seen to be of a scurril tongue, and over light-minded for the hearing of academick youth. Alas, alas!

M. Have you not then, Aristophanes! written plays which I have justly called 'books of grossest infamy' in my *Areopagitica*? (a treatise which I would commend to the Doctors of Oxon). Have you not us'd the stage to make a mock of your own gods (whom, though they were but demons, you might well have spared), and to arouse that laughter which is like to the crackling of thorns under a pot?

A. I have: but I have not been condemned by the University of Oxford.

M. And have you not, Master Shakespeare! offended all eyes and ears polite with the villainous conversation of an old fat man, looking on the wine when it is red even to drunkenness, and doing other shameful deeds whereof I would not even make mention?

S. Ay, marry: but I have not been condemned by the University of Oxford.—O, Master Milton! I fear me that thou art but little fit to be a *censor morum*. To think that all these years thou hast been no better than a naughty knave, and we knew it not! Yet mayest thou perhaps repent: forswear sack, John, and live cleanly: get thee to a—a monastery, John: go, go! . . . . . . O, Aristophanes, these Puritans!

For the 1897 *Taming of the Shrew* the costumes were lent to the OUDS, as often at this period, by Sir Henry Irving, whose Lyceum was the National Theatre of its day. On this occasion A. N. Tayler, who later worked with Nigel Playfair at the Lyric, Hammersmith, was the hapless OUDS member sent off to collect them. He recalled the experience all too vividly.

I duly presented myself at the stage-door of the Lyceum Theatre. I was ushered into the presence of the great man, who was then made up to resemble a Napoleon of Titanic proportions.

'Oxford,' I murmured.

'Eh, what?' he exclaimed, staring at me absently. 'What about Oxford?'

For a moment I felt as if the whole honour and credit of the University, from the Chancellor downwards, rested on my humble shoulders, instead of an insignificant coterie of undergraduates with histrionic propensities. But I pulled myself together and reminded Napoleon of his promise, and was duly authorized by him to take what I wanted from the Lyceum wardrobe. I got these finally packed into four baskets, and then the question arose, How was I to get them to Paddington? It was suggested that I should take them in a four-wheeler, but when they were piled upon the pavement my pride shrunk from

sitting amongst what was obviously four baskets of dirty linen. Besides, when they were got into the cab, there was no room for me. A crowd—the inevitable crowd—collected and stung me with facetious remarks. The suggestion that I was paying my annual visit to my washerwoman was accepted, of course, as an explanation of my presence there in the heart of the London traffic with four ponderous baskets. It was proposed that the difficulty might be solved if I were to get inside one of the baskets. I indignantly repudiated the idea. 'Put the cabby in, then, and drive yourself!' fared no better. Another waggish individual, inspired by Dan Leno, suggested my engaging two cabs, putting two baskets in each and 'running between'. The result was I did engage two cabs, seating myself in one, the baskets in the other, and at length took the train to Oxford with my precious cargo. But I was not going to run the gauntlet of Oxford in the daytime. As I deposited the baskets in the cloak-room and the attendant demanded sixpence apiece for them, I could not deny myself the pleasure of explaining their contents. I feared that he, too, might fancy they were dirty linen. I therefore mentioned, with a fine, careless dignity, that they held theatrical costumes. His face altered. 'Oh, theatrical?' he said. 'Why didn't you say so? That'll be fourpence the lot.' With that he handed me eight coppers, while I, with pride humbled and with a mien far from 'theatrical', stole out of the station and got back to my college.

I have only to add that I did not personally convoy those four disreputable baskets either to the theatre or back to London.

Philip Comyns Carr was one of the very few OUDS members before the First World War to produce plays himself. For most years between 1896 and 1914 the staging was in the hands of George R. Foss, who succeeded Alan Mackinnon as the Society's regular producer. Foss, who was in his late thirties when he began his OUDS stint, was an Old Marlburian who had gone on the stage professionally, working with Ben Greet and other touring actor-managers; by the time he began to assist the OUDS he had already produced in the West End, at the Old Vic, and for the Browning Society. He was obviously keen on working with young actors—he was an instructor at one of the London drama schools—but his OUDS productions did not generally reach a higher standard than Mackinnon's.

Part of the trouble lay in the methods of casting and rehearsal. The allocation of parts was in the hands of the Secretary, without auditions and simply on the basis of that gentleman's judgement. Usually his friends were given the best parts and the rest were handed to whoever happened to be around. When Nigel Playfair came up as a freshman to University College he wrote to the OUDS Secretary, asking to join,

and immediately received a letter back to say that he was cast as Sir Eglamour in *The Two Gentlemen of Verona*, a part to which he thought himself eminently unsuited; but it was 'the only one . . . still vacant'. Nobody in the OUDS had yet set eyes on him.

The producer, then, had no hand in the casting, and the earliest rehearsals were conducted by the Secretary too. And when Foss did turn up and take over rehearsals, the ladies taking the female roles were not at first present. By the 1890s these ladies were usually 'amateur' performers in name only, young women who had set their sights on a professional career and were gaining wide experience with dramatic societies before entering the business. For example Lilian Braithwaite played Anne Page in the 1896 OUDS *Merry Wives of Windsor*, and became a professional actress three years later. Performers such as her were not available for more than a few rehearsals, and George Foss himself would stand in for them. This was described by a correspondent in *Isis*.

In the rehearsals prior to the advent of the ladies . . . Mr Foss plays the female parts. These are his real master-pieces!!! I myself had played Benedick to his Beatrice, and even now my heart throbs when I recall that lily-white hand that so often pressed mine, that slender waist round which my arm passionately clung, and that peach-like cheek which oft reclined on my shoulder, and on which I had pressed a chaste salute! Ah! 'That was love indeed!'

Foss's annual New Theatre productions, like Mackinnon's, were in accord with the dreary stage fashions of the time, with endless changes of heavily painted scenes and incidental music to fill up the many gaps this entailed. Being a hardy annual at the New, Foss was of course on familiar terms with its stage staff; *Isis* describes 'the silvery tones of his mellow voice in supplication to "Alf" and "Electrician", who, it is whispered, are the Gog and Magog of the Theatre'. But Alf did not always serve him well. The 1898 *Romeo and Juliet*, with Frank Stevens and Lilian Collen in the leads, was marred by 'various ludicrous hitches in the raising and lowering of the scenes'. The occasion seems to have resembled the Marx brothers' *Night at the Opera*: 'Instead of the moonlight Balcony scene, Romeo found himself in the foreground of "the blasted heath" (in *Macbeth*), it taking the stage-manager an unconscionable time to set things right.' The New Theatre stage manager was accustomed to trouble; one OUDS member recorded that he 'had a peculiar and, I take it, fairly expensive habit, when

anything went wrong at rehearsal—not by any means an uncommon experience—of taking off his hat, dashing it on the floor and vigorously stamping on it!' On the last night of one OUDS production the cast, amused by this habit, presented him with 'a positive shop-load of "bowlers" of every conceivable size'.

Alf and his colleagues do not seem to have taken much trouble to sweep their stage. The *Oxford Magazine*, reviewing *Romeo and Juliet*, passed over 'the little accident with the scenery' as something that 'might happen to any one', but could not help observing that 'the dance in the first act . . . took place in a cloud of dust, raised by the busy feet of the dancers . . . As the dance proceeded the dust grew denser, until it screened the performers from the house as by a curtain.' Things were no better two years later, during the 1900 *Twelfth Night*; the reviewer in *Isis* wrote: 'It is a pity that the stage authorities think fit to bury the orchestra under a cloud of dust every time the curtain falls.'

Foss's production of *Romeo* restored Shakespeare's original ending, which was still something of a rarity (it had long been the custom to tinker with the text and provide a happy conclusion), and the general verdict was that this was 'thoroughly justified'. But otherwise there was little to be said in favour of the performance. 'On the humours of "Friar Lawrence",' wrote the *Oxford Magazine*, 'with his total inability to speak blank verse, and of poor "Paris", who never appeared to know what to do with his hands and feet, or why he was on the stage at all, it would be unkind to dwell, but the "Apothecary" was surely an unnecessarily ludicrous figure, while the "Prince" . . . irresistibly provoked a spirit of levity in the audience. If it be the function of the theatre to evoke laughter and tears, the performance of *Romeo and Juliet* must be held to have ably fulfilled that function.'

Romeo was a low-water mark, and nothing else produced by Foss was 'panned' so universally, but it is fairly obvious even from the bland praises churned out by most reviewers that during this period the annual OUDS Shakespeare was something to be endured by the audience rather than enjoyed. The function of the Society was chiefly to provide the University with a supply of popular heroes, who (like their opposite numbers in the sporting clubs and at the Oxford Union) were made the subjects of pen-portraits in *Isis*, under the heading 'Isis Idol'. These rarely gave any real picture of the character and attainments of the actor in question; a typical piece, about Charles Croker-King (Slender in the 1896 *Merry Wives*), remarks: 'There are some

who say he is conceited . . . We can say without hesitation that it is utterly untrue, and, that what strikes some persons as egotism is merely the result of a keenness to please and anxiety to know whether he has done so.' Actresses who took part in OUDS shows were sometimes idolized in *Isis* too; of Dorothea Baird the paper wrote: 'If you want an autograph, send her a tin of Three Castles tobacco (from which in "Trilby" she makes *her own* cigarettes).' The Senior Members were objects of interest as well; W. J. Morris, the Jesus College don who had been a Philothespian in the 1880s and gave the OUDS his support up to the First World War, was described as 'so versatile, so broad-minded, so handsome, so original . . . He looks like some "star" —some "legitimate drama" star—of the stage.' Morris, who affected the dress and manner of an old-style tragedian, was undoubtedly a Frank Benson *manqué.*

Succeeding generations of OUDS actors were featured in *Isis.* Among them was Harry Moncreiff Tennent of Wadham, who played Demetrius in the 1899 *Midsummer Night's Dream,* Aguecheek in the 1900 *Twelfth Night,* and Benedick in the 1901 *Much Ado,* as well as becoming Secretary of the OUDS and producing *Twelfth Night* in Worcester College gardens in May 1902—the first time that this outstanding setting was used for an OUDS Shakespeare. As H. M. Tennent he afterwards founded the famous West End production company. *Isis* called him 'a prodigy of energy and keenness', and mentioned 'the abnormal length of his legs' which served him well as Aguecheek. On leaving Oxford he went first into the music business and made quite a success as a songwriter—he had been a familiar figure at the piano at OUDS Smokers—and during 1908, 1909, and 1910 he assembled several old OUDS members, as well as other professional and amateur actors, and took them on a 'pastoral play tour' around the public schools, doing *Twelfth Night* and *As You Like It.* Among them was Freddie Grisewood, many years later to become famous as chairman of the BBC's *Any Questions* but then a Magdalen undergraduate noted for his singing. In his autobiography Grisewood recalled the opening of *Twelfth Night* in Oxford before it left for its tour—in fact back in Worcester College gardens. It was

a perfect summer night, soft and warm as velvet . . . Our music was supplied by a hidden orchestra, and during our evening shows our natural stage was lit by concealed limelights, which gave an entrancing effect of bright moonlight. Worcester gardens were ideal for our purpose, and I remember how thrilled I

was when our orchestra started up, then faded away into silence and Jack Gilliatt, looking really magnificent, as the Duke, began, 'If music be the food of love . . . play on . . .' then on my entry, hearing my voice echoing through the warm night in 'Come away, death', and seeing in the shadows outside the circle of our moonlit stage, the vague and nebulous figures of our audience.

Tennent had discovered something of the formula which Nevill Coghill was to use with such effect in his celebrated 1949 *Tempest*.

Sir Toby Belch in the 1902 outdoor *Twelfth Night* was Compton Mackenzie, then at Magdalen. The son of the actor-manager Edward Compton and the brother of Fay Compton (who adopted her father's professional surname), Compton Mackenzie was soaked in the theatre from his earliest years, and devoted a great deal of his prodigious energy to the OUDS while he was an undergraduate. He was the subject of an 'Isis Idol' portrait, which mentioned his appearances as Sir Toby, as the Duke of Milan in George Foss's 1902 New Theatre production of *The Two Gentlemen of Verona*, and as Gratiano in the 1903 *Merchant of Venice* (again Foss, at the New Theatre), and described his 'precipitous hair, keen and vivid features, yellow tie, green shirt and conspicuous attire'. By this time—February 1904—he was Business Manager of the OUDS (a fairly new post on the Committee), and also had a reputation as a prolific writer; *Isis* remarked: 'It is said that the British Museum is enlarging its accommodation for new books in anticipation.'

Mackenzie's final OUDS appearance was as Phidippides in the *Clouds* of Aristophanes, which was performed (instead of the annual Shakespeare) at the New Theatre in March 1905, in an English verse translation by Cyril Bailey and A. D. Godley. Bailey, a Balliol classics don, became a senior member of the OUDS around this time, and contributed an enormous amount to the Society; Godley, who taught at Magdalen, wrote comic verse for the *Oxford Magazine* and had several collections of it published. His and Bailey's witty *Clouds* had music by Sir Hubert Parry, and was one of the more successful OUDS productions in the early 1900s. The year after came another low ebb, *Measure for Measure* produced by Foss at the New Theatre and bowdlerized until it was virtually meaningless. North Oxford shrieked in alarm at the prospect of Angelo's attempt upon Isabella's virtue being depicted by undergraduates and actresses; there were 'letters to the local and even to the metropolitan press', and also a 'suggested boycott of the performance as indecent'. But Foss prepared an acting

version 'as seemly as the motive of the plot allows', depicting Angelo as 'one whose acts had hitherto matched his professions' and whose advances to Isabella were but a momentary lapse from virtue. This 'did much to exalt the character of the play', but most reviewers felt the whole thing had been an utter mistake.

Vague rumblings against the OUDS could be heard now and then. In 1904 a rival dramatic club appeared in the University, under the title 'The Olympians', and as well as mounting several productions it published a magazine which included a satire on the OUDS, based on 'The Walrus and the Carpenter':

> 'If seven scouts with seven boys
> Washed at the OUDS all night,
> Do you suppose,' the Squire said,
> 'That they could get them white?'
> 'I doubt it,' said the Sileger,
> 'Their day has gone by—quite.'

The Olympians, perhaps intending to show the OUDS how stuffy their style of production had become, invited Beerbohm Tree down to Oxford in March 1905 to give a *Hamlet* in the Town Hall that had no scenery and was adorned only with black drapes. But a few terms later this rival organization faded away.

Around this time the OUDS took to using fully professional actresses for the leading female parts, which did a little towards raising the standard of performance. Lilian Braithwaite seems to have been the first—she returned to Oxford in 1900 to play Viola in *Twelfth Night*. In 1907 Lily Brayton, wife of actor-dramatist Oscar Asche, played Katharina in Foss's production of *The Taming of the Shrew*, this being a part she had often performed opposite her husband in the West End. But some greater change than this was necessary to rescue the OUDS from its sorry artistic plight.

Another Greek play was performed in February 1909, this time the *Frogs* of Aristophanes in the original Greek, with Cyril Bailey producing. Freddie Grisewood was leader of a chorus whose members included 'A. C. Boult (Ch. Ch.)'—the future Sir Adrian Boult. Grisewood had got the part on his vocal ability rather than his knowledge of Greek, which was almost non-existent, and recalled in his autobiography (published nearly half a century later) that to learn it 'entailed such an effort that to this day it still remains with me and I can

sing almost all of it'. He made such a good job of it that Sir Hubert Parry, who was in charge of the music once again, told him he should become a professional singer—which eventually led (somewhat tortuously) to Grisewood's joining the BBC as an announcer. But few other people got much out of this 1909 *Frogs*. Bailey's production was neither in the authentic classical style nor genuinely entertaining. *Isis* remarked that 'the novelty of hearing Greek spoken wears off after ten minutes', and muttered about the 'hypocrisy and pedantry' which inflicted Greek plays on an undergraduate audience.

The fortunes of the OUDS were therefore still low when the twenty-fifth anniversary of its foundation was celebrated during the winter of 1909–10. In November 1909 Arthur Bourchier, together with Holman Clark, Gilbert Coleridge, Mackinnon, and other founder-members, organized a public reading of *Henry IV, Part 1* for old OUDS performers at the Aeolian Hall in London, and the twenty-fifth anniversary production the following February was *The Tempest*, staged by Foss at the New Theatre. Though the show was of Foss's usual low standard—the *Oxford Magazine* complained of the severe cutting of the text to make way for heavyweight pageantry, and of many small departures from Shakespeare's words—this production was notable for the first appearance of someone who was to play a vital part in the regeneration both of the OUDS and of British professional theatre, William Bridges-Adams. He was to become the director of the first resident company at the Memorial Theatre, Stratford-upon-Avon, after the First World War; Sally Beauman in her history of the Royal Shakespeare Company calls him 'that child of the new age, the producer or director', and points out how very far he was from being 'an actor-manager in the Benson mould'.

Bridges-Adams came up to Oxford from a 'progressive' education at Bedales, and took two major OUDS roles, Prospero in the 1910 *Tempest* and Leontes in *The Winter's Tale* in 1911. Prospero was really too much for him, considering his youth and his slight, shadowy appearance (he might have been better cast as Ariel), but he earned high praise as Leontes. He was to return to Oxford as a producer for OUDS after the war, when he did much to raise the Society's standards.

The part of Antigonus in *The Winter's Tale* was taken by Geoffrey Faber of Christ Church, the future founder of the publishers Faber & Faber, and according to *Isis* he 'made a most effective exit pursued by a

bear-skin'. He was Cassius in the 1912 production, *Julius Caesar*, in which the historian Philip Guedalla, then President of the Oxford Union and reading classics at Balliol, played Mark Antony. Faber's Cassius was judged by *Isis* to be the 'outstanding achievement' of the production; Guedalla's acting was described as 'original, careful, and at times exciting', but it was doubted whether the part really suited him. Foss was once again the producer but Bridges-Adams had been given the task of directing the crowds, and *Isis* commmented on his having achieved 'an atmosphere of keenness and reality such as has seldom been found within the walls of a theatre'.

Adrian Boult soon progressed from being a mere member of the chorus to conducting the music for several OUDS productions. His band was too loud on the first night of the 1910 *Tempest*; it was observed in *Isis* that Bridges-Adams as Prospero 'came off badly in his occasional contests with the Orchestra; but no doubt this will be rectified by "his own bolt", as Prospero calls him'. A few months later Boult sang Don Fernando in a production of Beethoven's *Fidelio* at the New Theatre, with Dr H. P. Allen of New College (later Sir Hugh Allen, founder of the Oxford Bach Choir and Principal of the Royal College of Music) conducting in the pit. A year later the same company, with Rosina Filippi producing, staged Weber's *Der Freischütz* with Boult as Zamiel. But while these enterprising experiments were paving the way for the Oxford University Opera Club, the OUDS remained fettered to its routine. 'We have had doubts at times whether these productions of Shakespeare in Oxford are really worth it,' remarked *Isis* in 1910; 'they challenge inevitable comparisons with . . . enterprises in London.' Yet the Vice-Chancellor's permission still had to be sought for any departure from the annual Shakespeare. In 1912 when the Society wanted to stage Greene's *Friar Bacon and Friar Bungay*, permission was only given on condition that Greene's text was changed 'to avoid some too topical allusions' (topical, one supposes, to the sixteenth century rather than the twentieth), and when no agreement could be reached Dekker's *Shoemaker's Holiday* was chosen instead, and performed in February 1913. C. K. Allen of New College—later Sir Carleton Allen, for many years Warden of Rhodes House—played the Shoemaker and was the producer. He managed to achieve a general standard of acting well above that of Foss's Shakespearian productions; the *Isis* reviewer considered it 'of a remarkably high level, much higher, I am inclined to think, than has been attained in the OUDS for many years'. This

upward turn in the Society's fortunes was maintained a year later when Cyril Bailey's third Greek production, the *Acharnians* of Aristophanes, was judged 'hugely entertaining' by *Isis*, even though it was in the original Greek; Bailey treated it as burlesque, and revived an old Oxford custom when he cast male undergraduates in all the female parts.

In the event this *Acharnians* provided a rousing finish for the OUDS before its activities were brought to a halt by the outbreak of war, and it was Cyril Bailey himself who had the task of informing the remaining Committee members at the beginning of Michaelmas Term 1914 that 'the Club . . . had been *permanently closed* for the duration of the war'. At first an attempt was made to keep the OUDS alive but comatose; Freeman, Hardy & Willis, owners of the shoe-shop over which the club-rooms were situated, agreed to accept half rent (£100 per annum), and a letter was sent to members past and present asking for subscriptions or donations to help retain the premises. Meanwhile the rooms were made available to the Belgian Club, a social group for Belgian refugees in Oxford; the few remaining OUDS members in residence used the Gridiron Club for their social life. There were no productions or dramatic activities of any kind.

By Michaelmas 1916 even the Grid had closed, and though one or two new OUDS members had been elected since 1914, Cyril Bailey judged that it was now 'clearly useless to attempt to continue the activities of the OUDS in any form'. The club-room lease expired, and Bailey (as he afterwards recorded in the minute-book of the Society) 'took on himself the responsibility of selling up the OUDS property', with the exception of the archives. The sale raised over £300 and enabled him to pay the wine bill—'which had been unsettled for the last ten years'.

Promptly after the Armistice the OUDS sprang to life again. No more than half a dozen men who had been members in 1914 returned to Oxford as undergraduates, but in the Lent Term of 1919 they formed a committee of management. At first they resolved high-mindedly (in the minutes) that the OUDS 'should devote itself to the study of dramatic art more consciously and enthusiastically, perhaps, than in the past; while the annual production of a play should be considered, as in past years, the main motive of its existence'. P. H. B. Lyon of Oriel, a future Headmaster of Rugby, was elected the first post-war President, and during his brief term of office it was resolved

'that the Club be restarted at once as a Dramatic Society, but not as a dining and social club with club premises'. These good resolutions were kept only briefly. During the following months, at meetings held in members' college rooms, there was a reading of Sheridan's *The Critic* and of Browning's *Strafford*. But members soon became determined to get the old club-rooms back, and the first public dramatic performance organized by the Society was a gala matinée at the New Theatre in November 1919 to raise money to furnish them. Arthur Bourchier and Fay Compton appeared in a one-act play about Dr Johnson, and Nigel Playfair and Holman Clark starred in A. A. Milne's recent West End success *Wurzel-Flummery*. Six hundred pounds were raised, but the OUDS could not get their old club-rooms back since Freeman, Hardy & Willis had let them to other tenants. At a committee meeting there was a fierce resolution 'to accelerate the departure of the present tenants' (it was not suggested what form of harassment might be adopted), but other premises opposite the theatre were soon found, and the former Daffodil Tea Rooms were quickly annexed to restore a dining-room to the Society. By the summer term of 1920 the OUDS was again doing a brisk business in dinners, drinks, and the supply of such facilities as telephone calls, headed writing paper, and the delivery of letters within the University (the OUDS had its own messenger). A surviving ledger for 1922 to 1924 records the running-up of considerable bills by many of the members, with such items as 'Supper 2/6, Bass 1/6, 2 Chartreuse 5/6, Telegram 1/–'; debts were as accepted a part of the Oxford way of life after the war as before it.

By the mid 1920s the OUDS was once again a formidable social body, not a little alarming to those Oxford undergraduates whose family background and education placed them apart from the elegant and well-off young men who provided the backbone of the Society. George Emlyn Williams, coming up to Christ Church at Michaelmas 1923 from a poor and semi-literate Welsh family, and propelled to Oxford largely through the benevolent efforts of a local schoolmistress, was warned on arrival that it was as well not to try to rush into the OUDS too quickly. 'Drake-Brockmann . . . asked me to tea in his rooms, crumpets and muffins under covers from the JCR . . . I mentioned the Dramatic Society. "Oh yes, the Ouds," he said, pronouncing it Owds, "rather special, I'm told with that sort it's best to wait till one's second term."' Williams duly delayed, performing in a

French Club play in the hope of getting noticed. The ruse worked: the stage manager was an OUDS member who 'told me he had been cast as First Sailor in the Ouds *Hamlet,* and would I like to be put up for the Club. I tried to welcome the idea without eagerness.' And when finally 'G. E. Williams' (who had not yet contemplated calling himself 'Emlyn' as a stage-name) acquired the right to saunter into the George Street club-rooms, the experience was a challenge as much as an enjoyment. In his first volume of autobiography, Williams recalls how, in the evenings,

after Hall, sick of swotting, I would walk up the Corn past the invisible townees, down George Street, past the toy-shop and up the stairs to the Ouds. In at the swinging door, plonk umbrella, hang gown and scarf, give a weary look at notice-board, glance at letters on the green baize to make sure those bores haven't tracked one down, then saunter into smoking-room. The feel of it was enough to give the form, either there were one or two dominant souls presiding plus-foured on the high shabby-leathered fender, knocking out pipes on the mantelpiece and toasting in liqueurs the closed circle of arm-chairs—'cheers Clive Bobbie Pat Michael'—or it was a dead loss, a couple of dim aspirants like oneself humbly turning the pages of *Variety* to read how many dollars *Abie's Irish Rose* had played to in Mamaroneck. Nothing in between.

On the good nights one did not attempt even a side-seat, one oozed into the back room to lean over *La Vie Parisienne* as if seeking a telephone-number. For one was eavesdropping . . . But eavesdropping was better than nothing. 'Rowley Patsy Monty Chris, benedictine? Peacroft, five, and would you put a call through to the Queen's stage-door, Miss Compton's room?' . . .

Then an aimless walk over to the *Hamlet* photographs, newly framed. Voices were being raised. 'Yes, but stage realism *qua* realism'—'Ah but what about Freud's "Technique of Wit" '—I longed for Noël Coward to breeze in and blow us all away. It was ten-thirty . . . A last blasé look at the letter-board as I gowned and brollied myself . . . and hurried down, anonymous, into the night. Walking, I felt the weariness of the demoralized: of my own free will, I had spent an hour overhearing the prattle of the stage-struck. Did I not even belong in the Ouds?[1]

Not surprisingly, Williams's club-room bill for 1924, his first year in the OUDS, is one of the smallest in the book: one telephone call, one supper, one glass of beer.

And yet the conversations on which he eavesdropped were about

---

[1] Emlyn Williams, *George* (Hamish Hamilton, 1961), pp. 307–8.

stage technique. Alongside the increased sophistication of the club-room life since the war, there was a growing interest in the theatre, and when the annual major productions began to take place once again they were very different in character from those before 1914. The first play chosen was Thomas Hardy's *The Dynasts*, an epic survey of a war (the Napoleonic) which no doubt seemed a suitable subject for those recently returned from the trenches. Certainly it relaunched the OUDS spectacularly at its performances in February 1920, no fewer than a hundred and twenty actors being required for its long series of historical scenes. This was also the first occasion on which the OUDS had performed a work by a living author. It was organized largely by Maurice Colbourne, who had been an Oriel undergraduate in 1914 and returned to Oxford after the war to complete his degree with the determination that 'his first work would be the revival of the Club'. (He afterwards became a professional actor and director, performing for Bridges-Adams at Stratford, and eventually a governor of the Royal Shakespeare Company.) He and his successor as OUDS President, Charles Morgan (Brasenose), arranged for *The Dynasts* to be produced at the New Theatre by A. E. Drinkwater, an old member of Merton who was a professional actor and playwright. The cast was by no means untalented; it included the future film actor Raymond Massey, Canadian born and then at Balliol. But the more candid reviewers acknowledged that *The Dynasts* was scarcely a play, more a series of tableaux vivants. Raymond Massey observes in his autobiography: 'I doubt if the best professional cast in the world could have handled Hardy's leaden verse.' Massey was so put off by this experience of OUDS that he dropped out of it in his second year and organized his own play-reading group in Balliol, which met fortnightly to tackle such stuff as Ibsen and Galsworthy. 'We got more out of our nameless little group than the OUDS ever offered.'

Thomas Hardy attended a performance of *The Dynasts*, and during his Oxford visit was granted an honorary degree. This was due to efforts by Dr H. E. Counsell, an Oxford general medical practitioner who became a supporter of the OUDS on his arrival in the city in 1897. Counsell was not then a graduate of any university, but in the midst of his medical work and bringing up a family he decided to read History at New College, in such little spare time as he could find. This qualified him to join the OUDS, and he was a member from 1910, soon finding himself a role as prompter in the New Theatre productions, and

earning the nickname 'Doggins'—this being the current Oxford slang for 'doctor'. Emlyn Williams described him as 'a loved Oxford figure in cloak and eye-glass who for years had sat in the prompt-corner of Ouds productions happily holding the book, open at the wrong page, dreamily appreciative of all he watched'. Osbert Lancaster writes in his memoirs of 'the venerable and dearly loved Dr Counsell, with his broad-brimmed hat and Inverness cape, who lived in what were generally held to be the Duke of Dorset's old lodgings opposite the Roman Emperors [the stone busts outside the Sheldonian Theatre] . . . whose medical knowledge might not quite have kept pace with the advance of science but who was universally acknowledged to have a magic touch with clap'.

In his own autobiography, *Thirty-Seven the Broad* (1943), named after the address of that house opposite the Emperors, 'Doggins' describes how, during the production of *The Dynasts*, he acted as ambassador from the OUDS to the University authorities, bearing the suggestion that it would be a good idea to give Thomas Hardy an honorary D.Litt. The Vice-Chancellor told him to put his case to Sir Herbert Warren, the President of Magdalen and current Professor of Poetry. Warren was at first rather icy, remarking that Hardy already had an honorary degree from Cambridge, and 'Oxford does not like following in the wake of Cambridge'. Counsell, knowing Oxford's monstrous egotism, suggested that 'greater honours always follow the less', and this gross flattery worked, Hardy duly being given his degree in the Sheldonian before the performance. The OUDS members, however, were not present, being detained by the later courses of 'a colossal lunch at Christ Church'.

If *The Dynasts* sat heavily on most stomachs, the production which followed was altogether lighter fare—*As You Like It* in Wadham gardens, with Nigel Playfair returning to Oxford to produce ('expenses paid' says the minute-book; clearly he and other professional producers for OUDS at this time received no fee). Playfair was now an accomplished professional director, who had stunned Stratford audiences with his avant-garde production of *As You Like It* in 1919—Lovat Fraser costumes, a formalized set, and a brisk treatment of the text quite unlike the old Frank Benson style at Stratford. In June 1920 he repeated it in Oxford, using the Fraser designs and music by Arthur Bliss. Gerald Gardiner (Magdalen), an energetic young man who forty-four years later became Lord Chancellor, played Orlando,

and E. Martin Browne of Christ Church, later to make his name as a religious drama producer particularly associated with T. S. Eliot's plays, took a walk-on part as a servant.

Playfair's *As You Like It* proved to be the first regular OUDS summer production. Early the next year a 'New Charter' was granted to the Society by the Vice-Chancellor, which allowed the performance of a maximum of eight plays in four years—in practice two per annum. Fifty per cent of plays in each four-year cycle were to be by Shakespeare, one must be in Greek, and the remaining three were left to the discretion of the OUDS, 'on condition they were plays of at least thirty years standing'. In fact there were to be only three more obligatory Greek productions, the *Rhesus* of Euripides and the *Clouds* of Aristophanes, produced by Cyril Bailey in 1923 and 1928, and *Oedipus Tyrannus* by Sophocles, performed in 1932; but forty years were to pass before the work of contemporary dramatists found a secure place in the OUDS repertoire.

Shakespeare continued to dominate, his plays often being chosen for both the Lent Term 'major' production at the New Theatre and the summer show in a college garden. Given this sameness of repertoire, it is an indication of how far English theatre had travelled since 1914 that the post-war OUDS Shakespeare productions were invariably vigorous and imaginative.

The OUDS, of course, could call on old members now working in the professional theatre to come back and direct, and the next was William Bridges-Adams, who since the summer of 1919 had been struggling to run, on the slenderest of means, the first resident company at Stratford. Though hideously overworked there—he frequently had to rehearse six or seven plays in five weeks, and was his own set and lighting designer—he somehow found the energy to make three excursions to Oxford during 1921 and 1922 and produce for the OUDS. Bridges-Adams was by no means the most innovative director of his generation; he was not averse to old-style Benson-type acting if it was done well and saved him rehearsal time. But compared to Mackinnon and Foss he was a revolutionary. He came to the text with a fresh eye and a determination to eliminate the clutter of would-be realistic scenery and crude lime-lighting that had characterized the Edwardian stage, and he worked (as far as was possible, given the limitations of his time and budget) to the high standard of Shakespearian production set by Harley Granville-Barker and William

Poel, the pioneers of the new methods of staging. A withdrawn, reserved man, still with the frail look he had had as an undergraduate, he was sympathetic to young amateur performers and was greatly liked by those who worked with him in the OUDS.

His first production for the Society was *Antony and Cleopatra*, staged at the New Theatre in February 1921. The policy of engaging professional actresses for leading roles continued—there were now plenty of women students at Oxford, but the OUDS did not yet invite them to act, remaining all-male in membership—and Bridges-Adams chose as his Cleopatra the thirty-two-year-old Cathleen Nesbitt. She had been on the professional stage since 1910, and would probably have married Rupert Brooke had he survived the war. Though much sought after, she had not attached herself to anyone else. Bridges-Adams could not find a suitable Antony within the ranks of the OUDS, so he turned to the Union, whose President, Cecil Ramage, met the requirements exactly and was immediately pressed into dramatic service. Ramage was twenty-six and had been decorated several times during his war service, from which he emerged with the rank of Captain. He was also strikingly handsome. It soon became apparent to the rest of the OUDS cast that he and Cathleen Nesbitt had fallen in love.

'I very much doubt if such love scenes . . . have ever been performed with more conviction,' wrote another performer in the production, Bruce Belfrage of St John's, later a famous wartime BBC newsreader. 'At rehearsal it was frequently necessary for Bridges-Adams to call time so that we could get on with the job.' The reality of Cleopatra's feelings communicated itself to the audience; the *Isis* reviewer wrote of Cathleen Nesbitt's performance: 'It was not acting, it was just Cleopatra.' And in his curtain speech after an ovation on the last night, Ramage remarked: 'I can't think what I have done to deserve this. My words were supplied by Shakespeare, my movements by Bridges-Adams, and my inspiration by Miss Nesbitt.' Yet according to Cathleen Nesbitt in her own memoirs, 'everybody seemed to have known it before we did ourselves . . . We played well together as lovers on the stage. Off-stage I don't think we had ever met alone. On the last night there was a farewell party and we danced together continually. I think we would have been dancing "cheek to cheek" as the popular song has it, but he was so tall that I could not reach up so far. During the last dance he kissed the top of my head and said: "Will you marry me?" and

I answered: "Yes. Oh! *yes!*"' They met at lunch the next day at the Randolph Hotel, each feeling that the whole thing had been a dream; but they went through with the marriage, despite parental opposition (he was merely a penniless would-be barrister, she was merely an actress) and her admission to such friends as Mrs Patrick Campbell that she was marrying him because he was the first man to fall in love with her who was not otherwise attached. The wedding took place a few months after *Antony and Cleopatra* in a predictable blaze of publicity which left the OUDS in a state of complacency.

Cecil Ramage received several offers from London theatrical managers, but turned them down. Talent-spotting at Oxford was going on as energetically as before the war. Nor was it only for actors; Charles Morgan, President of the OUDS at the time of *Antony and Cleopatra*, invited the *Times* dramatic critic A. B. Walkley to the last-night dinner, and was soon rewarded by getting a job as Walkley's second-string, not long afterwards succeeding him as principal critic—the beginning of a successful journalistic and literary career.

Anyone in search of new theatrical talent would have been well rewarded by a journey to Oxford in the mid 1920s. Bridges-Adams returned to produce a *Twelfth Night* in Wadham gardens in June 1921, and came back the following February for a New Theatre production in which there were several new names of note—Bruce Belfrage, Richard Goolden (New College), and a St John's undergraduate called W. T. Guthrie, who as Tyrone Guthrie soon became one of the leaders of modern English theatre. The choice of play was Ibsen's *The Pretenders*, and did not much please the candid critics; M. R. Ridley writing in *Isis* spoke of the cast gamely 'galvanizing such lethargic material into life'. He observed: 'Mr Guthrie was an impressive skald, though he occasionally used a facial expression which can only be described as a contorted grin.' Guthrie, who was a history scholar, intended to become a singer, and it was because of his music that he first took part in a play at Oxford. By the time of *The Pretenders* he had begun to take some interest in acting for its own sake, and little more than a year later he would find himself committed to a theatrical career.

The OUDS was now settling for nothing less than the best in its choice of professional producers. In June 1922 Barry Jackson, who had founded the Birmingham Repertory Theatre just before the war and was one of the most imaginative and open-minded figures in English theatre, directed Molière's *Le Bourgeois Gentilhomme* in New College

gardens. Gerald Gardiner and Tyrone Guthrie were among the cast, and Jackson, one of whose abilities was to spot outstanding talent in others, asked Guthrie to choreograph the dances. Unfortunately this and other summer productions of the period attracted much less notice than did the more heavyweight February 'major' OUDS shows in the New Theatre, and coming at the end of the summer term they were not usually reviewed in the *Oxford Magazine* and *Isis*, which had closed down for the long vacation.

Though the professionals who assisted in the 1920s were the chief cause of the vigorous and imaginative acting which Oxford audiences were now seeing, William Bridges-Adams, towards the end of his series of OUDS productions, speculated in an interview with *Isis* whether the Society might not soon do without professional help: 'One thing they still have to do, and that is to evolve their own producers . . . I believe and hope that some day the OUDS will be a wholly self-running concern.' Typically, for he was a man of foresight and vision, Bridges-Adams was anticipating what would not happen for more than twenty years. Nevertheless OUDS members were now being encouraged to do much more than just act. The design of sets and lighting was often being put into undergraduate hands, something that would have been inconceivable before 1914, though for reasons of expense the costumes were still usually acquired from some professional source, often the director's 'home' theatre. Make-up was not entrusted to the actors themselves or OUDS helpers, but was left in the charge of the London firm of Clarksons. The celebrated Willy Clarkson, who like his father before him provided wigs, crêpe hair, and false noses for amateur theatricals all over Britain, had been coming down to Oxford with his assistants since long before 1914; it was a favourite sport with the actors in Edwardian Oxford to try and lure 'Clarkson's men' away from their task, and one night Clarkson 'was rushing about all over the place trying to find them, and after about an hour I discovered them in one room, where they had been detained, against their will, by a certain gentleman, who had locked the door and would not release them until they had swallowed two magnums of champagne. Of course you can imagine they were not fit for much during that evening.' By the mid 1920s the Clarksons' representative was a lugubrious person named 'Gus', who told an *Isis* reporter that he 'prefers doing "character" to "straight" make-up. "Pick up lost time on the juveniles" is his motto . . . "I like to keep the young young," he said.'

77

The next professional producer was J. B. Fagan, whose *Henry IV, Part 1* was staged at the New Theatre in February 1923. Fagan had been at Trinity thirty years earlier and had belonged to OUDS, but had taken little part in it as an undergraduate; in 1895 he joined Frank Benson's company, and also acted with Beerbohm Tree before becoming a producer. He was Irish, extremely able, and the ideal person to direct the OUDS. Tyrone Guthrie, a fellow Irishman, described him as 'large and genial, with merry blue eyes and an amusing turned-up nose. He was very good with the young.' Watching him, Guthrie became fascinated for the first time with the way a play could take shape in the hands of a director.

'Undoubtedly their best performance since the war', was the judgement on Fagan's *Henry IV* of the *Isis* reviewer (Hugo Dyson, then reading for a B. Litt. at Exeter College, later to become a notable teacher of Shakespeare at Oxford). Eric Dance of Christ Church, who made quite an impression as the Soothsayer in the 1921 *Antony and Cleopatra*, was the King, and Dyson wrote that the 'centralizing influence was supplied by Mr Dance, for whose acting no praise can be too high'. A romantically handsome eighteen-year-old called Gyles Isham (a baronet's son from Magdalen) played Hotspur ('splendid' wrote Dyson), while 'the comic genius of Mr Goolden found all too little scope in the part of the First Carrier'.

Two months after *Henry IV* Goolden and Gyles Isham both took a prominent part in the first-ever OUDS overseas tour, organized by C. K. Allen, who had produced *The Shoemaker's Holiday* before the war and had now taken Cyril Bailey's place as the most active Senior Member of OUDS. He and his company visited Denmark and Sweden, presenting modern plays forbidden within the confines of Oxford—Galsworthy's *Loyalties* and A. A. Milne's *Mr Pim Passes By*. Goolden played Mr Pim; an 'Isis Idol' portrait of him at this period describes him as 'a small and wide-awake individual . . . whose nose is adorned by a pair of twinkling pince-nez, whose gait is more of a merry caper than a conventional walk'. The description recalls Arthur Rackham's drawing of the Mole in *The Wind in the Willows*, and Goolden eventually became the regular tenant of the part of Mole in Milne's *Toad of Toad Hall*, adapted from Grahame's book, still playing it on the London stage when he was over ninety. Obviously an old man from the day of his birth, Goolden was reported by *Isis* to have 'created . . . a sensation in Gothenburg and Copenhagen' during the OUDS

tour. Even more of a sensation was caused by Gyles Isham, who as the juvenile lead was said, according to a Scandinavian correspondent to *Isis*, to have 'caused an almost audible palpitation in the hearts of the young ladies in the stalls'.

J. B. Fagan, having arrived in Oxford to direct *Henry IV*, decided to stay. Perceiving that there would be a role in the city for a resident professional repertory company, he proceeded to create one on the slenderest of means, converting a disused big-game museum ('The Red Barn') at the junction of the Woodstock and Banbury Roads into a makeshift theatre which he named the Oxford Playhouse, and engaging a small company of actors on the lowest acceptable salaries. Among these were no fewer than three OUDS actors from *Henry IV*, who had just taken their degrees (in the summer of 1923) and so were available. These were Goolden, Guthrie, and R. S. (Reggie) Smith of Merton, who had played Falstaff. Goolden and Smith acquitted themselves well enough, but Guthrie proved such a hopeless actor that he was soon demoted to prompter/assistant stage manager. In his autobiography he recalled the atmosphere of this first Oxford Playhouse, whose former role as a museum 'meant that it was haunted by the ghost of a moose, an elk, and a lion, whose stuffed and mouldering corpses had been the melancholy sole exhibits; it also trembled and reverberated like thunder every time a truck or bus went past, that is about every six seconds'. Fagan had decided that, to achieve stark simplicity and also to save money, there should be no scenery and everything should be performed against a background of white. This, combined with the rumbling of traffic, made an evening at the Playhouse something of an endurance test for the audience, but there was an enthusiastic if small following. Among those who hurried up St Giles for the weekly first nights was Emlyn Williams.

Every Monday I would sprint from Hall dinner, long scarf flying, Carfax, the Corn, Martyrs' Memorial, just in breathless time to hear the clock on the little church strike eight. The adventurous drill-hall—unraked, no balcony—had an apron-stage, a novelty flanked by grey-white pillars: an imposing frame for tragedy which tended to overlay Mr Pim Passing By. The company had no money to spend, but offered a standard kept consistently high by the taste of a lovable unbusiness-like man of the theatre. At one draughty première after another, the backstage gong would clang out, darkness, and I would be a creaking chair among many; the reason they did not all creak was, alas, that they were not all occupied. The players were not always word-perfect: loyal

first-nighters began to notice that long speeches tended to be directed thoughtfully at the hidden backs of chairs, a habit which seemed to afford mysterious refreshment to the memory. I was to see a maypole named Tyrone Guthrie, as Vedio in *Monna Vanna*, his first serious role, hasten on with a message, trip, fall his improbable length, rise and deliver the line 'But sire, you are hurt—let me sustain you!' On the first night of *The Master Builder*, after Hilda had embarked on a couple of direct questions which seemed to puzzle Solness as much as they did me, I heard the prompter call, in a strangled voice, 'Get her back, she's in the wrong act!'

On the other hand I was to see in his first leading part, in *Love for Love*, a youth whose name in the programme caused a woman behind me to paraphrase my father on another occasion, 'Poor boy, how *does* he pronounce it, John *Jeel*-gud?' When he got going though, all nose and passion and 'dragging calves and unbridled oboe of a voice—no peering at the back of furniture for this beginner—the creaking stopped. But the *Isis* could not get his name right either, 'a very interesting performance by Mr Gielgerd'.[2]

Gielgud, who was being paid eight pounds a week, 'took a tiny flat in the High, almost next door to Hall's the shirtmaker opposite the Mitre'. He and other actors in Fagan's company were made honorary members of the OUDS, and 'enjoyed the privileges of eating in the Club (upstairs next to the George) and using their sitting-room whenever we liked, which of course delighted us'. The *Oxford Magazine* exulted over this new development in the city's drama: 'We have got what we wanted, a cheap Repertory theatre with a stage restful to look upon, which concentrates all one's attention on the acting, which has a caste of quite thrilling excellence.'

Gyles Isham still had another year as an undergraduate, and his good looks dominated the OUDS performances. For Cyril Bailey's production of the *Rhesus* of Euripides in the summer of 1923 (New College garden) Isham provided a handsome Hector, with Anthony Asquith, son of the Prime Minister and himself a future film director, as Paris. Herbert Asquith came down to see his son perform and disconcerted the cast by keeping his eyes glued to the Greek text throughout. It was the success of this performance, and of his Hotspur the previous February, that led Gyles Isham to agree to undertake the title role in the first-ever OUDS *Hamlet*.

'No performance of the Oxford University Dramatic Society during the last quarter of a century has attracted greater attention', stated *The*

---

[2] Emlyn Williams, *George* (Hamish Hamilton, 1961), p. 307.

Oxford theatre before the days of OUDS: a poster for the 'Vic' (Theatre Royal) *c.*1870.

At a meeting held in Mr. Bourchier's rooms in Christ Church on November 3rd 1884 —

Mr. Courtney in the Chair —

"It is desirable to form a new Dramatic Club & Society bearing the simple title of "Oxford University Dramatic Society"—

It was unanimously carried —

Those to whom the O.U.D.S. are chiefly indebted for its existence as an University institution — are many — but

to Mr. Bourchier it owes its actual being and organization

to Mr. S.S.R. Lane and Mr. Frank Oscar — its incorporation with Vincent's Club & the 'Varsity at large —

to Mr. Alan Mackinnon, its first dramatic success —

and

to Mr. W.L. Courtney of New College —

it owes more than it can ever repay — for he has acted as mediator with the authorities — protector from its literary & other prejudices, and counsellor & friend to the officers of the Club in all their many difficulties.

The minute recording the formation of OUDS in 1884.

The founding fathers of OUDS: (*above left*) J. G. Adderley as the Nurse in *Villikins and his Dinah*; (*above right*) Alan Mackinnon as Prince Hal in the 1885 *Henry IV, Part 1*; (*left*) Arthur Bourchier as Death in the 1887 *Alcestis*.

(*Above*) A typical pre-1914 OUDS production in the old New Theatre: George Foss's 1902 staging of *Two Gentlemen of Verona*; (*below left*) the first big OUDS romance: Cathleen Nesbitt and Cecil Ramage as the 1921 *Antony and Cleopatra*; they married a few months later. (*Below right*) OUDS golden boy of the 1920s: Gyles Isham as Hamlet in 1924.

The 1925 *Peer Gynt* company outside the New Theatre. The producer Reginald Denham (in hat) sits between Eva Albanesi and Clare Greet, to the left of the OUDS signboard. Gyles Isham is on the right of Clare Greet, and Robert Speaight stands immediately behind him, slightly to the right. Emlyn Williams is third from the left in the back row.

(*Left*) Emlyn Williams as the Lean Person in *Peer Gynt*, and (*above*) as Yvette in a 1924 Smoker.

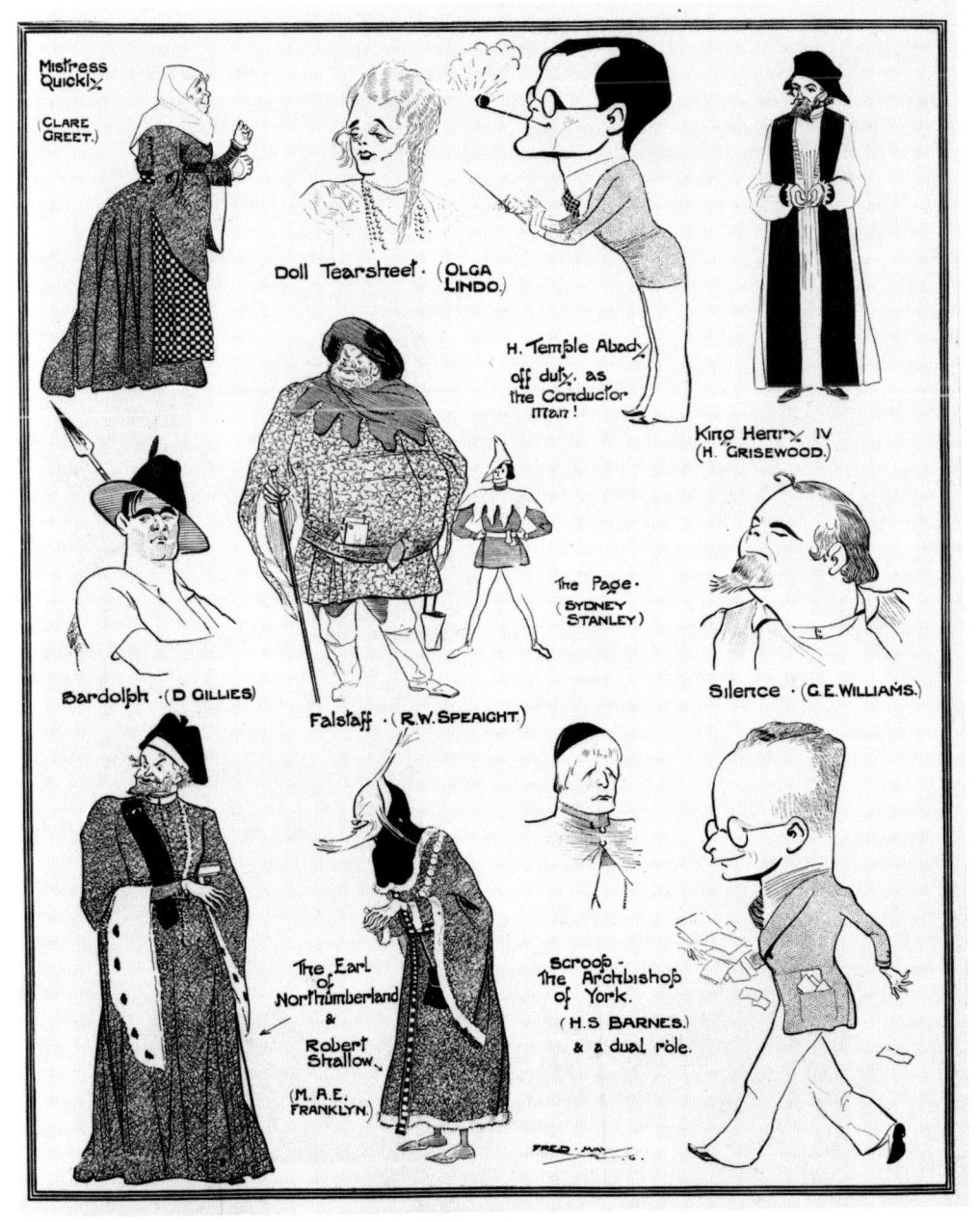

The society papers lavished attention on OUDS in the 1920s. The *Tatler* printed this page of cartoons of the 1926 *Henry IV, Part 2*.

A real rehearsal of *A Midsummer Night's Dream* in Magdalen Grove, 1926. J. B. Fagan (in hat) directs John Maud (centre, with arms outstretched) as Bottom, and John Betjeman (left of Maud) as Starveling. John Fernald stands on the extreme left.

John Betjeman's fake rehearsal photograph, printed in *Cherwell* in February 1927.

The 1932 *Romeo and Juliet*: Peggy Ashcroft and Christopher Hassall in the title roles. John Gielgud directs the rehearsal.

The balloon goes up at Oxford gasworks on 15 March 1930. Left to right: Sir Nigel Playfair, Hugh Speaight, Tallulah Bankhead, Giles Playfair.

Times with complete truth. *Hamlet* had never before been performed by a university cast, either in Oxford or Cambridge, and this undoubtedly contributed to what would now be called the 'hype' in Fleet Street. But the real attraction for the press was Isham himself: young, handsome, and the heir to a title—the very opposite of Irving and the other great Victorian Hamlets, but perhaps exactly what the play needed.

The build-up before the performance was considerable, and discussions of Isham's talents, character, and appearance eclipsed virtually every other actor in the cast—which was a pity, since it included Gerald Gardiner as Horatio, Robert Speaight (Lincoln) making his first OUDS appearance as the Player King, and the eccentric John Sutro of Trinity (friend and crony of Evelyn Waugh) as the First Gravedigger. J. B. Fagan had found time to spare from his Playhouse work to be the producer.

Isham virtually had to barricade himself from reporters during the days before the first night; an emissary from the *Evening Standard* managed to get into his rooms at Magdalen, where he found Isham in bed but interviewed him nonetheless; and Isham was persuaded to write a piece on 'Conceit—and Success' for the *Daily Express*. Arthur Bourchier resurfaced on the OUDS scene, telling reporters that it was at his suggestion that Isham was taking the part.

Fagan, unlike the Edwardian actor-managers, had decided to make as few cuts in the play as possible, removing no more than six hundred lines, so that it ran for over three hours. His designs were imaginative; John Gielgud was struck by 'Düreresque costumes and a pearl-grey dawn after the Ghost had vanished'. The supporting cast was versatile, Robert Speaight earning particular praise from the more discerning critics. But of course it was Isham himself who attracted almost all the attention.

'Wonderful New Hamlet: Genius of Oxford University' shrieked the *Express* after the first performance, and the general tone was of lavish praise, Isham being compared favourably to Irving. However, there were more sober critics. George Gordon, Merton Professor of English Literature, agreed to review the production for *Isis*, and judged it 'a very fine performance', but there was a certain reserve in his tone. The *Oxford Magazine* observed that Isham 'misses Hamlet's hardness' though he 'has all Hamlet's charm'. *The Times* praised Isham in rather vague terms ('well-considered and in many respects remarkable'), but the *Daily Mail* declared, 'Often he was astonishingly good, and

often he was depressingly bad.' A few critics, irritated by the super-
latives of their colleagues, were positively hostile. Probably the most
balanced judgement of Isham was that made by James Agate in the
Sunday Times: 'He was just an extremely gracious and graceful young
man tackling each line intelligently as it came along.' Agate wondered
whether Isham really knew or understood the play very well, or had
seen many performances of it, but conceded that his good sense kept
him on the rails most of the time, though he lacked power in the great
speeches.

The programme for the February 1924 *Hamlet* states that the
prompter was, as usual, 'H. E. Counsell (New Coll.)'. But in fact
'Doggins' had to drop out at the last minute, and the cryptic message
'Doggins is out' was sent to the enthusiastic freshman Emlyn Williams,
who had just been 'put up' for the OUDS and had no expectation of
seeing *Hamlet* from any closer vantage point than a humble seat in the
stalls. Williams, picked to take over the prompt-book, was 'to report at
seven, curtain up at eight. Tonight. The first night.' In his autobiography *George* he gives an account of what followed, so striking that it
deserves to be quoted in full.

It was as if I had been offered a leading part which I already knew: there was
all the excitement and none of the apprehension. A sandwich in the
JCR—'hello Byam Shaw, odd time to be eating but I'm due at the New stage-
door, bit of a crisis!'—and I hurried off, past the lighted front of the theatre, to
the little long-forbidden door. I found myself straight on the stage, in the
shadow of a great cyclorama and under a glaring working light; workmen
hammering, stage-hands sweeping, young men in shirt-sleeves and plus-
fours dusting cardboard goblets. I hung my gown on a nail and tiptoed to the
stool in the prompt-corner, getting up when Lockhart-Smith the stage-
manager hurried down—shirt-sleeves, plus-fours—with a Temple
Shakespeare, 'Christ, it hasn't got the cuts . . .' He stood with a blue pencil,
consulting his own copy—pages gummed on to a foolscap volume with
hundreds of notes and diagrams on each—and swiftly excising from mine.
When people ran up to him he was 'Ken' to them all, but as sternly composed
as a sea-captain of fifty, 'There's an extra gelatine on the o.p. side, but tell
Bobbie or Greville to pop over to the club and ask J.B. first.' The Christian
names scattered like sparks, 'Reggie, have you tested the warning light under
the stage—and Frank, check that the Ophelia mad wig is back and tell Bert I
want a word with him about that bloody awful make-up he put on Patrick, J.B.
said it turned Osric into something out of the Insect Play.' Then, to me,
'Williams—is that right—the one thing, Williams, you must do as a prompter

is—*don't prompt*, unless there's a dead emergency, which you'll soon spot if you've done some acting, Willie says you have.'

He left me with my Temple; by craning I could see into the wings, otherwise my view was of three-quarters of the acting area. Lights were being turned off; the soft tread of many people passing upstage, whispered good-lucks in the shadows. My corner was two feet from the red plush curtain at which I had stared longingly from the pit, and I could hear the audience drifting in; as the activity near me simmered to orderly twilight, so out there the murmur feverishly grew. Suddenly there was the orchestra—playing Byrd, I found later—and our side of the curtain was a lilting pool of confident promise. Applause; then I guessed, from the multiple chatter swiftly fading out into silence, that the house-lights had dimmed. The curtain still down, the lights on stage came up slow and sure on the haunted battlements. Miles away in the Elsinore air, a great bell boomed the ominous twelve of midnight; then, two feet from me, with an imperious sweep, the curtain rose. From the upper darkness, a voice. 'Who's there?'

The first sight of Hamlet seated apart, six feet from me, black of hair and dress and mien, took my prompting breath away, so it was as well that he knew lines which he spoke with a moving simplicity. The scene with the Ghost, green-armoured and thrillingly resonant, ending on the steps in a slow icy dawn over the battlements, grew on me with each performance. Tirelessly I studied the professional Gertrude and Ophelia, and although I was for the whole week under a spell, I never missed one effect they made, one move or one pause, and every time waited for each one so as to mark its apparent spontaneity—as on 'Get thee to a nunnery', when Ophelia turned, unbeliev-ing, and slowly put her hands to her face . . . I was learning. The spell worked all-powerfully, because what I experienced was unique: not having attended one rehearsal, and not once—through five nights and three matinées—seeing one actor out of make-up and costume, I stayed under a continuous illusion and yet an integral part of that illusion.

I was at a play, and in it. Fortinbras would stand two feet from me, I could see the pulse beat in his neck, smell the musty scent of the costume, the tang of spirit-gum—then he was on, 'Where is this sight? . . . This quarry cries on havoc . . .' As for the Ghost—the only character I would have been shocked to find next to me—I was in luck: it appeared and disappeared on the other side, and I never once saw it out of its weird light. Rosencrantz and Guildenstern would creep up behind me for their entrance—by Thursday I was waiting for them, as with dreamlike inevitability they would form out of the darkness, dabbing at a beard, twitching at the crutch of a doublet—but even at these moments (almost more) they eluded me completely—and yet I can touch them! Not once did I wonder which colleges they belonged to, who they were. And in the interval, stretching my numbed neck in the wings—hark to the

safety curtain, 'For Thine Especial Safety, *Hamlet*'—I would have rebuffed any know-all of a stage-hand informing me that impassioned snub-nosed Laertes—A. Tandy (Magd.)—is the spit of his little sister Jessie who is going on the stage, or that Osric the butterfly is the Hon. J. P. D. Balfour (Magd.) and the future Lord Kinross, or that the First Gravedigger, J. R. Sutro (Trin.) is going into films, Horatio, G. A. Gardiner (Magd.) into law and the Player King, R. W. Speaight (Linc.) and a Messenger, J. W. Counsell (Exeter) into the theatre. I wanted nothing of reality to impinge on a timeless time of trance and romance.

Outside the theatre, I lived a shadow among shadows, for the only students I knew were from Wittenberg: my room a chimera, my bed a kip between one Elsinore and the next. It was only when I sank into my corner and heard the orchestra climb and climb to 'House Out', that the people I knew—Bernardo, Francisco—swam into flesh-and-blood focus. Life began, for me, on the stroke of stage midnight. Wednesday, one p.m., sitting in the J.C.R. with coffee, sandwich and *Daily Mail*—'he was a boyish Hamlet'—I looked round at two blazered men accoutred for the river and thought, if only I could wear something that told the world I have a matinée! A pair of gold-laced Greek buskins? a make-up towel negligently round the neck? I looked at the clock and left for Denmark.

Saturday night I ate in Hall, in my dinner-jacket. The width of the lapel and my Edwardian pumps were off-set by my being able to remark that after my performance I had the Ouds Supper, in the Town Hall; even without my new wealth, I would have paid the astronomical price. The long and merry night—special permission—was doubly entrancing, for not only was Fagan there with his regal wife Mary Grey and the Playhouse company in the flesh, but I was identifying, from *Hamlet*, players whom I had watched for over thirty hours; it was strange to see the raven-haired organ-toned Prince as a blond stripling with high boyish notes. Sipping my champagne and tweaking my black tie, I made friends with a high-spirited youth who turned out, incredibly, to be the Ghost. The banquet was long and hilarious, with speeches and programme-signing (enviously I saw 'With admiration Lila', 'God bless, Tim', 'Love Gyles') followed by the Ouds custom of 'toys', the cheaper the better, with attached a single punning line from the recipient's part, to be passed up and down with whoops of laughter; opposite me, the Second Gravedigger was brought a mangled celluloid doll, with a label 'The crowner hath sat on her'. It was the custom to stay up all night, the favoured ones finishing up at Doggins' house, 37 the Broad, for story-telling and tipsy turns and even breakfast; but I knew I was too unfledged to tag on to this, and went sighing home. A bewitched and irrevocable week was over.[3]

[3] *George*, pp. 321–4.

5

Golden Age

━━⟨⟩━━

IN June 1924, four months after the Gyles Isham *Hamlet*, the OUDS summer production was *Love's Labour's Lost* in Wadham gardens, with H. K. Ayliff from the Birmingham Rep directing. Like almost everyone else, Emlyn Williams, fresh from his experience as prompter, hoped for the part of Berowne. He had to put up with Dull the constable. As usual the play was 'blocked' in the OUDS dining room in George Street before rehearsals continued out of doors. Soon 'the dressing-tents were going up behind the trees. "Bert" arrived from Clarksons' in London, with costumes and wigs, and made us all up; the scent of flowers and trodden grass mingled with the smell of hot canvas and grease-paint and moth-balls. A telegram, my first, "Good luck Emlyn . . ."' (he had now decided on his stage-name). The weather had been terrible, but it cleared up just in time. 'On Saturday night, under a marvellous sky, we sat enchanted at the OUDS performance', wrote a London reporter. Mercifully, Williams did not go unnoticed in the reviews. 'Mr Williams as Constable Dull made a small part large by a rich suggestion of the well-intentioned lackwit hopelessly at odds with a world of scholars', said the *Manchester Guardian*. 'It was hard to attend to the sweet parting song so perfectly was Dull gazing in clownish adoration, a rapt oaf on whom beauty was descending through the chinks in an empty skull.' And Ivor Brown in the *Saturday Review*: 'Played by Mr G. E. Williams, this Dull became a monstrously agreeable compound of simple loyalty to the social order, of the translated oaf's fierce pride of place, and of the bumpkin's humble faith that all the palaver of his betters had really got some meaning and pertinency within its high-flown composition.'

'Doggins' was back in his prompter's chair for this *Love's Labour's Lost*. Although already notorious for his inattention to the prompt-book, on this occasion he excelled himself, as he recalls in his autobiography.

During the first performance of *Love's Labour's Lost* in Wadham garden one of the actors 'dried up'. From behind the bushes where I was concealed I gave him his line but he merely strode up and down looking desperately in my direction. Thinking that perhaps he had not heard me, I raised my voice and gave him the line again, yet still without any effect and he merely looked more hot and bothered. This was indeed a crisis. Had the poor man lost his voice or had mine lost its power to carry in the open air? Now ever since Laurence Housman taught me how to throw my voice to the back of beyond during the great Oxford Pageant, I have been rather proud of its carrying power so I tried again, and this time I sent Shakespeare's line rocketing to the tree-tops above actors and audience. The actor, however, only gave me a look of anguish and I was just beginning to think that he really must be ill when there came a shout from the back of the garden, 'Oh, that's all been cut, Doggins!' This left me helpless in a complete fog, but fortunately it seemed to strike a spark in the actor's memory, and skipping valiantly over the cut, he went on.

Because *Love's Labour's Lost* concerns a group of young men who forswear the company of women, the gossip-column of the *Morning Post* chose to describe it as 'a play with no small topical interest for our bisexual university'. The OUDS, though by no means composed chiefly of 'Aesthetes', was far more in the 'Aesthetic' camp at Oxford in the mid 1920s than in that of their opponents the 'Hearties', and the OUDS Commemoration Ball at the Town Hall at the end of the summer term became an occasion for the finest display of peacock-plumage by Harold Acton, Brian Howard, and their celebrated set, whose antics later supplied their friend and contemporary Evelyn Waugh with much 'copy' for *Brideshead Revisited*. The June 1924 ball was the first of a splendid series. The *Oxford Chronicle* described it gleefully:

Several of the ladies, taking advantage of the fact that their hair was of the 'bobbed' variety, had turned themselves into very chic page boys . . . Mr Gyles Isham was in ordinary attire, but had conceded a red flower in his buttonhole as an indication of special festivity . . . Mr Harold Acton, in a cross-buttoned blue coat and close-fitting trousers, favoured the fashion of a century ago.

The Town Hall was decorated with streamers and coloured drapes and the band lit with limelight, and guests in fancy dress preferred not to arrive by cab but to walk through the Oxford streets, displaying their costumes to curious townees. By 1926 the OUDS Ball had reached a peak of celebrity; a London paper described it as 'probably the most brilliant and certainly the most crowded ball the Society has held'.

Such things were not within the means of poorly-off OUDS members like Emlyn Williams, who slipped away from Oxford before it.

Harman Grisewood, a cousin of Freddie Grisewood (and like him later a BBC stalwart), who came up to Worcester College at Michaelmas 1924, argues in his autobiography that Oxford was not class-conscious, 'a stronghold of privilege and so on. I noticed nothing of this sort when I was there. Oxford, I believe, has done far more to bring men of different backgrounds together than it has to separate them.' But Grisewood came from a well-off family and had been to a public school, Ampleforth. The process of bringing-together could be painful for those from less privileged backgrounds. Emlyn Williams had just settled comfortably into OUDS membership when 'Tim' Abady (H. Temple Abady), the then reigning pianist and songwriter for OUDS Smokers and the undergraduate who had put his name up for the OUDS, called on him to say with some embarrassment 'that a couple of people have noticed that you are tending to call people by their Christian names a bit more than is warranted . . .' Williams was greatly distressed by this 'club snub', which he called 'my first and last brush with public-school punctilio'. As a result he spent the *Love's Labour's Lost* period taking immense care to brandish surnames, and by the autumn term of 1924 found himself on firmer ground socially. He was invited to take part in the Smoker, on its 'tiny curtained stage rigged up at one end of the dining room', with an upright piano hammered by Tim Abady while 'sketches of the crudest ribaldry were directed at an audience of cackling undergraduates and daringly tipsy dons'. Williams played a ragbag of parts, but had his own moment in a 'drag' number ('lyric by G. E. Williams') in which, in a purple velvet dress and cloche hat borrowed from somebody's sister, he impersonated one of the tarts he had encountered in summer journeys around France (he was reading Modern Languages):

> Je m'appelle Yvette,
> Yvette des trottoirs,
> Tous les soirs, je m'arrête . . .

Slowly but distinctly he found himself making social headway in the OUDS. He gave a small dinner party for Abady, Ken Lockhart-Smith the stage manager, and 'Willie' Wilson Wiley, the Secretary. By the spring of 1925 he had the confidence to sit in one of the armchairs in the club-room, no longer an eavesdropper. 'It wouldn't be long before

I'd be on the fender, I had even bought a pipe and had half my heart in trying to smoke it.'

'Willie', the rest of the Committee, and Gyles Isham (who was now the OUDS President) set their hearts on doing a modern classic for the next major production, in February 1925. Shaw's *Caesar and Cleopatra* was contemplated, but they were told that the Vice-Chancellor's rule about not performing plays of less than thirty years standing was still in force. They had hopes of producing *Cyrano de Bergerac*, but Rostand's play was still in copyright and negotiations over the English rights broke down. Their final choice was no less ambitious, Ibsen's *Peer Gynt*, which had only been given one full-length production in England, at the Old Vic in 1922 with Russell Thorndike as Peer. The news that the OUDS was now to attempt it caused a minor sensation in the press. 'The part of Peer Gynt is far longer than that of Hamlet,' declared the *Daily Sketch*. 'Only people with a Thorndikish memory can tackle it . . . The brave undergraduate who is taking it on is R. W. Speaight of Lincoln College.'

Robert Speaight, a year older than Emlyn Williams, had acquired some public reputation as an actor even before arriving at Oxford. While still a schoolboy, he and some friends mounted an amateur production of *The Merchant of Venice* on the Sussex coast, Speaight playing Shylock, and it got a good notice in *The Times*. He tried to repeat this success by acting Macbeth in the town hall at Hatfield where his family lived—and got rapped by the critics for his presumption. Would he overreach himself again as Peer Gynt?

The OUDS Committee chose as producer Reginald Denham, who had been directing for J. B. Fagan at the Oxford Playhouse since it opened. Casting was undertaken much more carefully than by previous generations of committees: three 'casting readings' were held well in advance of the first rehearsals, and the Society's officers conferred at length with the producer before the final choice was made. Emlyn Williams got a series of walk-ons (Wedding Guest, Troll, Lunatic) and one important part, the Lean Person—the devil in disguise. In the same scene Harman Grisewood was cast as the Button-Moulder who wants to melt Peer down. Williams started his rehearsals and quickly made friends with another bit-part player, John Maud of New College —the future Lord Redcliffe-Maud, Master of University College. Williams liked this 'gangling high-spirited boy', and the two of them took a great interest in the professional actresses who soon arrived from

London to fill the female parts. 'There were two shy walkers-on named Mary and Ann, the daughters of Sybil Thorndike and Lewis Casson; but they were aged eleven and nine and therefore invisible.' Clare Greet (no relation to Ben Greet), an old hand at character parts, was to play Peer's mother; Williams found her 'a giggly asthmatic bundle of Cockney', and when the production opened the critics said she brought too much of the Bloomsbury boarding-house into the Norwegian fjords. Eva Albanesi, sister of the popular actress Meggie Albanesi whose recent death in her twenties had caused national heartbreak, was cast as Anitra. Then there were Solveig and Ingrid—'Joan Maude, daughter of Nancy Price, just seventeen with auburn hair, a face made more perfect by freckles, and a heart-stirring lisp: and Lilian Oldland . . . a warm brunette. They were nice enough to be anybody's sister and also had sex-appeal, a formidable combination . . . John and I decided that Lilian was the charmer, while Willie and Boy Malcolm [W. S. Malcolm, another walk-on] fought openly over Joan, who exercised wide-eyed diplomacy.'

Reginald Denham treated the play briskly, cutting a good deal of Ibsen's philosophy out of the later scenes, and using a cyclorama and a minimum of scenic effects to speed up the changes. (On the other hand Grieg's incidental music was played almost in full, by a big orchestra.) Clare Greet, used to Bensonian sets with backdrop and wings, was puzzled by the cyclorama, which made it impossible to come on in some of the usual places. One night she failed to make her entrance in the wedding scene, and everyone began a frantic search for her. 'Doggins', who was prompting as usual, records that she was 'found on her hands and knees trying to crawl under the heavily weighted cyclorama cloth which she had forgotten prevented entry to the stage except from prompt corner or O.P.'

Most of the property-making and such scene-painting as was required was done by OUDS members. Alec Penrose (elder brother of Roland) had been brought in by Denham as designer, and he provided grotesque masks for the Trolls which rather hampered clear speaking but were wonderfully effective visually. As the first night approached the production was the talk of Oxford. The *Oslo Aftenavis* even sent a reporter over from Norway, an Oxford graduate named Nordahl Grieg (related to the composer), who wrote afterwards:

The OUDS ruled Oxford that week. Rowing, football, tennis, fencing, cricket, golf—all disappeared for some days as topics of conversation, and for

a few days wherever two or more flannel trousers met they talked of Ibsen, and agreed that, like Peer Gynt's, their souls were onions and that the button-moulder's ladle was their real destiny.

A better public Ibsen has never had than that which filled the theatre the first evening; in the front seats all the leading critics of England; then all the splendid youth . . . and, at the back, Indians—small nervous young men, so tremendously western in all their opinions, but with that far-away, mysterious look in their eyes . . .

Backstage, Emlyn Williams had thrown himself 'into the endless wonderful sandwiches-and-coffee dress-rehearsal, with masks and chaotic changes, patiently quickened by Mr Denham—"Reggie" by now, but I was taking no chances—and great beams of light and the orchestra suddenly, thrillingly, beating out the Grieg music'. Then the first performance. 'I caroused as a Wedding Guest, gibbered as a Troll, drooled as a Lunatic, then prepared calmly for the Lean Person. This was my real indoor test: a sustained scene late in the play. Standing in the wings, in stockinged feet with cloven hoofs fitted over them, I was suddenly conscious of the packed darkness beyond and of the fire of light into which I must soon walk alone. Suppose I were to . . . I felt my heart begin to knock, loud. "Be still, look up at the moon and the stars . . ." I calmed, and stepped forward into the blaze, and was secure. All went a little more than well.'

It went more than well for Robert Speaight, too, who had to carry nearly the whole weight of the production. No one doubted that the part of Peer was really beyond a performer so young, but virtually all the critics (even those who misprinted his name as 'Spright') felt it a huge achievement to come as near it as he had. W. A. Darlington in the *Telegraph* was impressed far beyond his expectations:

Mr Russell Thorndike played it at the 'Old Vic', well, but not supremely well . . . Mr Speaight plays it, according to the length (the shortness, rather) of his experience, exceedingly well. Whether in the future he will ever fill out to the stature of the part is a question that only time can answer. Mr Speaight is an interesting actor. He is chock-full of that peculiar dynamic quality called 'temperament'. When I first saw him act it was as a schoolboy who had suffered from being over-praised, and had consequently got it into his head that he only had to let his temperament have its way to achieve immediate success. The result, as I saw it on that occasion, was horrible—but full of promise. Last year Mr Speaight was cast by the astute J. B. Fagan for the Player King, a part in which he could rant to his heart's content; and in

consequence he had a small but unmistakable triumph. This year Mr
Speaight is older, more experienced, surer of himself, less dependent on his
power of turning on the emotional tap, but he is still at his best in those scenes
where flamboyance can be accounted to him as a virtue. It is true that he
cannot quite bring off that scene at Ase's death-bed (the scene which, above
all others, lives in the memory as Mr Thorndike played it)—that most difficult
scene where Peer pretends to drive his mother up to the gates of Heaven; but if
he had done so at his age it would have been something like a miracle. As the
older Peer Mr Speaight plays quite soundly, without particular distinction; but
I personally find this side of his playing more interesting than the other, since
it is symptomatic of the growth of something which he lacked before, and
without which he could not hope to go very far.

Ivor Brown in the *Saturday Review* was upset by Denham's cuts, which
he said destroyed the philosophical purpose of the play and treated it as
a fairy-story. He also differed from Darlington in his view of Speaight,
whom he called

a light-weight Peer, far better in his tender moments than when driven
through insolence to taunting and defiance of gods and men. He seemed too
lovable, too good a sort . . . [But] what he could give the part, he gave in full.
He had no rest during a performance of three and a half hours and never
faltered for a word. In Gynt's quiet moments he was delicate and charming.

James Agate, probably the shrewdest critic at this date, wrote in the
Sunday Times that the play was really unactable, but called Speaight
'magnificent' (though like Brown he thought him 'too lovable'), and
continued: 'The impetuosity, the vanity, the adventure, the *excitement*
of living were all admirably suggested.' Harman Grisewood, whose
'persuasive irony' as the Button-Moulder was commended by the
Morning Post (the same critic praised 'Mr G. E. Williams's admirable
impersonation, momentary but highly effective, as the devil in pious
garb'), includes in his memoirs a considered account of Speaight's
performance as it seemed from behind the footlights. It was, he said,

remembered by those who have forgotten many others of more recent date. It
has lasted, I believe, because of qualities which only youth can give. You could
never see such a performance except in an amateur production. No young
professional would be given a part which makes such heavy demands upon
maturity. But in one aspect it is a young man's play; the thoughts and
imaginings about maturity and old age are those of a young man, not an old
one. Bobby Speaight's conception of the part was exactly attuned to Ibsen's.

Speaight himself, in *The Property Basket* (1970), described his own feelings during the production.

I went through the week—eight performances in five days—in a daze of fulfilled ambition . . . My chief anxiety was the vocal strain, which I was far too inexperienced to avoid. But I have often noticed that a voice which has apparently disappeared in the daytime mysteriously returns to one on the stage. I got through the week on 'Bismarck'—a mixture of stout and champagne—and at the end of the week I had leave from Lincoln to go down to Sussex with a friend to recuperate.

Emlyn Williams finished the week in a state of elation—'there was the Supper: champagne again and programme-signing and congratulations, but this time I was part of it. Toys arrived for me; at 2 a.m., elevated by bubbly . . . I went along to Doggins' with the rest, John Sutro told stories, Willie did a piece as a yokel, John and I talked to Lilian about the vac, there was coffee and we saw in a sunny February dawn . . .'

With John Maud, Williams was now elected to the OUDS Committee, 'which was satisfying as it was exactly as far as I wanted to go, in Oxford, socially'. Tim Abady succeeded Isham as President, while Isham, who had already edited *Isis*, completed the hat-trick by becoming President of the Union. Williams was now a confident man-of-the-theatre, popping over to the OUDS for a quick sherry in the interval of New Theatre shows ('a chic custom') and telling the diners what he thought of that week's visiting production: 'Rubbish, but expertly projected . . .' His Welsh accent 'seemed to be rubbing off, I said "Yes indeed" only when I meant to'. In the next Smoker he had a big handful of parts; as usual the 'book' was pepped up with more and more blue jokes during the three nights of its run, 'and by the end even I was rather ashamed of the inanities in the way of double-entendre'. Richard Addinsell from Hertford College had taken over Abady's seat at the piano (he became a successful light music composer, and after the war was Joyce Grenfell's accompanist), and he and an OUDS lyricist scored a hit with 'Jumper Boy', a number which guyed the Harold Acton fashion for polo-neck jumpers—

> In pinks and reds and yellows,
> Just like Ivor Novello's . . .

The song 'had a bite of professionalism which we badly needed'.

June 1925 saw a Wadham gardens production of an Edmond Rostand double-bill, *The Two Pierrots* and *The Fantasticks*. William Armstrong from the Liverpool Playhouse directed, and Emlyn Williams (playing small parts) was amused by his camp old-maidish manner: 'My dear boys, don't *breathe* such limericks down the neck of an old prude from the frozen North—no, don't laugh at me, beastly new-born creatures . . .' Then, in the Long Vacation, there was a tour of *Twenty-One*, a revue concocted by Tim Abady and 'Willie' Wilson Wiley, with Williams in the company and acting as business manager—'a strenuous job . . . a different village or town hall every night'. It ended with a big party which was nearly ruined for him by a letter from Miss Cooke, the schoolteacher who had got him to Oxford. What was he doing, she stormed at him, wasting so much time on acting? 'One-eyed nonsense, I've no use for slackers who can't stick it . . . Fooling about with amateur theatricals . . . You'll come a cropper . . .' Williams gulped champagne, then more champagne, then felt better. 'Slacker? But I was exhausted.'

Next term, Michaelmas 1925, found him a rather cynical elderly member of OUDS. 'By this time, I was on the fender, ordering a round of drinks.' He and Speaight (now the Secretary) helped to organize a competition for original one-act plays, to be written and performed by members. 'The idea was that the Ouds should explore the territory between Shakespeare and a smutty smoker.' The best three were to be performed in the club dining-room. Williams himself immediately wrote one. It was called *Vigil*, and its sinister but rather inexplicable plot concerned a benighted English traveller arriving at a lonely Welsh mansion whose sleeping owner has hypnotic powers over all who enter it. It was one of three judged good enough for performance; Speaight played the Englishman, and the producer was John Fernald, 'a bouncing fresh-faced head boy biting a pipe', who had just come up to Trinity. He was afterwards a professional producer and Principal of the Royal Academy of Dramatic Art. 'Marvellous,' he said to Williams, 'your first play, my first production.' Sixty years later he writes: 'It was doing this play that made me realize where my theatrical ambitions lay. From the moment in rehearsal when I realized what a wealth of emotional expression could be evoked by a dramatic pause, I realized too that I had discovered how and where I could be of use in the theatre. I am afraid that this put paid to any question of working for a degree.' Williams and Leslie Nye made up the rest of the cast; J. B.

Fagan came to see it, and told Fernald he would have liked people in London to watch it.

Henry IV, Part 2 was the next major production (February 1926), and Speaight rather anticipated that he would be cast as the King. Bridges-Adams was invited back again to produce, and the usual casting readings were held, with parts being freely interchanged. Then came the final Committee meeting of Michaelmas Term 1925, on a Sunday morning. (The Committee always met on Sundays at this period, after a big Sunday breakfast in the club-rooms—a favourite habit with members since the early 1900s.) To Speaight's astonishment he was told that Bridges-Adams wanted him to play Falstaff. 'At the OUDS we did as we were told in these matters, and I prepared with no little diffidence to meet a tremendous challenge.' Over Christmas he ran into James Agate, who told him 'that I was mad; that although I might give an excellent lecture on Falstaff, I couldn't possibly play him; that I could easily get out of the part if I wanted to; that it was mere vanity on my part going on with it; and that since he had no wish to be rude to an amateur about to turn professional, he would refuse to see the show. I defended myself as best I could but, if he felt like that, I was relieved to think he would not be in the audience. We parted coolly, and once rehearsals started I gave the matter no further thought.'

Bridges-Adams was busier than ever, handling a London production of *Much Ado* as well as the OUDS show; he stayed at the Randolph Hotel in Oxford and took a morning train up to town each day, returning for undergraduate rehearsals in the evening. Towards the end he could not be in Oxford at all, and one of his oldest and most experienced Stratford actors, Randle Ayrton, took his place. 'It was not an ideal arrangement,' writes Speaight; 'we liked to have our producers on tap . . . But Bridges was no stranger to tight schedules. There was enough of the undergraduate left in him to know what could, or could not, be done with us; and he had a wonderful way with a stage crowd.'

Clare Greet came back to the OUDS as an ideal Mistress Quickly, pure Cockney, and Olga Lindo provided a real uninhibited harlot of a Doll Tearsheet. Together, said Speaight, they 'recreated an Eastcheap in which the spirit of the OUDS "smoker" was allowed to mingle with the spirit of the OUDS play'. Harman Grisewood was an adequately solemn King, Leslie Nye was Hal, Emlyn Williams doubled as Morton and Silence, Douglas Cleverdon (Jesus), later an outstanding BBC radio producer (he was responsible for *Under Milk Wood*), was among

the walk-ons, and Wart, one of Falstaff's mouldering recruits, was played by 'J. Betjemann (Magdalen)'.

Betjeman, not yet wholly convinced about the dropping of the final, German, 'n' in his surname, had just arrived at Magdalen and was proving a pestilential if intriguing pupil to his tutor C. S. Lewis. Emlyn Williams judged him from his sense of humour to be 'a fourth-former . . . a zany wiseacre with a protruding tooth'.

At the suggestion of Charles Morgan, now writing drama criticism for *The Times*, the Committee took the unusual step of inviting the press to attend the dress rehearsal, 'in order to facilitate the writing of their notices'. The gamble paid off: the critics had more time to compose their pieces, and they almost unanimously voted *Henry IV*, *Part 2* the best OUDS production to date, surpassing even the Isham *Hamlet* and Speaight's *Peer Gynt*.

The real surprise was Speaight as Falstaff. S. P. B. Mais in the *Daily Graphic* called it quite simply 'one of the finest pieces of acting ever seen in Oxford or anywhere else'. Ivor Brown deplored the Falstaff costume, but thought the performance quite magnificent: 'The belly deceived nobody, but the brain's counterfeit was not to be denied. The voice was not that of elderly grossness, but the mind dripped fatness.' Above all it was James Agate who poured plaudits on Speaight's head. At the last minute he had reconsidered his decision not to attend, and sent a telegram asking for a seat to be reserved at the dress rehearsal. By that time Speaight

had gathered enough self-confidence to be less troubled by this news than I might have been. Encased in putty and padding, I went on to the stage feeling as well as looking about six times larger than myself. 'Boy—what says the doctor to my water?'—from the first word of the outrageous opening the laughs came easily. At the interval, which was placed after the great scene in the Boar's Head tavern where Falstaff has Doll Tearsheet on his knee and for a few moments the shadow of mortality darkens the stage, Gyles Isham came round to my dressing-room. 'I thought you would like to know', he said, 'that I have just left Agate weeping in the foyer.'

Agate afterwards told Speaight, 'You are the best Falstaff I have seen since Louis Calvert', and he considered Calvert's performance immortal. In the *Sunday Times* a few days later he called the Oxford *Henry IV* 'quite extraordinarily satisfying', and described Bridges-Adams as 'a producer of genius'. He then turned to Speaight's performance: 'Mr Speaight confounded even his best friends. There

was nothing of amateurishness . . . It was a triumph to stir one so deeply alike at the words "I am old, I am old" and in the unutterable dumb dismay of the end, to give us not only the large stomach but the brain in which it "snows of meat and drink".' Happily for another member of the cast, Agate added: '. . . and I think I spy an actor in Mr G. E. Williams, who gave the small part of Morton very well indeed.' He was not the only one to pick out Emlyn Williams from the large cast; Mais said that Silence's 'astringent terseness was quite wonderfully brought out by G. E. Williams'.

Agate wrote about this OUDS production again, some time later in an article in *Playgoing*. He spoke of other great versions of *Henry IV, Part 2*—that with Calvert as Falstaff, one in which Laurence Irving played Shallow, and a few others. Then he continued:

But it is possible, I suggest, for virtuosi by their brilliance to overlay the piece they are performing. Shakespeare's greatest comedy, and if not greatest certainly most human play, was brought nearer to the heart by a performance at the O.U.D.S. in 1926. There was a moment then when I became sensible of the greatest effect of which the art of the dramatist is capable—the Pisgah-like view of human life. The scene was the Eastcheap tavern; the musicians were playing; the Prince and Poins had entered in disguise; and Doll had asked her whoreson little Bartholomew boar-pig when he would leave fighting o' days and foining o' nights, and begin to patch up his old body for heaven. From the fat knight's 'Peace, good Doll! Do not speak like a death's head; do not bid me remember mine end' down to his 'I am old, I am old', it seemed that night at Oxford as though the world stood still and the English centuries were spread beneath one like a map.

Agate was guest of honour at the OUDS Supper after the last performance of *Henry IV*, and in his speech, recalling that he had implored Speaight not to attempt Falstaff, he said he now felt like a physician who had told his patient he only had six months to live, and was a touch mortified to find him still alive a year later! A few days later Agate was put up for honorary membership of the OUDS, a privilege that at this period was extended to various well-known men of the theatre as well as distinguished former members. The proposal was made with Agate's own knowledge and consent, indeed partly at his own suggestion, which was unfortunate, since it was rejected by the Committee on the grounds 'that it was considered inexpedient and unadvisable [*sic*] to elect a dramatic critic to honorary membership'. The consequence was that when Agate met Speaight in later years he

was markedly unfriendly. 'It seemed as if he had forgotten, or wished not to remember, the encouragement he had given me.'

Hamlet, Peer Gynt, and *Henry IV, Part 2* provoked three years of very wide press coverage of OUDS productions, and this led to complaints about undergraduate drama being so enthusiastically publicized. The first grumbler was one Walter Frith, who wrote to *The Times* on 15 February 1926 (just after the *Henry IV* notices had appeared) to

protest against the undue prominence given in the London Press (only in the last few years) to the theatrical performances of undergraduates—mainly, it seems, at Oxford. Parents and guardians (probably without exception) do not send their charges to the university with any idea of their one day adopting the profession of acting; nor can excessive and highly injudicious praise of efforts which must actually be extremely immature bring anything but future disappointment to the recipients, urged thereby, as in some of the papers I have seen, at once to go upon the stage. The profession is already densely overcrowded; further to embarrass it with purely amateur talent is only to invite discomfort and very often distress for all concerned, not only the amateur himself and those responsible for his welfare, but, may I add, the already long-suffering audience.

If in future it may be thought necessary to intrude these young geniuses on our notice in London, will not the veteran *cliché* of the provincial Press be sufficient?—'Where all were so good it would be invidious to select any for especial praise.' Not very illuminating, perhaps, *quâ* criticism, but, at any rate, harmless.

The name Frith does not feature in OUDS activities at this period, so that one may suppose the writer of this letter to have been, like Arthur Chandler in the 1890s, one who never saw an OUDS production but was convinced *a priori* and *a posteriori*, that they were bad. However, a letter of support for Frith, which appeared in *The Times* a day later, came from someone with a more personal concern in the matter, one William Farren. He declared that 'it is hardest of all on parents who in many cases have had to pinch and save to give their sons the years at Oxford or Cambridge'. It might have been supposed that he was one such parent. In fact, as a later correspondent pointed out, Farren was an old professional actor who was forever trying to keep amateurs out of the business.

'Willie' Wilson Wiley replied for the OUDS on 22 February, producing some facts and figures. During his four years' membership, he said, 'some 270 undergraduates have passed through the Oxford

University Dramatic Society, and of these only nine have adopted or intend to adopt the stage as their profession. Of the 15 that I may select as having received "excessive and highly injudicious praise" of their efforts, four have taken the call—the remaining 11 adopting the Law (five), the Church (one), Literature (four), and Commerce (one).' On the same day and the same page *The Times* printed a leader on the matter, which from its tone and content was obviously written by Charles Morgan.

To suppose that undergraduate actors, or indeed any good amateurs, take all praise at its face value is to mistake their attitude of mind . . . The compliment that they most desire is sincere criticism of a high standard, and it is hard to understand why, when they deserve it, they should not receive it.

The leader argued that acting societies

are not to be regarded as being chiefly, or even in any considerable part, recruiting grounds for the professional stage. To most of their members they are a department, and a very pleasant, legitimate, and intelligent department, of university life.

There the matter came to an end, at least in the columns of *The Times*. Certainly the University authorities were thought by the OUDS Committee to be rather anxious about the amount of time and energy that leading OUDS members were devoting to their theatrical activities, and some tactful approaches were made to the Proctors to sound out their views in case trouble was imminent. But it was chiefly the Smokers that concerned the Proctors, because of their known impropriety, and, to the relief of the OUDS, they only requested (rather absurdly) that there should be two performances of the Smoker rather than three—a concession that the Society was willing to make.

It was of course ingenuous to pretend that many OUDS members did not have one eye on the acting profession. New recruits to the George Street club-rooms were constantly struck (as both Compton Mackenzie and Emlyn Williams had been) by the very un-Oxford atmosphere, the familiarity with West End stars and producers. The OUDS imported professional directors and actresses largely to make useful friends, and many people were helped into their first jobs by contacts made at Oxford. But, as Robert Speaight remarks in his autobiography, a contact was one thing, experience was another:

To be sure a number of us had our eyes on a theatrical career. We imagined,

quite wrongly, that the publicity which attended our performances, and the professional guidance we got from them, would dispense us from going through the mill. We little realized how uneasily we could stand on our own feet. We cherished our contacts with the profession and wasted a great deal of time in theatrical 'shop'.

When Speaight went down from Oxford, a few months after his triumph as Falstaff, he was able to get straight into a high-class 'rep' at the Liverpool Playhouse. But he soon discovered 'that star parts at Oxford, even under expert guidance, were no substitute for a systematic training at a drama school, or for a year or two finding my feet in a humbler repertory, or on tour'.

After *Henry IV* the OUDS finances were in a fairly secure position, the production having made a profit of £257 (expenses £985, takings £1,242). The professional producer was now being paid (£75 was about the average, much less than he would have earned for a West End show), but the actresses often gave their services free in return for hospitality and the invariable adulation of OUDS members. The ladies always praised Oxford, its beauties, and the friendliness of their fellow actors—to the extent that *Isis* parodied their remarks.

In fact the OUDS survived largely by not paying its bills. In 1926 H. M. D. Parker, a Keble don who was currently Senior Treasurer, offered his resignation in protest at the club's debts and lax credit to members, and was only persuaded to withdraw it after promises of reform. These were not kept, for no one could seriously contemplate giving up a system which allowed members to live like gentlemen. The club-room had a full-time Steward named Callow who lived in a house belonging to the OUDS (which at that time owned several properties in the vicinity of George Street); it was reported in the minutes that he and his family were crammed into one bedroom, and that the building was in a sorry state of repair. Resolutions were made to do something about it. There were several waiters, who were expected to come up to scratch; one minute records displeasure 'with the little smiling waiter who was as yet unable to distinguish between hors d'oeuvre and savoury' and who treated admonitions 'in too jovial a frame of mind'. The little smiler was eventually dismissed for attending a football match when he should have been at work.

Club-life continued unabated throughout the University year, and at the end of the 1920s the custom began of having an OUDS Rugger Match against Balliol, at which the OUDS usually made a good

showing. On the other hand there was a cooling of relations between the Society and the 'Old OUDS', who were being kept going energetically in London by Gerald Gardiner. John Fernald, OUDS President in 1927, had a letter from Gardiner asking him to attend an Old OUDS Committee meeting, but Fernald told his own Committee that he 'did not consider that the Old OUDS served any useful purpose, save the providing of tickets for the winter play to old members of the club. It had been founded in a spirit of sentimental comradeship on the part of immediate post-war members, a sentiment that no longer existed among present members.' An acrimonious correspondence ensued between Fernald and Gardiner.

The General Strike, falling conveniently between the winter and summer productions of 1926, had no effect on OUDS activities, and in May Fernald led another Scandinavian tour, taking productions of *Heartbreak House* and *The Rivals* to Denmark; the cast included Speaight, Emlyn Williams, and John Maud. Meanwhile Bridges-Adams's theatre at Stratford had burnt down just before he was due to begin his summer season; undeterred, he went ahead with his productions, staging them in the local cinema—and used Tim Abady's musical score for *Henry IV, Part 2* for his Stratford version of it. Arthur Bourchier, by now a doyen of actor-managers, keeping Victorian traditions alive in the post-war professional theatre, helped out by lending props to replace those destroyed in the fire.

The custom continued for the OUDS Smoker each March to parody February's New Theatre production, and in March 1926 Emlyn Williams was given the job of getting up a mock *Henry IV*. The show that he organized, and largely wrote, was an indication of how much the OUDS sights were nowadays set on London, for it was a musical comedy in miniature, with elaborate score and lengthy programme. The front page of the programme (*facing*) parodied those of big West End shows (or was it entirely parody?). The cast included characters such as 'Tumour, a prologue', 'Flagstaff, a cabaret king', and 'Dolga, the darling of the Prater', the latter played by Emlyn Williams himself, who sang such numbers as 'Bad, Bad Woman'. It was a five-week job for Williams—'getting numbers composed, producing and writing most of the dialogue, work not only gruelling but worthless in view of the low level, in every sense, expected of the book'. His academic work suffered more than ever. And then 'John Fernald bounced into the Ouds with a letter, Mr Fagan had arranged for us to

DENYS BUCKLEY presents

'Country Life,'

A MUSICAL COMEDY.

Book by Emlyn Williams, Patrick Monkhouse, Maurice Green, Allan Michelsen, Jim Courage, and others.

Lyrics by Rowland Leigh.

Music by Dick Addinsell.

Additional musical numbers by Tim Abady.

Produced by EMLYN WILLIAMS.

Musical Director: **DICK ADDINSELL.**

Dances and Ensembles by **ROWLAND LEIGH.**

Choreography of Ballet by **Emlyn Williams.**

Music of Ballet by **Tim Abady.**

At the Piano: **Dick Addinsell.**

Programme Cover by **Allan Michelsen.**

Wigs by **Potterton.**

King Henry dressed by **Walters.**

Spotlight kindly lent by **Morris Garages.**

Stage Manager   -   -   -   - **J. Malcolm McIntyre.**
Assistant Stage Manager   -   -   - **Cyril Mundy.**
Front of House Manager   -   -   - **John Counsell.**
MANAGER   -   -   - **MICHAEL HANKINSON.**

play *Vigil* in front of a couple of people in London, at the Fortune Theatre.' The 'couple of people' were in fact Sybil Thorndike and Lewis Casson, who gave it a kind reception; in consequence it was nearly impossible for Williams to tear his mind away from the theatre and work for his final Schools, which were due in June. He had a nervous breakdown, brought on by this and a complex emotional relationship with another male undergraduate, an OUDS member. At the crisis it was to 'Doggins' that he ran.

Crossing the Turl and passing Blackwell's—books, books, I shrank as if the rivers of print had wafted me a bad smell—I rang a bell where it said 'Dr Counsell'. His eyesight was already failing, and he was not sure who I was at first. I sat down, told him I wanted to die, and could he give me something. The dear old man—he had his own problems—blinked, sat next to me, put his arm round my shoulder and said, 'Now, tell old Doggins all about it.'

Sedated, Williams was taken away from Oxford back to his uncomprehending family in Wales. While there he wrote a play, *Full Moon*, which J. B. Fagan put on at the Oxford Playhouse. (Soon afterwards John Fernald directed it at the Arts Theatre in London.) Williams quickly fled his Welsh home and went to London, where it was Fagan who gave him his first job on the stage, a walk-on—'On one condition . . . As an old Trinity man, I insist that you take your Schools and get a respectable Second, a degree never did anybody in the theatre any harm.' Williams soon fulfilled this condition.

The OUDS had meant everything to him at Oxford, yet it had never discovered that he had anything of the tragic actor in him; as an undergraduate he was usually cast in comic roles. The Society was better at discovering comic talent than serious acting. In June 1926 Fagan produced *A Midsummer Night's Dream* in Magdalen Grove, and John Maud was cast as Bottom, filling the role very adequately. Among the 'mechanicals', John Betjeman was given the part of Starveling; John Fernald recalls that Betjeman 'had a nice line in comic old men and his Starveling was extremely funny. He could certainly have become a professional actor had he so wished.'

Isis reported of this production:'Mr Fagan has a scheme for laying seductive trails of food across the grassy sward of the stage, so as to bring in the local colour of the Magdalen Deer at opportune moments.' The plan failed—*Isis* pointed out that 'these deer are too fat to walk at all'—but otherwise the natural scenic effects were stunning. Fagan got

hold of a set of golden dresses for the fairies—played by schoolchildren—which had been used by Harley Granville-Barker in a celebrated pre-1914 production (they were now owned by John Masefield and used in his private theatricals on Boar's Hill), and W. A. Darlington was rapturous about the results: 'The effect of the gold against the green, as the two delightful bands of fairies approach from the shadows of the Grove, might inspire a pen less prosaic than mine to lyric flights.' The weather was wet until the opening night, whereupon the sky miraculously became cloudless; the last performance was on Midsummer Night at full moon. Charles Morgan in *The Times* was as lyrical as Darlington:

For *A Midsummer Night's Dream* it would be hard to find or imagine a lovelier setting. The great trees, the wide spaces, the prolonged distances belong to mortals lost or sleeping and fairies on the march. Here Puck may put a girdle round about the earth as he never can in a theatre, and here Titania approaching from afar with an escort so small in stature that the grasses are almost a forest to them, may cast over all who watch a long increasing spell, so that, when she stands at last before you, you may see in her not a sudden apparition, not even a creature of fairy-tale, but a queen quietly moving through a realm that has always been her own.

Jean Forbes-Robertson was the professional Titania, an actress with a cold, rather remote beauty who made a huge impression the next year as an eerie Peter Pan, a role she was to play regularly until 1939. 'Doggins' describes her Oxford performance: 'Jean Forbes-Robertson played Titania with a fey charm that truly seemed to belong to the world of fairies. No one fortunate enough to have seen it on the nights of the full moon can ever forget its unearthly beauty.' Robert Speaight, who was watching the production, recalls her rather differently: 'There was nothing airy-fairy about her Titania; rather, a grave and tranquil "otherness", a kind of literal magic, which compelled your unquestioning assent. Peter Pan and Titania are not easily interchangeable roles, but in her case they proved to be so.'

The only reviewer to mention John Betjeman's performance as Starveling was a Danish reporter, presumably sent to Oxford because of the OUDS' frequent visits to his country; he recorded that 'Starveling was represented as an old, half-dead fool'. By this time Betjeman had begun to make his mark on OUDS. There is a cryptic reference in the minutes for 23 May 1926 to 'Mr Betjemann refusing his resigna-

tion under rule 47'. Unfortunately it is impossible to discover what rule 47 was. Betjeman must have proved recalcitrant, for on 30 May it is recorded that 'The Secretary and Mr Fernald said they would see Mr Betjemann concerning his resignation.' Since he was not sacked from the cast he must have made his peace with the Committee. A set of pen-portraits of OUDS members in the recently-founded undergraduate weekly *Cherwell* on 19 June included this entry: 'J. Betjeman. He is the club naughty boy. He could be a poet if he took the trouble.'

With Isham and Speaight gone, not to mention Emlyn Williams, the OUDS acting talent was somewhat depleted by Michaelmas 1926, Harman Grisewood being the only performer of stature to remain. In these circumstances the Committee made a particularly daring choice of producer for the coming February production, engaging someone whose presence and style of direction would almost certainly make up for a lack of solid acting ability. Theodore Komisarjevsky, born into an aristocratic Russian family, was the director of the Imperial and State theatres in pre-Revolutionary Moscow, and Chekhov considered him to be an outstanding interpreter of his plays. He came to England not long after the Revolution, and his fiery unpredictable talents made much impression on the discerning. Rather surprisingly, he had not yet tackled Shakespeare. The OUDS invited him to direct *King Lear*. The play was then generally regarded as unactable, and was treated warily by most producers; it had not been performed in London since 1910, and Bridges-Adams fought shy of it at Stratford. There was a chance that Komisarjevsky's approach would be so fresh as to change the popular view entirely.

John Fernald writes of Komisarjevsky's impact on British theatre at this time.

It is difficult to explain and do justice to the excitement caused when he astonished us all in the autumn of 1926 with his productions (in a sleazy converted cinema in the suburb of Barnes) of three Tchekhov plays and an adaptation of *Tess of the d'Urbervilles*. We had never seen acting so 'real' and so deeply felt. Several decades later I was asked to give a memorial lecture on him at King's College, London, and this is what I said in the introductory paragraph:

For the first time since Granville Barker we began to look at ourselves, our theatre and our acting through the eyes of an artist whose values were conditioned by the idea of the non-commercial theatre. We were suddenly able to see acting not as a system of exploiting the appetites of audiences

through a tricksy compound of personality, experience and technique, nor as a means of reproducing an author's argument, but as a process of continuous distillation of thought and feeling to which the audience made its contribution but did not dictate the terms.

Something of the kind had been felt by all of us in *King Lear*, we found ourselves giving better performances than we thought we were capable of—and hardly understood why until many years later, when our perceptive capacities had grown up.

Komisarjevsky opened his work on the OUDS production by remarking characteristically to his company: 'A professional cast would need three months to rehearse this play: you, three years: and you have three weeks. So we cannot act the play. We must just try to speak it.' He was scarcely exaggerating: reviewers were to make the point of later OUDS Shakespeare productions that they stood or fell on the verse-speaking. On the other hand Komisarjevsky does not seem to have been condescending about working with amateurs; in *Myself and the Theatre*, published two years after the OUDS *Lear*, he remarked of amateur performers: 'I must say that they take their work much more to heart and are much less selfish than professionals, and the results of the work with them are usually much more fresh and sincere.'

The press began to take an interest in his Oxford *Lear* long before the opening night. It was reported that 'Rigid simplicity is to be the keynote . . . The stage will be built of platforms and rostrums at various heights . . . By the combination of two lighting systems and a gold panorama cloth the heath can immediately be transformed into the interior of the palace without any change of scene.' The 'two lighting systems' meant an augmentation of the New Theatre's somewhat limited electrical resources, and an OUDS minute records the Committee's anxiety 'as to whether there would be enough electric current available'. Strand Electric was called in to make good any deficiency. Meanwhile the cast nicknamed Komisarjevsky's up-and-down set of rostrums and narrow steps 'The Mappin Terrace'.

Komisarjevsky predictably chose Harman Grisewood for Lear; Denys Buckley, now the President, was to play Gloucester, Leslie Nye was cast as Edgar, and Gabriel Toyne, a fencing blue, was chosen for Edmund. Rehearsals were held partly in the University fencing school, so that the fights could be as realistic as possible. Others took place as usual in the dining-room of the club in George Street. John Betjeman in *Summoned by Bells* describes the scene:

We'll thread the hurrying Corn and George Street crowds
        To the unlovely entrance of the OUDS
                And hear
How Harman Grisewood, in the tones which thrill
                His audience in *Lear*,
        Orders a postcard and a penny stamp . . .
And in the next-door room is heard the tramp
        And 'rhubarb, rhubarb' as the crowd rehearse . . .

Among that crowd was Osbert Lancaster, who had just come up to Lincoln College. After a grim week or two trying to row for his college he 'cast in my lot with the aesthetes, laid down my oar and joined the OUDS'. As a new member he was first cast in 'the anonymous ranks of Goneril's drunken knights', but soon found himself promoted. This is how he relates the incident in *With an Eye to the Future* (1967):

It so happened that *The Cherwell*, the less reputable but by far the livelier of the two undergraduate magazines, was at that time edited by John Betjeman who published a cod photograph, with a ribald caption, of the O.U.D.S. rehearsing. The club, which in those days took itself very seriously, was furious and both Denys Buckley, the president, and Harman Grisewood, who was playing Lear, insisted on the poet's immediate expulsion. Unluckily this resolute but rather hastily considered move involved a major reshuffle of the cast less than a fortnight before the first night, for Betjeman was playing the Fool, a major rôle which had now to be taken over by John Fernald, who relinquished the part of the Duke of Cornwall to Peter Fleming, until then only the Duke of Cornwall's servant, to enact whom I was now promoted.

Apparently the unembroidered facts were slightly different. Betjeman was originally chosen to play the Fool but (according to Fernald) was then 'forbidden to do any more acting because of interdiction by his college, and I, who had been warned that I might have to take over the part from him, did so'. The picture appeared in *Cherwell*, but not until just before the opening night. Captioned 'A Last Minute Rehearsal of the OUDS', it exactly catches and parodies the atmosphere of the real thing.

Peter Fleming, later a travel and real-life adventure writer, had just come up from Eton to Christ Church, and loved amateur theatricals. His favourite part was Bulldog Drummond, with whom he closely identified; he had once impersonated Sapper's hero in a performance at the Electric Cinema, Newport Pagnell; on this occasion Frank Pakenham (the future Lord Longford, then a New College undergrad-

uate) had what Fleming's biographer Duff Hart-Davis calls 'a sort of Third Murderer part—his stealthy movements being reminiscent of an immature pachyderm which had fallen unexpectedly into a morass'. Unfortunately the OUDS did not acquire the services of the pachydermic Pakenham, but Fleming quickly became an ambitious member. Meanwhile Osbert Lancaster had to cope with the acrobatic demands of Komisarjevsky's set:

Keen Shakespeareans will readily recall that the Duke of Cornwall's servant, although not a very large part, has one highly important and spectacular scene of which, I flatter myself, I made the most. The honest fellow, appalled by his master's treatment of the unfortunate Gloucester, bids him stay his hand, is promptly set upon by the incensed Duke and, after a prolonged sword-fight, slain. Thanks to the Mappin Terraces with which Komisarjevsky had filled the entire stage—a device which in those days, at least in England, was looked on as revolutionary—the sword-fight, for which we had received special training from the University sabre champion, became one of the highlights of the production and each night I confidently awaited the horrified intake of breath with which my dying fall from the topmost ledge was regularly greeted. That I survived a week of this, relatively intact, was due to luck, careful timing and the maintenance of strict precautions in the matter of body-armour; others were not so fortunate, or so careful, and Peter Fleming, ever impetuous, on one occasion, when he had scorned to put on his helmet, received a nasty crack on the head from my four-foot blade (steel, not papier-mâché) and on another, having forgotten his mail gauntlet, received a wound which lent dramatic emphasis to his exit-line, 'I bleed apace!' Nor was he the only victim, for one night as I swung Excalibur over my left shoulder a loud groan signalled that I had dealt an effective back-hander to one of those old men whom Shakespeare so frequently leaves hanging about the stage, invariably in one of the pools of darkness without a superfluity of which no continental producer can possibly make do. The very next evening my trusty weapon finally failed, snapping off smartly at the hilt, flying across the stage, tearing through a flat and, after narrowly missing Miss Martita Hunt who was playing Goneril, buried itself in the prompt-side wall.

Such excitements tended to distract attention from Harman Grisewood's attempt at Lear himself. When the production opened, reviewers were quick to identify the central weakness.

Sincerity, restraint, a sense of verse, a personal subtlety of intellect and imagination will carry Hamlet far [wrote Charles Morgan in *The Times*, remembering Isham three years earlier], but they can avail little to make the madness of Lear emerge clearly from the tempest's madness . . . Lear is, in the

highest sense, the most theatrical of the great Shakespearian parts. Natural genius, without technical knowledge, particularly if its struggle for illusion be hampered at every turn by the voice and gesture of extreme youth, is scarcely more valuable on the heath than in command of a three-masted ship in a hurricane . . . M. Komisarjevsky's proper genius . . . does not make him a quick tutor of undergraduate actors playing Shakespeare in English, nor, indeed, are his qualities of a kind to minimize their defects.

Morgan, however, allowed himself a little cautious praise of Grisewood: 'His opening scene was a flurry of impetuous anger, and on the heath, when his voice was inevitably strained, tumult beat the meaning out of his words; but at the end, when he might be quiet with Cordelia, there was a genuine depth in his quietness. Lear is beyond his present range, but good acting most certainly is not.' One of the difficulties was the contrast of experience between the undergraduates and the professional actresses; on this occasion the latter almost swamped the former. Morgan praised Martita Hunt and Dorothy Green as Goneril and Regan, and was especially complimentary about Cordelia, played by a beautiful dark-eyed young actress named Elizabeth Greenhill, who he said 'shone with lucid accomplishment'. But he judged finally that 'the most loyal friend of the OUDS and the warmest admirer of M. Komisarjevsky's work could not but confess that, on this occasion, the Society had seriously over-reached itself'.

James Agate in the *Sunday Times*, however, took a characteristically subtle view of Grisewood's performance. He accepted that the part was virtually unactable, and argued that most professional Lears got in the way of Shakespeare's words. But

at Oxford you could see *through* the actor to the character, whereas in roles of greater attainability your eye stops at the performance . . . In friendliness to Mr Grisewood, and to show him that one was paying attention, one might tell him that his gestures were too young, that he did not mark the crescendo of lunacy, that when he awoke from his last sleep but one it was with the alacrity of a midshipman bidden to show a leg. But I prefer to pay this thoughtful young actor the compliment of saying that at his loudest he never got in the way, and that in the quiet passages he helped you to re-create your own Lear . . . The staging was so completely successful that one forgot all about it, and thought only of the play.

Despite the enormous improvement in the quality of OUDS productions since the war, undergraduate behaviour at performances had scarcely mended itself, and there were often tipsy latecomers. An

attempt was made one year to shut them out until the first interval, but the only result was a great deal of noise in the foyer of the theatre, a battle with the staff to gain admission, and a cheer raised when this was achieved. Even during the Komisarkjevsky *Lear* audience behaviour was sometimes terrible.

On the last night there was the usual OUDS Supper, with Komisarjevsky in the place of honour. He gave a speech in Russian, which was translated by the popular novelist Maurice Baring, another guest; according to Robert Speaight it began as follows:

Komisarjevsky: «Король Лир» очень плохая пьеса.
Baring: King Lear is a very bad play.
Komisarjevsky: Я очень хороший режиссёр.
Baring: I am a very good producer.

After the Supper came the invariable last-night party at Doggins's, attended on this occasion by Osbert Lancaster:

After the last night of the run it was customary for a large party to be held, allowed by the Proctors to continue till dawn, in Dr Counsell's house in The Broad. It was attended not only by the whole cast but also by former members of the Society, some of whom were already firmly established in the London theatre. The principal entertainment was provided by musical members past and present repeating the numbers which they had composed for OUDS smokers, many of which—such as 'How now brown cow'—had, after some slight modification of the lyrics at the request of the Lord Chamberlain, reappeared in West End revues. On the first occasion on which I was present we had to wait a long time for this ritual treat as Komisarjevsky, whose temperament was exaggeratedly Slav, despite his local triumph and the long and favourable notices in the London press and his successful seduction of the leading lady, was suddenly overwhelmed with gloom and retired to a corner where he monopolized the piano for hours on end playing a melancholy and interminable Russian folk-song with one finger. For me the evening was also rendered unforgettable by my first cigar which combined with an all-night session, sustained on alternate draughts of whisky and mulled claret, to produce my earliest and most horrible hangover.

The fun of the last-night parties, remarks Lancaster, 'was in no small measure due to the presence of the actresses; this was the result not so much of their professional glamour as simply of their sex, for in those days in Oxford women played a very small part in our lives.' Though there had been female students in the University since the 1870s, and women had been allowed to take degrees since 1920, no

suggestion was made that they should participate in the OUDS. The few women up at Oxford who had a serious interest in the theatre therefore found life hard. An Australian girl named Helen de Guerry Simpson came up to Oxford Home Students (late St Anne's College) in 1920 to study music, but she was devoted to acting and the writing of plays, and left before completing her degree 'because the university objected to her taste for the stage'. In June 1924 her play *The Cautious Lovers* was given a club performance at the Lyceum, and the *Daily Graphic* reported that while at Oxford she was 'the first president of the women's section of the OUDS'. It seems highly improbable that she held any such office, which would not have been countenanced in George Street; her theatrical activities at Oxford chiefly took place at John Masefield's home on Boar's Hill. Later she collaborated with Clemence Dane in the writing of plays, and also produced detective stories.

At Cambridge attitudes were even more reactionary at this period; actresses (professional or otherwise) were not allowed at all in the ADC or the Marlowe Society, and male undergraduates took all the female roles. (On the other hand the Cambridge societies were allowed to do modern plays without restriction, and Harold Acton, reviewing an ADC production of Pirandello's *Henry IV* for *Cherwell* in 1924, compared the quality of their productions favourably with those of the OUDS: 'They do not secure fungoid producers from London to do their dirty work.') Even in Oxford, as late as 1926 the idea came up in an OUDS Committee meeting, when the performance of one-act plays was being discussed, 'that, as a last resort, it might be possible to allow members of the club to play female parts'. In fact a year later the barrier was temporarily lifted, and for the first time women undergraduates took part in an OUDS production.

This was *The Tempest*, directed by Reginald Denham in Worcester College gardens. *Isis* reported in May 1927 that 'a startling innovation . . . will be the performances of an undergraduette in a female role'. John Fernald, who was largely responsible for the decision, remembers it as 'really a sort of publicity gimmick: we thought we might acquire some merit in the eyes of the ladies' colleges by taking them more seriously than we ever had before'. An announcement was made of auditions for ladies, though it was stipulated that the OUDS reserved the right to engage a professional actress should no suitable local candidate be found. This provoked complaints among the more

militant young women at Oxford, who declared that the whole thing was a put-up job—the OUDS would say they couldn't find a good enough Miranda, would hire a professional, and would declare that this proved the inadequacy of Oxford's women. There were strongly-worded denials of this from the OUDS. A female correspondent to *Isis* ('Eve') also reported that 'some among us have taken up a nasty carping attitude. "Parlourmaids? Who is going to make application to enter the OUDS domestic service; a good appearance and pleasant voice required?"' But there were twenty-four female applicants, and the Committee, evidently feeling they were on to a good thing, chose not one but two Mirandas, Dulcie Martin and Molly Blissett. Both were from Somerville. Blissett was to play the part at six out of the eleven performances and Martin at the remainder. Osbert Lancaster says that Dulcie Martin was the belle of her year, 'with whom many were in love and to whom not a few were engaged'. However, John Fernald remembers that her 'charm withered somewhat when she tried to act, as her voice was thin and un-"produced". Molly Blissett, on the other hand, was far better but also far plainer!'

The newspapers reported that 'Miss Fry, the principal of Somerville, has lent her two students her private garden in which to practise open-air voice production.' Meanwhile the OUDS Commit-tee, apparently feeling that they had done quite enough to satisfy female ambitions, decided that Iris, Juno, and Ceres, the only other women's parts in *The Tempest*, should be played by men. The Vice-Chancellor refused permission, whereupon their appearance was cut from the play.

Osbert Lancaster landed the part of Sebastian, and Peter Fleming hoped to get Prospero. He was unlucky, for it went to Julian Hall, a fellow Old Etonian who had come up to Balliol. Fleming complained bitterly to his friend Rupert Hart-Davis:

I have as bloody a part as you could wish to find—Alonzo, King of Naples, who wears a beard and indulges in conversation as limited as it is irrelevant. I missed getting Prospero by the breadth only of the most attenuated capillary attachment: all the other fairly amusing parts I might easily have got had by that time been filled with histrionic riff-raff, so I find myself confronted with the depressing prospect of saying 'Peace, prithee', or, alternatively, 'Prithee, peace', at intervals of 100 beautiful lines.

In fact there was another cast reshuffle, and Fleming ended up as

Antonio, a part which gave some scope to his Bulldog Drummond personality. He was also allowed to understudy Prospero, and nearly had his chance when Julian Hall was injured in a car crash; but it was decided that Harman Grisewood should step in and read the part.

The production was not very exciting. 'The storm was dropped out of the play,' reported the *Telegraph*, 'and the only sign that it had ever raged was an upturned boat lying so far down the stage that it was obvious that the lake had nothing to do with putting it there.' There was also 'the noise of shunting engines and peripatetic motor bicycles' to disturb the play. The same reviewer felt that Molly Blissett's performance as Miranda 'showed a certain self-consciousness not unnatural in the circumstances, but was very intelligent'. John Fernald felt that the experiment of using her and Dulcie Martin was a failure, 'and for those of us who were serious about acting it was a great loss, for we seemed to have forgotten how much was gained in OUDS productions by being able to learn from our professional guest artists'.

After this 1927 production women undergraduates were not invited to participate in OUDS productions again for many years. In the meantime the women's colleges mounted their own productions with all-female casts. Anne Scott-James, who was at Somerville in the early 1930s (and who is now married to Sir Osbert Lancaster), felt that 'it was a bit tough that all those callow OUDS undergraduates should swan about on stage with Peggy Ashcroft and what not while we weren't allowed to'. To add to the unfairness, local women amateurs who were not undergraduates were frequently used to swell the crowds in OUDS productions, while some of the so called 'professional' actresses scarcely deserved the name. Daphne Levens, whose husband was a don at Merton College, remembers auditioning for an OUDS production in the late 1930s and finding a throng of women queuing in the hope of getting roles: 'There were girls from drama school, desperate to get a speaking part; socialite sisters of OUDS members down from London; "elderly" local ladies in their thirties wanting walk-ons. Everybody wanted to get in.'

Plenty of local ladies (excluding undergraduates) were needed for the crowd in *The Fourteenth of July* by the contemporary French author Romain Rolland, performed by the OUDS at the New Theatre in February 1928. Komisarjevsky was invited back to direct. 'As M. Rolland is a living author, this constitutes a break with the OUDS tradition', reported the *Yorkshire Post*. The choice of play was John

Fernald's; *Cherwell* described it as 'a rather bad play about the French Revolution', but to Fernald 'it appeared to have a splendid blend of revolutionary and nationalistic fervour, tempered with philosophy and generalized sentiment that in a revolution it is "all the people" who suffer'. Moreover there was 'a huge cast and nice rousing speeches we could all get our tongues around'. Peter Fleming was given the reasonably large part of Pierre Augustin Hulin, Osbert Lancaster played Marat, and a Christ Church freshman named Valentine Dyall (son of the actor Franklin Dyall) appeared as 'a Mason'. But the chief actor, as everyone concerned with the production was keen to point out, was the crowd. Fernald's programme note explained: 'The author has attempted to paint one character, and one alone, the People of Paris . . . Thus individuals do not matter.'

The OUDS minutes record that a few days before the performance 'there were murmurings at the hanging of red flags out of the club windows—which were a little quieted by the President's assurance that it was only done to get them dirty'. Reviews were rather cool. Even the genius of Komisarjevsky did not manage to inject much life into the crowd, who according to *Isis* 'never quite succeeded in stirring the audience'. But they managed to stir each other, according to Osbert Lancaster who was in the thick of it, and who alleged that casualties were even higher than in *Lear*.

The ambulance was almost permanently at the stage door. This was largely due to the thoroughness with which the women of Paris, recruited from the frustrated daughters of North Oxford, rendered almost hysterical by the glamour of the footlights and their first gin-and-limes, armed with broomsticks, flails and rolling pins, stormed the Bastille. In the rôle of Marat I was in a particularly exposed position as Monsieur Rolland had apparently convinced himself that I could stem the onrush and prevent a general massacre by hoisting a repellent child on to my shoulder and saying, 'Listen to our little sparrow!', an invitation which the women of Paris understandably disregarded. That the child in question survived the holocaust to score a notable success as *Alice in Wonderland* in London the following Christmas I held to be entirely due to my presence of mind and total forgetfulness of self.

Peter Fleming got good reviews as Hulin and was elected President of the OUDS. At the end of March 1928 he produced three one-act plays at the Playhouse for the National Union of Students Congress —*Five Years*, of which John Fernald was co-author, Emlyn Williams's *Vigil*, and *King's Evidence*, a political thriller by Fleming himself, set in

'a prison cell in the capital of Auraine, a third-rate European power'. Meanwhile it became apparent that the OUDS charter had been transgressed, since no Greek play had been performed for more than four years. Hasty discussions were held, and a general meeting of the Society revealed that most members would gladly do without a Greek play. But it was pointed out that if the OUDS refused to put one on, another society might well be formed to stage it, and this would then exist in rivalry; moreover the OUDS 'could not afford to divorce itself entirely from academic interests'. In consequence Cyril Bailey was invited to produce the *Clouds* of Aristophanes in Greek at the New Theatre in June 1928, with an all-male cast. Maurice Bowra, classical tutor at Wadham College and unofficial Senior Member to the Harold Acton circle, made a rare excursion into drama as Bailey's assistant producer. In other respects the production was unremarkable.

By 1929 the era of Acton, Brian Howard, and the rest of the *Brideshead* generation at Oxford had come to an end, and many OUDS celebrities had departed too. Peter Fleming was highly ambitious, but the theatre was not really his forte. For the major production during his presidency, at the New Theatre in February 1929, he and the Committee selected *Othello* and chose as director Brewster Morgan, an American Rhodes Scholar at St Edmund Hall. The notion of having an undergraduate director was Fleming's own—he proposed it after the original choice, Raymond Massey, had proved to be unavailable—and much publicity was made out of this departure from tradition, the press stating that it was the first time an undergraduate had produced for the OUDS. This was scarcely true; moreover Brewster Morgan was scarcely an undergraduate in the common understanding of that word. Older than most of his contemporaries and already armed with an American degree, he had worked in professional theatre in Kansas and claimed to have been a pupil of Max Reinhardt. He entertained on a lavish scale and went around with a bodyguard of disciples.

He was not a good producer; *Cherwell* described his *Othello* as being on 'conventional lines'. The title role was given to Valentine Dyall, then in his second year at Christ Church. Very tall and already possessed of the sinister *basso profundo* that would make him famous as 'The Man in Black' (not to mention his appearances in *The Goon Show*), Dyall nevertheless lacked the qualities of a memorable Othello. However, Maurice Bowra, reviewing the production in *Isis*, was fairly polite: 'Mr Dyall . . . is not afraid to let himself go. He sweeps over the stage, he

roars and moans with the confidence of an old hand . . . He possesses a naturally low voice, and at times it becomes inaudible simply because it is an octave lower than the voices of the other actors.' *Cherwell* was equally bland: 'To speak of Valentine Dyall's performance as Othello is nothing but a pleasure . . . He was at his best in Othello's moments of hysteria.' The same reviewer was also good-mannered about the production's Iago—Peter Fleming himself, who as President could at last get a really good part: 'Peter Fleming's portrayal [of Iago] as the perfect melodrama-villain was perfectly right . . . after all, the pure spirit of evil has a somewhat Bullingdon-Eton attitude.' But the truth, as Duff Hart-Davis makes clear in his life of Fleming, was that Fleming was playing Iago as Bulldog Drummond:

These careful and on the whole eulogistic assessments diverge strikingly from the memories of Peter's contemporaries. To them, *Othello* was a disaster, a shambles pulled through only by Martita Hunt's highly professional Emilia. Nor is it easy, now, to see how Peter's acting can have won such acclaim, for his friends remember him as being quite embarrassingly bad . . . To Osbert Lancaster, Peter's renderings of Bulldog Drummond and Iago were indistinguishable. Many of his friends thought it almost pathetic that someone could be so passionately keen on acting and yet so frightfully bad at it.

6

Battles and Balloons

WHEN Peter Fleming's term of office ended in the spring of 1929, Brewster Morgan took over as President, with Valentine Dyall as Secretary, and J. B. Fagan was invited to produce Beaumont and Fletcher's *The Knight of the Burning Pestle* in Magdalen Grove. The production, Fagan's last for the OUDS, was unmemorable. The OUDS had reached a state of flaccidity. It soon acquired two members who injected fresh energy into it; but thanks to them most of the OUDS dramas over the next couple of years took place off-stage rather than on it.

At Michaelmas 1929 George Devine came up to Wadham. He was the son of a bank clerk and a woman who had gone insane; consequently at Oxford, in the words of his biographer Irving Wardle, 'he played the part of a self-created character with a mysterious background'. Solid-looking and very untheatrical in appearance, he had nevertheless acquired plenty of stage experience at Clayesmore, a public school founded by his talented but eccentric uncle Alexander. He expected to inherit the school, and intended to work hard and get a good degree which would qualify him to run it. But he also joined the OUDS, and according to a contemporary (T. R. Williams) 'made a big impact very quickly. He looked and behaved like a man among boys; and it seemed inevitable to us lesser mortals that this chap would become President'. After a few terms Devine's uncle died, whereupon it transpired that there was no school to inherit—Clayesmore had been established on insecure finances—so that Devine began to consider the theatre as an alternative profession. He became determined to secure the OUDS presidency, and thereby came up against Giles Playfair.

Nigel Playfair's heir had been brought up in the centre of the theatrical world, and both enjoyed and resented being 'My Father's Son'—the title he afterwards gave to his memoirs of childhood and

Oxford. Heavily built like his father and possessed of an almost permanent scowl, he had a self-destructive streak which compelled him to do outrageous things as publicly as possible. At Harrow he had cultivated unpopularity as if it were a virtue to be considered a 'bounder'. Now he began to do the same thing at Oxford, and to do it largely within the walls of the OUDS. His surname quickly got him elected to membership, and he was cast in a largish part in the next major production, in February 1930. This was *Macbeth* at the New Theatre, and Brewster Morgan was once again to direct.

Playfair immediately detected (or thought he detected) that the OUDS was dominated by 'a spirit of ungovernable conceit'. It seemed to him, after a few visits to the club-rooms, that the Society was divided into three ranks, which he dubbed 'ruling class', 'aristocracy or prefects', and 'working class'.

The 'ruling class' consisted of the officers and the members of the committee [he writes in *My Father's Son*[1]] . . . They had a serious appreciation of their onerous duties. Every Sunday they met in the strictest privacy to decide future policy. The secrets they discussed weighed heavily upon them for the rest of the week. And no wonder! For they alone had prior information of the name of the famous actress who was going to be honoured with an invitiation to undertake the part of Lady Macbeth or some other mighty part . . . The aristocracy or 'prefects' were scarcely less convinced of their own importance. They regarded the OUDS more as a social centre than as a play-producing society, for they did not act themselves. But they were loyal members nevertheless . . . The despised 'working class' seldom appeared excepting when rehearsals of *Macbeth* were actually in progress. They filled the minor and walk-on parts and it was obviously necessary that they should do so, since the officers were fully occupied with the leading roles and the prefects did not care to act. But apart from this, their co-operation was not encouraged and their presence in the club-room was unwelcome . . . Yet they did not complain. For they, too, had been hypnotized by a slogan which was common to every loyal member of the OUDS, 'Isn't Brewster wonderful?'

Giles Playfair did not think that Brewster Morgan was wonderful. 'His talents appeared greatly over-rated and it was difficult to regard him as a professional man of the theatre.' Playfair was cast as Malcolm in *Macbeth*, and he soon detected Morgan's 'deficiencies' and began to mount an attack on him. 'The louder his praises were sung, the more acutely I felt the call to arms!' He managed to get some support from

---

[1] Geoffrey Bles, 1937.

the 'working class', and was consequently soon under suspicion as an insurgent. Morgan meanwhile did not care for Playfair's performance: ' "Oh, Playfair," he said in American, "can't you understand? I know those lines rhyme, but for Christ's sake don't let the audience realize it!" ' Playfair did not improve, and consequently was hauled up before one of the 'prefects', who (he claimed) told him: 'Brewster is offended and offence must not be caused him. He has been very worried lately. His work on *Macbeth* has proved a severe tax on his nervous energies. I know that you, Playfair, have your own ideas. You have been brought up in the Shakespearian tradition. But Brewster does not wish to make *Macbeth* Shakespearian. He wants to make of it a real, live, human drama. Please to understand you must obey him implicitly, otherwise you will be relieved of your part.'

Playfair continued to be rebellious and, though not relieved of his part, found his unpopularity increasing. He prophesied that *Macbeth* would be a failure, and by the standards of productions in the Speaight era it certainly was. Valentine Dyall was no more remarkable as Macbeth than he had been as the Moor, and though Gwen Ffrangcon-Davies delivered a competent Lady Macbeth, *Isis* judged the whole thing 'rather a triumph of production and setting than of acting'. The London critics were blandly polite. Peter Bayne, then the junior treasurer of the club, production manager for *Macbeth*, and President-elect, told Playfair: 'Now you understand how wrong you were. All Oxford is talking about *Macbeth*.' To which Playfair replied: 'Anyone can make Oxford talk. I bet you that, within three days, *Macbeth* will be completely forgotten and that an activity of mine will be the centre of attention.' He fulfilled his boast.

This was the age when undergraduate hoaxes were the rage at Oxford, and were reported eagerly by the London press. (For example Tom Driberg and friends had mounted a hoax concert entitled 'Homage to Beethoven'.) Playfair and Robert Speaight's brother Hugh, who had just left Oxford and was working as a reporter on the *Morning Post*, now devised one. Speaight's plan, says Playfair, was simple. 'He and I became the founders of an Oxford University Balloon Union. True, we never had members. But from the beginning we had enterprise.'

They wrote a letter to the *Daily Mail* announcing the formation of the Balloon Union, and were immediately 'besieged by reporters' to whom they announced plans for a nationwide 'Back to Balloons'

campaign. The press lapped it up, and the columns of Fleet Street became full of the doings of the non-existent Union. The *Oxford Mail* editor Charles Fenby, wise to the hoax but knowing a good story when he saw one, had Playfair and Speaight photographed in a laundry basket which appeared to be suspended from ropes, and printed the picture over the caption 'The founders of the Oxford University Balloon Union out practising'. Speaight ordered a thousand sheets of notepaper printed with the Balloon Union's name, and even enlisted Doggins—'Medical Officer of the Union, Dr H. E. Counsell'. Osbert Lancaster, then co-editing *Cherwell*, published a leader headed 'Buy British Balloons!'

At this point, somewhat to the surprise of Messrs Playfair and Speaight, a real balloonist materialized, one Captain Percival Spencer, and the Oxford Gas Company agreed to provide the means of inflation for an ascent under the auspices of the Union. A date was fixed (Sunday 15 March 1930), and Speaight sent out notices to the press 'that Miss Tallulah Bankhead and Sir Nigel Playfair have signified their intention of ascending in the official balloon'. Reporters were also informed 'that on the day of the ascent Oxford housewives would be compelled to eat a late luncheon, as the inflation (lasting all morning) would cause a general shortage of gas throughout the city'. Hall Brothers, the fashionable Oxford gentlemen's outfitters, agreed to design and produce a 'ballooning hat', and a message of goodwill to the Union was sent by the Prime Minister, Ramsay MacDonald.

The day dawned, a luncheon party was held by the Playfairs with a grandly worded menu (*Huîtres Montgolfier . . . Dindon à la Ballonière*), and the guests of honour set out for the Oxford Gas Works.

I shall never forget the sight that greeted us [writes Giles Playfair]. In the middle of a vast, black-grounded area, Captain Spencer was standing by his fully inflated balloon. Near him, hundreds of reporters, feature writers, photographers and news-reel men were hustling each other for pride of place. Farther away, three thousand members of the general public, who had all paid sixpence for admission, formed a circle of silent spectators. And in the distance there was a view of the red gasometers.

As soon as we appeared, a concerted rush was made at us. We gave hurried interviews, we posed for innumerable photographs, and we spoke for British Movietone News . . . Tallulah released the balloon, but she did not ascend herself . . . The ascent, indeed, was only made with difficulty. The gas was not of the right quality to withstand too heavy a load, and after three abortive

attempts to take off, a reporter, who had offered a handsome price to be a passenger, and I both renounced our places. Speaight and his pilot (Captain Spencer) alone were left. To the accompaniment of loud cheers from the crowd, the balloon finally rose from the ground, narrowly skirted the top of a gasometer, and disappeared into the distant skies.

The event earned Playfair a place in *Who's Who in British Aviation* and, more important to him, made him famous throughout the University. But not everyone viewed such self-publicizing with pleasure. One of Playfair's OUDS contemporaries, Lionel Hale, later well known in Fleet Street and the theatre, thought the whole thing outrageous: 'While the ascent from the Oxford Gas Works had been in progress, he had sat in the OUDS, a solitary and embittered figure, furiously telephoning an abusive story about the Balloon Union to the offices of the *Daily Mail*.' Hale was on the staff of *Isis*, and did his best to attack Playfair publicly, accusing him of decamping with the large funds belonging to the Balloon Union (there were no funds). Few other OUDS members were so actively hostile, and when Playfair stepped in at the last minute to fill the role of Sebastian in *Twelfth Night*, replacing another actor who was ill, the Committee thanked him. 'But I was, by no stretch of the imagination, forgiven. I was still carefully left uninvited to the various "official" parties which took place after the evening performances, and I was treated more as a prisoner, temporarily released on parole, than as a prodigal son returned to his home!' He retaliated by founding a dramatic society in his own college, the Merton Floats, and staged Massinger's *A New Way to Pay Old Debts* with his father directing and Hermione Baddeley in the cast; Giles Playfair himself appropriately played Sir Giles Overreach.

The *Twelfth Night* production, in Wadham gardens during June 1930, had George Devine as Sir Toby and was directed by Gyles Isham, who since leaving Oxford had become an actor at the Old Vic. (He continued to be a popular figure in the theatre throughout the 1930s, but after service in the Second World War, having inherited his father's baronetcy, gave up acting to run the family estate in Northamptonshire.) For its next major show, at the New Theatre in February 1931, the OUDS decided to attempt the spectacular and mount a production of James Elroy Flecker's exotic verse-play *Hassan*. This could not be done without paying for the services of Basil Dean, who had staged the first London production some eight years earlier and who had the exclusive rights of presenting it. Moreover Dean,

though billed as 'supervising' the OUDS production, did not bother to attend more than a couple of rehearsals, and left the whole thing in the hands of his stage manager Gibson Cowan.

Rather surprisingly, in view of his behaviour towards them, the OUDS Committee (with Peter Bayne as President and Lionel Hale as Secretary) invited Giles Playfair to play Hassan—'they were convinced', he says, 'that no other member of the club had the necessary histrionic qualifications'. George Devine was cast as the Caliph. Two other undergraduates who were to become professional actors, William Devlin (Merton) and Ernest Thesiger (Magdalen), had parts, and two young professionals, Peggy Ashcroft and Thea Holme, were engaged as Pervaneh and Yasmin. Peter Howard, a huge Wadham undergraduate whose prowess on the rugger field was so remarkable that he was already captaining England, agreed to play a Negro executioner. Later to become a leading figure in Moral Rearmament, he was photographed holding the limp body of Thea Holme as if it were a rugger-ball.

The production was a disaster. Darlington in the *Telegraph* declared that the OUDS had 'this year fallen very far below its own best standard . . . Bad speaking is prevalent . . . If Mr Basil Dean, instead of merely supervising *Hassan*, had actually produced it, I should probably not have had to write these strictures. But he left nearly all the work to Mr Gibson Cowan, who evidently cares nothing whatever for good speaking. The result is disastrous.' In fact Cowan had worked very hard, conducting rehearsals for up to twelve hours a day, and earning the nickname of 'Back on it' Cowan because he made the cast speak lines again and again; but Playfair could 'only think of a dozen actors on the London stage who could do passing justice to Flecker's poetry', and asserted that not even a Granville-Barker could have trained OUDS up to the required standard.

George Devine had contracted what his biographer calls 'an infection' on an overseas trip, and was frequently absent from rehearsals to receive painful injections at the Radcliffe Infirmary. (There were constant murmurs of 'Where's Devine? He ought to be on the divan.') He was determined to secure the OUDS presidency in the election that fell just after *Hassan*; at that time it was the custom of the retiring Committee to nominate their successors, and Devine managed to secure nomination as President. Giles Playfair was nominated as Secretary; according to him, this was in the hope that by being given

office he would cease to be a destructive influence in the Society. But he could not be so easily pacified: ' "There is no doubt at all", I thought, "that I have a better claim to the Presidency than George Devine. My membership of the club is of longer standing than his by two whole terms. I have played Malcolm in *Macbeth*, Sebastian in *Twelfth Night*, and Hassan in *Hassan*. He has only played Sir Toby Belch in *Twelfth Night* and the Caliph in *Hassan*. Moreover my theatrical connections in London would be of enormous benefit to the Society while he has no experience of the professional theatre. I shall refuse to be put down by prejudice. I shall fight this injustice." '

Playfair, whose surname must by now have seemed very inappropriate, took the irregular step of instituting a counter-nomination and securing the support of two members of the retiring Committee, and the OUDS was soon a hotbed of canvassing, bribery and corruption. 'It was fought with wild fury and concentrated bitterness', recalls Playfair. 'Personal feeling and vindictiveness ran far higher than in the average election of parliamentary campaigns.' The Devine supporters were what Playfair called 'the old order'—those who had admired Brewster Morgan, the 'prefects', and the more conservative elements in the Society who would not forgive the Balloon Union. Playfair managed to get the support of the 'working class', who hoped that if elected he would give them a better deal. He also cajoled the Senior Librarian on to his side; Devine netted the Senior Treasurer. Lionel Hale in *Isis* backed Devine with partisan leaders; *Cherwell* put its support behind Playfair.

Members who had paid subscriptions but never bothered to turn up were hastily contacted and told whom to vote for. Detachments went round the colleges to gather support, and hired cars were sent to outlying parts of Oxford to fetch those who lived in far-flung lodgings to the actual poll. On the day no fewer than ninety members crowded into the George Street club-rooms.

Fifty per cent of them had faces which were quite unknown to the steward and the regular waiters [writes Playfair]. They were eyed anxiously by the leaders of both parties. Which way would they vote? As Peter Bayne rose for the last time from his presidential chair to announce the result of the count, the atmosphere was electric. 'Order, order!' he cried confidently. 'Mr Devine is elected President with 48 votes. Mr Playfair polled 45 votes.'

The remainder of his remarks were scarcely audible. A few of my supporters, who were standing nearby, whispered sympathetically 'Bad luck',

and simultaneously began to shake hands with their erstwhile opponents. The battle was over, as far as they were concerned . . . The time had now come for a general reconciliation. But I only knew that I had been defeated by the narrow margin of three votes. To say that I was disappointed would do scant justice to what I felt. I thought then that I had failed to achieve the one thing in life worth achieving, that I was 'finished', that I must say 'good-bye' to all hope of success not only in Oxford but elsewhere, that I had better go and bury myself . . . I left the club-room determined that I would never return there again.

In a sense Playfair was right. Devine's presidency gave him the best possible entrée to the theatrical world and proved to be the beginning of a distinguished career, which led eventually to the founding of the English Stage Company at the Royal Court Theatre in the mid 1950s. Playfair remained 'my father's son', achieving no great distinction in the world. But in fact at Oxford his pride healed quickly; he helped to edit *Cherwell*, ran a successful campaign to oust Lionel Hale from *Isis*, and even continued to use the OUDS club-rooms. Seated on the fender there, he felt himself to be 'a respected "politician" who had fallen from power and who had elected to remain leader of the "Opposition"!'

Meanwhile George Devine set about rescuing the reputation of the OUDS after the débâcle of *Hassan*. The summer production of 1931, *Much Ado About Nothing*, was scarcely an improvement. Christopher Hassall, recently come up to Wadham, was an adequate Claudio, and Hugh Hunt, subsequently a director at the Old Vic and at that time a Magdalen undergraduate, played Leonato; but Balliol Holloway who had been brought from Stratford and the Old Vic to direct was an Edwardian-style 'leading man' rather than a *metteur-en-scène*, and the production was unremarkable. In the autumn Devine cancelled the annual one-act play competition, declaring the entries not up to standard; they included a piece by a second-year Trinity undergraduate named Terence Rattigan. This play (according to its author) was 'a highly experimental piece, rather in the vein of Constantin's effort in *The Seagull*'. Devine was 'very kind' about it, and told Rattigan: 'Some of it is absolutely smashing, but it goes too far.' Rattigan consoled himself by performing in the Smoker as 'Lady Diana Coutigan', a feline drag-queen who made some sharp comments about other OUDS members.

Devine's real reason for cancelling the one-acters seems to have been so that he could play the lead in his own production of Chekhov's

Ivanov, of which the OUDS gave some nominally 'private' performances during the Michaelmas term of 1931. Chekhov was coming into
fashion, largely thanks to Komisarjevsky, and to J. B. Fagan's outstanding *Cherry Orchard* which, originating at the Playhouse, was taken to
London with huge success in 1925. Fagan knew how to stage Chekhov,
but Devine as yet did not, and OUDS members were reduced to
helpless laughter by the sight of him as Ivanov in an enormous,
implausible black beard. William Devlin played Borkin, and remembered it as all 'very rushed, no chance of proper rehearsal with clothes
and props: bashing away at the audience, what there was of it'. Matters
were made worse at the end of the play when Ivanov shoots himself, for
the pistol entangled itself in Devine's trouser pocket and burnt a nasty
hole in it. T. R. Williams, sitting in the audience, 'literally fell on the
floor, rolled on the floor in agony with laughing so much'.

Devine's talent as an actor was patchy, and as yet he had little idea of
how to direct, but he made a brilliant choice of professional director for
the next OUDS winter production, in February 1932 in the New
Theatre. John Gielgud's reputation was steadily increasing: after
several years of outstanding classical performances he was making a
success in the commercial theatre, and was currently acting in the
long-running adaptation of Priestley's *The Good Companions* in the
West End. But he had never yet directed. Devine conceived the idea of
asking him to take charge of an OUDS *Romeo and Juliet*, a play in which
Gielgud had more than once made a great mark as an actor.

During the Christmas vacation, accompanied by some of the Committee, Devine called on Gielgud at His Majesty's Theatre and put this
proposition to the twenty-eight-year-old star. Gielgud was not impressed by Devine's appearance; many years later he recalled the OUDS
President as 'rather ungainly and gross. Very greasy, spotty, and
unattractive. But he had great humour, great charm; and he was
immediately very intelligent.' Gielgud 'jumped at the opportunity' of
directing *Romeo*, and shortly afterwards came down to Oxford for
casting readings.

The first thing that struck him when he arrived at the OUDS was the
rivalry between Devine and Playfair, who were each putting up
candidates to succeed Devine as President. Nor was the business of
casting altogether without tensions; Gielgud was happy to accept the
handsome Christopher Hassall as Romeo, but Devine wanted to play
Mercutio himself, and Gielgud (according to Irving Wardle) 'did not

think much of the heavyweight bespectacled President's chances' in the part. William Devlin was chosen for Tybalt, Hugh Hunt was to double as the Chorus and Friar Lawrence, and Terence Rattigan got a small part as one of the revellers who discovers Juliet's death. Peggy Ashcroft, who had been almost the only good thing in *Hassan*, was an obvious choice for Juliet, and Gielgud secured not only her but also Edith Evans as the Nurse—though this final piece of casting was not made until a fortnight before the production opened, Evans just then returning to England from a flop on Broadway.

No special effort was made with regard to the set-design, a group of arches backed with drapes which were plain and unintrusive, if a bit cheap-looking. On the other hand Gielgud made an inspired choice for the costumes. He had become friendly with three Home Counties girls, ex art students who used to turn up at the Old Vic, sketch the company, and sell the results to the actors for a guinea or two. They also earned some money by making fancy dresses for the shops at Christmas. Their names were Elizabeth Montgomery and Margaret and Sophia Harris, and they worked under the label of 'Motley'. They jumped at the chance of making the *Romeo* costumes for Gielgud, 'rushed out and hired a couple of people to sew for us', but 'did most of it ourselves'. The resulting costumes seemed, it has been said, to have emerged from a quattrocento painting. Thereafter Motley was to become a leading name in the theatre. George Devine had tried to dissuade Gielgud from engaging the girls, arguing that the usual OUDS dressmaker ('Joan' of George Street) should be left to cope with the production. But when Motley turned up Devine was immediately attracted to one of the team, Sophia Harris, and soon began an affair with her.

Gielgud brought firm ideas to the production; Irving Wardle observes that it was 'a first sketch for the famous version he directed three years later in his New Theatre [London] season, alternating with Olivier as Romeo and Mercutio'. He used methods he had absorbed from Harcourt Williams at the Old Vic, who in turn was influenced by Harley Granville-Barker. This meant purging any rhetorical tendencies among the cast, achieving a fast-moving action uninterrupted by scene changes, and paying a great deal of attention to design. But most of all he set out to teach the OUDS how to speak verse. Devine afterwards recalled that Gielgud 'really *taught* us rather than produced us: the right method for intelligent undergraduates with flexible

voices'. His manner was that of a headmaster rather than a theatre director, and this found a counterpart in the headmistress-like Edith Evans, who would issue stern reprimands to late-comers at rehearsal, and insisted that the cast took bracing walks with her up Port Meadow to Godstow. She would also burst into the smoky atmosphere of the OUDS club-room and cry in her best Lady Bracknell tones: 'All this frousting about!'

The circumstances were not totally propitious for a good production: Gielgud had to rush back to London every evening to act in *The Good Companions*, and the presidential election was as bitterly fought as the previous year's. As it became imminent, Playfair attempted to kidnap Hugh Hunt, Devine's candidate, and Devine had to hide him in his digs in Bath Place. But Gielgud did at least manage to get the night off from His Majesty's to see his *Romeo* open, on 9 February—and 'nearly died with anxiety and mortification' when there was a hitch between scenes.

He need not have worried: the production was an outstanding success, reaching heights not achieved since the Robert Speaight Falstaff. David Cecil has called it 'easily the best performance of the play I have ever seen: straightforward in interpretation but fresh with youthful lyrical rapture, so that it seemed wholly in tune with Shakespeare's intention and yet as if it had been written yesterday'. The London drama critics were almost as enthusiastic. The OUDS, declared Darlington in the *Telegraph* after the opening night, 'have cared to speak verse again, and have learned to speak it. By this their work is transformed.' He judged it 'their best balanced and most satisfying performance of recent years', and gave particular praise to Devine as Mercutio. The director's influence was easily detected: 'It happens again and again in this production that one seems to hear Mr Gielgud's voice on the stage—which means, not that the undergraduates are slavish imitators, but simply that they are indeed learning to speak verse and are sensitive enough to recognize a master when they hear him.' But the highest honours, in Darlington's opinion, went to the two professional actresses. Ashcroft's Juliet he thought quite outstanding.

Above all, this Juliet is in love—not rehearsing phrases, but passionately in love . . . Miss Evans meanwhile is busy with a contributory masterpiece. She has the walk of an old woman; the hands of a sly one; and all the Nurse's experience of ribaldry and affection are in the curious tortoise-like move-

ments of her head . . . Not to see Miss Evans and Miss Ashcroft together . . . is to miss a part of the history of this play.

The only failure in this remarkable production seems to have been Terence Rattigan. He had just one line, 'Faith, we may put up our pipes and be gone', and proved quite incapable of saying it to anyone's satisfaction, least of all Gielgud's, who remembers giving 'endless demonstrations of disapproval'. On the first night Rattigan spoke it at the solemn moment after Juliet's death had been announced—and to his horror raised a laugh from the audience. Edith Evans glared at him and spoke the Nurse's next words with particular vehemence: 'Honest good fellows, ah, put up, put up; For well you know this is a pitiful case.' He tried it with a different emphasis the next night, but the audience still laughed. Word got around that he was having trouble, so that by the end of the week he could only avoid causing mirth by delivering the line so quietly that it was entirely inaudible. Some years later in his play *Harlequinade*, set backstage during a provincial *Romeo and Juliet*, he included the character of a bit-player who has the same trouble with this line.

Despite his flop on stage, Rattigan found the OUDS *Romeo* to be a turning-point in his life. He was taken up by the writer and actor John Perry, with whom Gielgud was then living, and in the 'fast' set to which Perry introduced him he began to come to terms with his growing homosexual feelings. The complications of his own emotional life led him to write his first successful play. It was called *First Episode*, and Rattigan worked on it in collaboration with another undergraduate, Philip Heimann, to whom Rattigan was attracted but who was having an affair with a professional actress. Rattigan and Heimann made this emotional triangle the subject of their play, setting it during a student *Romeo and Juliet* much like the OUDS production, and disguising themselves in the characters of 'Tony', who loves the actress ('Margot'), and 'David', who is deeply attached to Tony. The play soft-pedalled the homosexual theme, but even the heterosexual element in it was considered somewhat *risqué* at the time, and when it was produced professionally in a small theatre in Kew in September 1933 the Proctors of Oxford University became somewhat concerned—not least because the newspapers fastened greedily on this evidence of loose living in the University. It was a box office success, and transferred to the Comedy Theatre in the West End, with the homosexual element virtually eliminated. But Paul Dehn who was then

editing *Cherwell* was forbidden by the University authorities to print any review of it, and there seems to have been general relief in official circles at Oxford when Rattigan decided to go down without taking his degree, on the strength of this, his first West End success.[2]

George Devine left Oxford just as precipitously, and as a consequence of the OUDS *Romeo*. He had made a surprising success of Mercutio; Gielgud thought him 'suddenly remarkably good in a part I hadn't thought he would be very good in', while Rattigan perceived him to be miscast but 'pretty damn good all the same'. Peggy Ashcroft judged him to be 'dangerous and quick-witted: he had a lightning mind'. Ashcroft's first marriage, to Rupert Hart-Davis, was nearly at an end, and she was involved with Theodore Komisarjevsky, whom she married two years later. He came down to see her in *Romeo* and to renew his acquaintance with the OUDS, and was sufficiently impressed with Devine to give him a part in one of his forthcoming London productions. Devine decided to abandon Oxford before taking his final Schools, and left soon after relinquishing the OUDS presidency to Hugh Hunt—who had been successful in the election despite the Playfair opposition. Devine moved in with Sophia Harris and the other two Motley girls, and married her a few years later.

Before the *Romeo* company broke up they gave a final performance in London, on a Sunday at the New Theatre, by invitation of Bronson Albery and in aid of Lilian Baylis's Old Vic–Sadler's Wells fund. A cheque was to be handed to her at the conclusion of the performance and Hugh Hunt as President arranged for it to be written out, but his costume as Friar Lawrence contained no pockets so he asked Devine (who as Mercutio had 'died' and gone off stage before the end of the play) to look after it and hand it to him during the curtain calls. Devine forgot all about it and when Lilian Baylis, attired in the Honorary MA gown and hood which she loved to parade, came forward to take it from Hunt, he had to press an empty palm into hers in the pretence that it contained the cheque. The indomitable Miss Baylis was not having any of that, and said in a sarcastic voice that carried well into the stalls, 'Come on dear, where's the cheque?'

---

[2] *First Episode* has never been published, but a copy of the typescript is with Rattigan's agents, Dr Jan van Loewen Ltd., who kindly let me see it. It is a naïve, rather crude piece of work which the mature Rattigan understandably disowned, but it contains some accurate portrayal of the atmosphere of OUDS productions at the time, particularly the actress Margot grumbling at everybody asking her how she likes Oxford: 'Lord, you're not going to start that, I hope . . . Everybody I meet asks me the same question: "How d'you like the town, Miss Gresham?" '

The Greek play came round again in the summer of 1932—Sophocles' *Oedipus Tyrannus*, performed in Magdalen Grove with Alan Ker (a fellow of Brasenose and former OUDS member) producing, and William Devlin in the title role—but this was the last OUDS Greek production for many years. The minute-books for this period do not survive, but somehow future Committees managed to divest the Society of this obligation. Meanwhile the film world made an overture to someone in the OUDS. Leontine Sagan, German director of the celebrated *Mädchen in Uniform*, had just come over to work for Alexander Korda's London Film Productions company at Denham, and decided to make a film about Oxford life—perhaps in the hope that it would yield the sort of *risqué* material which had featured in *Mädchen* (which was about lesbianism in a boarding school). Had she known much about the private lives of, say, Rattigan and Devine, she could have produced something quite salacious. In fact she lumbered herself with a trite Hollywood-style story about an ugly undergraduate disappointed in love. There were reports about the film in the newspapers, and Giles Playfair, seeing them, 'conceived it a foolish impertinence that anyone should have contemplated a film about Oxford life without first consulting me', and demanded a part. Sagan decided he was ugly enough for the hero, and asked him to come to Denham for a screen-test. But Playfair was taking his final Schools (he got a Second in Jurisprudence) and failed to turn up on the appointed day. Given one more chance, he set off from Oxford by car early in the morning, but the car broke down. When he finally reached Denham late in the day he was mistaken for a journalist and thrown out. In the end the film seems never to have been made.

Playfair had slightly more success with his next dramatic venture, a Concert Party tour made up largely of OUDS members, augmented with professional actresses, under the name 'The Oxford Blazers'. They had a successful week in a tiny hall at Seaford in July 1932, and subsequently played at Brighton, Lowestoft, Hammersmith, and Wimbledon, concluding in the West End with a brief run at the Little Theatre. By Playfair's own admission their material was not very good and they had poor houses, but the BBC invited them to perform for an hour on the National Programme, and they were given star billing in the *Radio Times*. The programme's producer assured Playfair that listeners would write in to give their opinion, and made an appointment for him to come back to the studios a week later and read the letters,

adding the caution, 'They won't all be complimentary.' But when the letters actually appeared he cancelled the appointment: 'I'm afraid you'd find it rather painful.' Presumably they took the same line as the radio critic who judged the Oxford Blazers 'weaker than I had supposed possible'.

Playfair's final contribution to Oxford theatre was to co-produce, with Hugh Hunt, Shakespeare's *King John* in February 1933 at the New Theatre—the last OUDS production to take place in that building, for shortly afterwards it was demolished to make way for an extensive and modern theatre of the same name on the same site. Despite Playfair's presence the production went smoothly; Felix Felton (Balliol) played Hubert, and Devlin was the King. Playfair called it 'the incident of my Oxford career which I remember with most pleasure'—even though it coincided with his second defeat for the presidency of the Union. Shortly afterwards he left Oxford to read for the Bar. Oxford must have seemed more peaceful without him.

7
The Coghill Era

FROM 1933 to 1939 the history of the OUDS might be described as a
trough with a few peaks, a generally low standard of productions with a
few notable exceptions. The first of these, in June 1933, was Max
Reinhardt's *A Midsummer Night's Dream*. Reinhardt had just departed
from Germany in the wake of Hitler's coming to power, having made a
huge reputation there and elsewhere in Europe with his innovations as
a producer—a thrust stage, stylized scenery, and rhythmic crowd
movements. Above all he did things on a big scale. 'No place was too
vast for him', remarks Phyllis Hartnoll. Oxford indeed was too small
for him; or rather he was not content to do things on the scale of the
usual OUDS open-air summer production. Rejecting all college
gardens as too cramped, he insisted that the Society acquire the use of
South Park, a huge meadow on the slopes of Headington Hill. Here his
Dream was staged.

Early rehearsals were in the hands of Felix Weissberger, who played
a kind of John the Baptist role to 'Professor Reinhardt' (as the great
man was always known), arriving in Oxford some time before Reinhardt and giving interviews to the undergraduate papers about his
master's doctrines. The OUDS President was then Felix Felton
(Balliol), afterwards a radio actor (perhaps best remembered for his
comic performances in *Toytown* on Children's Hour). Felton, who was
playing Bottom, had to put up with criticism for allowing Reinhardt and
Weissberger to cast some parts from undergraduates who were not
OUDS members. But really the casting scarcely mattered, for it
became evident that the actors would be entirely dwarfed by the
gigantic scale of the 'set'.

'A huge stand was erected for the audience, an electric cable was laid
on from the city main and every tree was lit with many lamps.' So writes
'Doggins' in his autobiography; the old man still served as OUDS
prompter, despite Reinhardt's attempts to oust him ('Reinhardt did not

like me and tried to prevent me from attending rehearsals, but he did not succeed'). He continues:

Then a lake was constructed simply to enable Bottom to see his own reflection and psycho-analyse himself in horror at his grotesque appearance. Nothing but [Reinhardt's] own costumes from Berlin were good enough for him, and when they arrived the Society had to pay import duty on them. One morning, an agitated manager came to ask me if I knew where he could hire four boar hounds as Reinhardt wanted them. I told him to go back and tell Mr Reinhardt that he could go on wanting them as far as I was concerned, for I was already horrified at this appalling extravagance.

But the boar-hounds were found, for photographs of the production show them taking a bow with the rest of the cast.

No one [continues Doggins] seemed to make it his business to curb the undergraduates' prodigality nor their producer's soaring ambition. To some extent he was the least to blame, as I discovered afterwards that he had been left under a complete misapprehension as to the source of the Society's finances. They depend, of course, on undergraduates' subscriptions and the proceeds of the plays, while Reinhardt imagined that he was helping himself out of the University chest. When it was at last suggested that there must be some limit to expenditure, I believe he replied, 'Is this not a University club and is not the University very rich?' Someone ought to have enlightened him before he came to England, but I doubt whether a German should have been asked to produce such a play as *The Dream*. To him, Puck was a devil and he gave him a cloven hoof. When a feeble protest was made he replied, 'He is, you say, an imp, and is not an imp a devil?'

But Doggins admits that Reinhardt 'did two good things: he made every actor perfectly audible, and he brought over from Copenhagen an exquisite little Danish dancer'. This was Nini Theilade, a seventeen-year-old whom Reinhardt had discovered; she played First Fairy and directed such dancing as the *Dream* required. Contemporary photographs show her to have been truly *fée* in appearance, and Doggins lost his heart to her: 'One day, during a rehearsal, this lovely little fairy broke away from her dance and ran towards me. There was a loud bellow from Reinhardt, "Go back to your place," but she finished what she had to say to me and gave me a parting kiss before returning to the stage.'

The acting space was vast, though according to one story not vast enough for Reinhardt, who is said to have surveyed the site and said:

'Very nice. But—' indicating the Headington rooftops in the distance—'that village over there must be removed!' Field telephones had to be installed to ensure co-ordination of entrances, and Reinhardt's extravagances also included digging holes in the ground so that Puck could appear and disappear as if by magic. Fortunately the books just balanced: the production expenses came to £1,548 and the takings, despite bad weather, totalled £1,589. Moreover on the first night all the effects worked superbly well. 'At the foot of the audience,' wrote *The Times*, describing the scene in South Park,

a bank rises sharply for some 20 yards, set with elm and beech and may. Beyond the great trees the incline is less. The prospect widens and flattens into what appears as a vast circle of grass, set about with distant woods.

In such a theatre there is nothing the faeries [*sic*] may not do. Puck may mock his victims from branches above their heads or from the swift invisibility offered him by a hole in the ground; Oberon's troop and Titania's, advancing from opposite woods, may meet by sudden chance and vanish, when their encounter is over, like the legions of a dream; from far away, while the lovers in the foreground are disputing the confusions of the night, a solitary faery may come through the late dusk, come for no reason of ours and depart beyond our knowledge, having miraculous business of her own.

The customary emphasis of the play has thus been changed. No longer is it a story of mortals in this world behind whom an enchantment has arisen; it is a tale of sprites and goblins pursuing the natural life of their own dwelling-place, into which men and women have blindly wandered. That it has been Professor Reinhardt's purpose to enforce this emphasis to create an illusion of immortal intimacy becomes increasingly clear as the evening passes and his lighting, which is masterly in its restraint and its gentle use of foliage, begins to have its full effect.

As to performances, *The Times* judged Nini Theilade 'the only outstanding individual', and said that actors 'have been subordinated to the mass'; moreover, 'the spoken poetry is sometimes weak, and the clowns have been dangerously given their heads'. However, in general, 'it is a production to take the breath away'.

The Reinhardt *Dream* brought the OUDS a lot of good publicity, and membership increased; but the momentum was not sustained. Gyles Isham produced *Dr Faustus* for the Society in February 1934, with Felix Felton no more than adequate in the lead, though Peter Glenville (Christ Church) scored a hit as Mephistopheles; Ronald Waldman (Pembroke), a future luminary of the BBC's Light

Entertainment Department, was Gluttony. With the New Theatre closed, *Faustus* had to be staged in the Town Hall, where Gyles Isham employed the organ for incidental music—there were some eyebrows raised at its being used to accompany 'Is this the face that launched a thousand ships?' Helen of Troy, whose appearance is both brief and entirely silent, was portrayed by Miss Primrose Salt, 'deb of the year', whose face graced the pages of the *Tatler* several times during the OUDS production.

The rebuilt New Theatre, a vast example of brash Art Deco, advertising itself as 'England's Finest Theatre' but really more notable for hugeness than good taste, opened only a few days after the OUDS *Faustus* had closed. It would have been perfectly possible for the OUDS to have inaugurated the new building, just as they had opened the old one in 1886; but significantly the management (the Dorrill family) elected to open with a Drury Lane musical, *Wild Violets*, which would show off the theatre's extensive technical apparatus. This included a large revolving stage which (according to *Isis*) 'was seen to greatest effect when the [chorus] rush through a wood and the audience watch their peregrinations from every angle as the stage slowly turns'. The story is told of the New Theatre 'revolve' that a certain Oxford stage manager was making advances to a chorus girl in the prompt corner when she, struggling to free herself from his clutches, knocked against the lever which controlled the revolve; it began to turn, bringing the entire set down with it. The revolve was in fact more a gimmick than a useful device; by the 1950s it was rarely used, and twenty years later its curious-looking mechanism lay moribund beneath the stage.

University verdicts on the new New Theatre were cautious. 'An enormous edifice has been built to house enormous shows', said *Isis*, which called the decorations 'standardized, vulgar and lacking in individuality', though it concluded: 'We cannot but admire this theatrical enterprise as a whole.' It was perceived from the outset that the enlarged building, which could seat 1,700 people, would for the first time put Oxford on the circuit for big touring shows, and could be used for West End try-outs. The question remained: what could the OUDS do with it?

They had their first chance in February 1935, the fiftieth anniversary of the first OUDS performance; and for the 'jubilee' production the Committee chose *Hamlet*. Nevill Coghill was invited to direct.

Coghill, born in 1899, was the younger of two sons of an Anglo-Irish baronet; after service in the First World War he took his degree at Exeter College, Oxford, and in 1924 was elected Fellow and English Tutor of that college. As a teacher he inspired pupils more through enthusiasm and insight than any great degree of scholarship; his most celebrated published work, a modern English version of Chaucer's *Canterbury Tales*, irritated many of his more conventional Oxford colleagues. He married when he was very young and had a daughter, but soon separated from his wife—with whom, characteristically, he remained on the friendliest of terms—and got most of his social pleasure from the male company of his pupils and his undergraduate actors, though he could also sometimes be seen in C. S. Lewis's 'Inklings' circle. He was both adventurous and traditional, and hated making enemies (which he rarely did). His artistic talents were originally musical rather than theatrical—he said that but for the First World War he might have become a professional violinist—and he was drawn to the theatre almost by accident. An American undergraduate remarked in an essay for him that 'Milton was not dramatic, that *Samson Agonistes* would never play'. Coghill thought it would, so he had produced it in Exeter College gardens. (Charles Brandreth, father of Gyles Brandreth, played Manoa.) That was in 1930, and he was soon much in demand in Oxford theatre.

He remains vivid in the memories of those who were tutored by him or took part in his productions. He was already a legend when still a comparatively young man. *Cherwell* wrote of him in 1947: 'Is it possible to imagine Exeter without these rooms—books all over the chairs and couches, designs for sets on the floors—and their tall, tough, typically Irish tenant—grizzled somewhat at the temples now, with a pullover to match—stepping over everything with a brontosauric grace in his anxiety to find you a cigarette or give you a goblet of Bristol-blue beer?' (Coghill was a collector of Bristol glass.)

Robert Robinson describes him at about the same period:

The porter pointed across the quad and said, 'If Mr Coghill's your tutor, that's him.' And I saw the tall gaunt figure, this larger-than-life feeling I'd had about him ever since I'd heard . . . the *Canterbury Tales* he'd been doing on the Home Service was suddenly augmented, and I thought, 'Crikey, he *is* Chaucer.' But at the same time there was something fearfully unheroic about the man's hair—a sort of grey, wind-torn upland—not to mention the tweed trousers rising steadily towards half-mast (a good six inches of four-ply sock was visible

above shoes that at some stage in their lives may well have been suede) that revived the other feeling that I was an orphan who was at last going to be taken care of . . . When I left Oxford, I hoped the world might be full of such men. But it wasn't.[1]

Coghill's skills in the theatre were not those of the conventional director, neither was he a Komisarjevsky. His productions were often short on good verse-speaking and careful 'blocking', and he preferred to leave these things to an assistant director, usually an undergraduate. Yet, as Daphne Levens puts it, 'he worked with undergraduates in such a way that he made the best of what they could do well. If someone walked badly, for instance, Nevill might make him enter on his knees. He minimized all those jolts you usually see in amateur shows. You felt he wouldn't *let* anyone give a bad performance.' John Schlesinger, who acted for him after the Second World War, agrees: 'He always picked on the more positive sides of our performance, and encouraged us to do more.'

Coghill's greatest talent was for startling and beautiful visual effects. Never really at home on an indoor stage, he would create some stunning outdoor *coup de théâtre* in a college garden or quadrangle simply by considering the possibilities of the setting—trees, water, a tower, or some other feature. Schlesinger says that 'Nevill's great strength as a director was his visual imagination.' Dacre Balsdon, a fellow don at Exeter, recalled an early example of this when Coghill produced the medieval *Noah's Flood* with a group of young unemployed Welshmen at a camp organized by the University, alongside the Thames at Pinkhill Lock. 'What wiles did you employ on the lock-keeper', Balsdon asks, 'to produce . . . the flood itself, when he opened the lock gates?'

By the end of the 1930s, as Daphne Levens says, 'almost no college production would dare to face an audience without first asking Nevill to come and have a look, and give advice'. Some undergraduates resented his influence over Oxford theatre during this period; Lindsay Anderson, up at Oxford during the 1940s, thought that by then the OUDS was 'too whimsically dominated by Nevill Coghill. He was my tutor for a term . . . but I was never one of his favourites. Like many Oxford "characters", I thought him less entrancing than his reputation would suggest.' Moreover Coghill's flirtation with the professional theatre during this period of his life was not a great success. David William,

---

[1] *The Dog Chairman* (Allen Lane, 1982), pp. 80–1.

who acted for him at Oxford in the 1940s, recalls that 'For a while the theatrical establishment in London smiled on University drama. Nevill and George Rylands (Cambridge) were recruited under the H. M. Tennent banner to direct some plays for John Gielgud's season at the Haymarket. The results were unhappy. Academe's resources were over-extended: fine and deep thoughts about *A Midsummer Night's Dream* and *The Duchess of Malfi* were of little avail without the craft and technique to communicate them to players and thence achieve an articulate context.' However, at Oxford Coghill 'was one of the few Eng. Lit. dons at that time who recognized that Shakespeare wrote for the stage and not for Examining Bodies'. He was also the first don to throw himself utterly into the task of producing for OUDS, with an enthusiasm that always equalled and often surpassed that of his undergraduate cast. In most respects he was therefore far better for the Society than many of the professional producers who handled OUDS shows between the wars.

For the 1935 *Hamlet* he cast Peter Glenville (then President) in the title role, with David King-Wood as Horatio, Thea Holme returning to the OUDS as Ophelia, and Richard Buckle, future ballet critic, playing Rosencrantz and designing the costumes. Edmund Blunden wrote a special prologue to mark the jubilee, and a Jubilee Dinner was attended by two hundred and fifty people.

Glenville, afterwards a successful professional actor and producer, was praised in the highest possible terms by University critics. *Isis* declared that he 'has confounded the pessimists and amazed those critics who came expecting to see no more than a capable undergraduate performance', and even compared his interpretation of the part favourably with Gielgud's, concluding: 'Another half-century may elapse before Oxford sees another such production or possesses another such actor.' Similarly Michael Barsley wrote in *Cherwell*: 'Peter Glenville possesses a magnificent assurance . . . No scene was ordinary when [he] was on the stage, and his performance will long be remembered.' In fact the undergraduate reviewers were somewhat dazzled by the fact that it was the jubilee, and (as with Gyles Isham) the mere attempt on Hamlet by one of their number was sufficient to earn praise. A more detached view came from *The Times*, which called Glenville's performance 'a Hamlet which seemed only to live fully in moments of violent perturbation'. Moreover the *Times* critic felt that Coghill did not really know how to direct Glenville: 'Whenever the

producer tried to draw Hamlet out of the play he seemed to be creating more problems than Mr Glenville was prepared to solve.' In particular he objected (as did Barsley) to Coghill placing the 'To be, or not to be' soliloquy in front of a drop curtain, which rose at its conclusion to reveal Ophelia, listening behind it. And not surprisingly there were hints that the enormous stage of the new theatre—with its 45-foot-wide proscenium arch, twice the size of that in the old building—was unsuitable for an OUDS Shakespeare.

At least one member of the audience had never seen *Hamlet* acted before. This was W. H. Lewis, a retired army officer and brother of C. S. Lewis, whose diary records his impressions:

My goodness! Coghill was the producer, and had I thought done his work well, though some of the critics didn't appear to think so: the costumes I liked. There is one admirable character in this play, Polonius (very well acted I thought), and whenever he was on the stage I enjoyed myself: his scene where he explains to the King and Queen what he thinks is wrong with Hamlet is capital fun: but alas, all too soon he was killed, and from that point onwards I was desperately bored. As for Hamlet I have rarely conceived such a sudden antipathy to any character, and there was an intolerable deal of him: every few minutes all the characters would hard-heartedly sneak off and leave us at the mercy of this snivelling, attitudinizing, platitudinizing arch bore for hundreds of lines at a stretch, and I could have screamed. In fact if I had not been fortified by a double whiskey and soda half way through, I would not have stuck it to the end . . . What dramatic merit the play had, seemed to have been supplied by Coghill and not by Shakespeare. The murders in the last ten minutes would have disgraced a Punch and Judy show.

Despite the local success of the jubilee *Hamlet*, Coghill did not produce again for the OUDS until the war. But he was responsible for a good many college productions during the 1930s, including a Worcester Buskins version of *The Tempest* in Worcester College gardens in June 1934 which anticipated his celebrated 1949 OUDS production of that play; the *Oxford Magazine* mentioned 'the quiet beauty of the painted barge setting out across the darkening lake'.

The OUDS open-air shows in the 1930s after the Reinhardt *Dream* were rather dreary affairs. In June 1934 *Richard III* was performed in Christ Church cloisters with Peter Glenville as the King and Leontine Sagan directing—the first woman to take charge of an OUDS major. The creator of *Mädchen in Uniform* does not seem to have done anything remarkable with Shakespeare, though at Reinhardt's invi-

tation the production afterwards visited his Salzburg Festival, as well as playing at the Regent's Park open-air theatre in London. In June 1935 a Stratford actor named John Wyse directed *Julius Caesar* in New College cloisters, with David King-Wood as Brutus and an enormous troupe of Roman citizens—no fewer than forty-eight of them! King-Wood, writing in *Cherwell* a year later, judged this and *Richard III* to have constituted 'two years of depressing historical tragedies, essentially unsuited to open-air production', and there was an attempt to liven things up in June 1936 with Thea Holme (whose husband Stanford Holme was then running the Playhouse) directing *As You Like It* in Magdalen Grove. Michael Denison, who had just come up to Magdalen from Harrow, 'destined for the diplomatic service', walked away with most of the honours as Orlando; King-Wood called him 'a romantic hero, who . . . looks splendid, and shows a delightful flair for comedy' (the diplomatic service was never to acquire him). Nova Pilbeam, then aged seventeen and already a successful film star, provided a gamine Rosalind whose transformation into a boy was judged entirely credible. During rehearsals, John Witty, who was playing Oliver, galloped in on a horse whose hoof cut into a high-voltage electric cable; the horse fell dead instantly, and Witty would probably have been electrocuted had he not been a bad rider—at that moment he was making no contact with the saddle, and he was merely flung clear. *Twelfth Night* in June 1937 in Exeter College gardens was directed by another actress, Esmé Church, and received an unusual repeat performance in an enormous pub on an LCC housing estate in south London, at the instigation of John Masefield, who lived just outside Oxford and was a friend of Coghill.

John Gielgud returned to the OUDS in February 1936 to direct *Richard II*, with David King-Wood in the lead and Vivien Leigh making a visit to Oxford to play the Queen; Gielgud again chose Motley as his designers (this time of set as well as costumes), and engaged the young Glen Byam Shaw, who had been acting at the Oxford Playhouse, to help him with the production. But the results were not as remarkable as Gielgud's 1932 *Romeo*. Vivien Leigh was no Peggy Ashcroft; Michael Denison recalls her 'bringing ecstasy to those whose invitations she accepted and anguish to those whom perforce she had to refuse', and *The Times* praised her beauty; but its critic said that 'she has yet to make herself at ease with Shakespearian verse', while *Isis* called her 'no more than adequate'. In Gielgud's memory the most remarkable feature of

the production was the casting of the Duchess of Gloucester. He writes:

I had a sudden brain-wave. Max Beerbohm and his wife were both living in England at the time, and Mrs Beerbohm, well known in America before her marriage as Florence Kahn, a fine exponent of Ibsen, had recently played Ase, Peer Gynt's mother, in a production at the Old Vic, with William Devlin as Peer. I told the OUDS Committee that if we could persuade Miss Kahn to play the Duchess of Gloucester (one short scene only) we could surely persuade Max Beerbohm to speak at the OUDS dinner, and both these suggestions came to a successful outcome. It was fascinating to watch Beerbohm descending the staircase at the Randolph, dressed in a white suit with a flower in his button-hole and straw boater in his hand, looking exactly of his period, jaunty and debonair, and to escort him to the rehearsal in the theatre nearby, where his rather formidable-looking spouse, clambering up the ladder which crossed the orchestra pit, began to rehearse the Duchess's lines with an old-fashioned declamatory passion. The very short boy who was playing John of Gaunt shrank back in dismay, alarmed still further by repeated admonitory gestures from the lady as she towered above him, intended (though of course he had no idea of their significance) to enjoin him to come down stage level with her. Beerbohm, huddled modestly in the stalls, watched the goings on with, I fancied, a scarcely concealed amusement.

The critics were amused too. David Cecil, in his biography *Max* (1964), writes: 'Those of a younger generation thought her style mannered and old-fashioned to a comical degree. In particular they were amused by her habit of accompanying every phrase with an illustrative gesture. If she spoke of her heart, she pointed a finger at her left breast; at the mention of a spear, she flourished an imaginary weapon in the air. This practice tended to slow down the pace . . .' At the last-night dinner Beerbohm made a characteristic speech, and (recalls Gielgud) 'his wife plucked a flower from the centrepiece and stuck it in her hair as if to contradict her rather awesome personality'. This was her last appearance on the stage.

Gielgud managed to cope with the vast New Theatre stage, but his successor the next year, in February 1937, was less fortunate. This was Hugh Hunt, who had done well in the theatre since leaving the OUDS, and was producing at the Abbey, Dublin. He tackled *Macbeth* with a cast that included Michael Denison as Macduff, and *The Times* commented that the performance was dwarfed by the gigantic stage: 'One receives an impression of a broken and often remote action . . .

What is needed is a smaller theatre with easier entrances and exits.'
The cast struggling over the big acting area seemed like 'amateurs . . .
mountaineering in the doubtful dusk'. Michael Denison, judged *The
Times*, was the only actor to hold the audience's attention, simply
because he spoke the words clearly and with feeling. A year later the
actor Leslie French directed a *Much Ado* at the New Theatre which was
so awful as to earn adverse criticism even from the usually bland *Oxford
Times*, which made such remarks as: 'Mr W. Robertson-Davies had a
notion of how to speak Dogberry's lines, but we can only hope that it
was not Shakespeare's.' The best reviews were earned by the future
professional director Michael Benthall (Christ Church) as Claudio. By
now there was a certain amount of public grumbling at the poor work of
many 'professional' OUDS producers (in fact most of them were not
producers at all but actors), and David King-Wood defended the
OUDS practice in *Cherwell*: 'Acting, like anything else, is a job, and
those who want to act must learn to do it well . . . The person to teach
them is the professional producer.' The truth was that at this period,
unless the producer was of the calibre of a Gielgud or a Fagan, the
professional hand was likely to be a dead one.

Happily the 1938 *Much Ado* proved to be the last OUDS production
in the New Theatre. The fortunes of the Playhouse had fluctuated
considerably since Fagan had founded it in 1923; after about five years
box office takings had fallen drastically, and all too few people were still
willing to make the trek to the draughty 'Red Barn' at the foot of the
Woodstock Road. After a very shaky year or two, the Playhouse closed
in 1929 and was converted into a miniature indoor golf course. But a
group of actors led by Stanford Holme managed to reopen it about a
year later, and in the period that followed many ex-OUDS professional
actors were seen there, among them Lionel Hale and Valentine Dyall.
In 1933 the theatre's closure was again announced, but money was
quickly raised by its supporters and the company which reopened it
included another old OUDS member, Eric Dance. Stanford Holme
soon co-opted him as joint director of the theatre, and Dance set about
raising money for the building of a new Playhouse in Beaumont Street
in the centre of the town, where it would stand a good chance of
rivalling the New Theatre. An appeal was launched, the money was
somehow raised, and with Dance in sole charge the 'Oxford Repertory
Players', as they were now called, prepared to make the move.

By chance, the OUDS gave just one production in the old Playhouse

in the Woodstock Road before it closed, in June 1938, when no college garden could be obtained for *The Taming of the Shrew*. Jack Hawkins produced, and the American actress Constance Cummings made a good Katharina. Then on 22 October 1938 the new Playhouse opened in Beaumont Street.

The *Oxford Magazine* called the building 'a triumph of simplicity and good taste'. The character of the street's Georgian façades was retained in the theatre's sober frontage, and inside the accommodation seemed positively lavish after the old Red Barn. The opening ceremony was performed by A. P. Herbert, Member of Parliament for Oxford University, and Irene Vanbrugh spoke a prologue written by Christopher Hassall (who had become Ivor Novello's librettist at Drury Lane). The play performed at the opening was the Oxford Repertory Players' production of *And So To Bed*, J. B. Fagan's own dramatization of the life of Pepys. Eric Dance held a large party on the stage afterwards. Interviewed by *Isis*, he remarked of his difficult times in the last few years: 'I continued to cling to the sinking ship—there was something about the Playhouse that made you want to do that sort of thing.'

In February 1939 the OUDS gave their first show in the new Playhouse, with Maurice Colbourne returning to Oxford to direct *The Duchess of Malfi*. The *Isis* reviewer observed that he had 'toned down the horror of the piece' and called his production 'one of great restraint'. Daphne Levens, later the drama critic of the *Oxford Magazine* and principal director of the Oxford city amateur dramatic group, made her first OUDS appearance as the Duchess's lady-in-waiting, Cariola, getting the part despite competition from professionals 'simply because I had bothered to learn the lines before the audition'. In June 1939 Leslie French directed *The Tempest* in Worcester College gardens, and then war was declared.

At its outbreak the OUDS faced exactly the same problem as in 1914—closure without warning, and an enormous debt to be paid off. This time the club had more than £1,000 worth of unpaid bills to Oxford tradesmen, and just as Cyril Bailey had done in 1914, Nevill Coghill now took it upon himself to wipe out the debt and keep the Society in suspended animation 'for the duration'. He led a deputation to the Vice-Chancellor, who fortunately was his friend and ally in the English Faculty, George Gordon, President of Magdalen. Gordon agreed that Coghill should form a benevolent dictatorship, should sell

off the assets of the George Street club-rooms, and should then raise money to pay off the remaining debts by producing plays and making a profit from them. Although there were few undergraduates in residence for any length of time during the war, many came and went while waiting to be called up, and after a while there began to be a supply of cadets billeted on the colleges to take 'short courses' before beginning active service. There was thus a reasonable supply of actors and audiences.

The wartime productions were given under the name 'Friends of the OUDS', and the first few were not a matter for self-congratulation. In February 1940 George Bradford, an undergraduate, directed Machiavelli's *Mandragola* at the Clarendon Press Institute in Walton Street. *Cherwell* wrote of the Friends on this occasion: 'They are the OUDS gone amateur and not liking it a bit . . . The majority of the cast cannot keep still, even when they are talking, and the general effect of restlessness is displeasing.' The following June Coghill himself produced *Timon of Athens* in Exeter gardens, a play which did not suit his style as a producer. 'Why the Friends of the OUDS chose to produce *Timon of Athens* is a mystery', declared *Cherwell*. 'Their version was copiously cut—which was perhaps a mercy as what they did give us was appallingly under-rehearsed . . . There were so many *little* things that went wrong. Scarcely anyone had thought of pulling his tights up before coming onto the stage, and the beards included some of the most precarious we have ever seen.' *Othello* in March 1941 was little better, even though it was given in the more congenial surroundings of the Taylorian Institute. An undergraduate, Reginald Barr, directed and played Othello. 'Is it wise for an actor to produce a play in which he is playing the lead? The answer is no', said *Cherwell*. 'Othello . . . in his first appearance wore a fearful turban, which made him look like the commissionaire at the Taj Mahal.[2] Mr Michael Flanders [Brabantio] was the best of the other characters.' Michael Flanders was at Christ Church, and had not yet been stricken by poliomyelitis; he acted professionally at the Oxford Playhouse before his call-up. Peter Bayley, then an undergraduate and later a Senior Member of OUDS, was what he recalls as 'an inadequate Duke' in this 'underpowered' production; he thought Flanders easily the best performer in it —'the most delightful and attractive chap I had ever met or was ever to meet, charming, amusing, considerate, disarmingly modest, a paragon . . .

___

[2] Oxford's oldest-established Indian restaurant, in Turl Street.

Years later, after the war, after his polio, it was distressing to see him on TV, an inevitably overweight podgy oldish bearded man in a wheel-chair.'

The first signs of improvement in the Friends' productions came in June 1941 when *Much Ado About Nothing* was performed in New College gardens, directed by Glynne Wickham, an undergraduate at that college; he later became the first Professor of Drama at Bristol, and played a leading part in establishing there the first Drama Department in any British university. He writes of his Oxford days:

I went up to New College in 1940 determined to try my hand at a production before being called up into the RAF. I tried the college dramatic society first; but when I had secured a cast for a production of *Much Ado*, the Warden told me he could not officially sponsor it as the society had been 'dissolved for the duration of hostilities'. As a last resort (and with small confidence) I made an appointment to see Nevill Coghill at Exeter re 'Friends of the OUDS'. His response was likewise negative. He told me 'Friends of the OUDS' had been formed to pay off the existing OUDS debt, but that the productions presented in its name had only added to the debt. This being the case there was virtually no prospect of funds or of being able to use any society's name for the production. I retreated, depressed, to talk things over with my prospective cast for *Much Ado*. In doing so it occurred to me to wonder what response we might get if we dropped the request for funds and only asked for the Friends' name. Being possessed of a small legacy invested in the Post Office Savings Bank, I thought we could at least fund the production from that. When I put this proposition to my friends, they urged me to go back to Coghill and put the idea to the test. This I did. Coghill's response was tough, but optimistic. He promised to take the proposition to the Proctors provided I would sign a written agreement to pay all production costs; if the production made a profit, Friends of the OUDS would receive the profit, but if it made a loss I would cover that. I signed. A few days later we had the necessary Proctorial permission to present *Much Ado* in front of New College Library. The weather smiled on our efforts and we made a handsome profit of more than a hundred pounds. Coghill was so encouraged by this result that he decided to use this profit to finance a production of *Hamlet* at the Taylorian in the autumn term. Auditions were held, and I found myself offered the part of the Prince. This too made a profit.

The 1941 *Hamlet*, directed by Coghill, did not make the spectacular impression of those before and after the war, but in its quiet way it was a major achievement. John Bryson, a Balliol don who gave a lot of support to the Friends of the OUDS, wrote in the *Oxford Magazine*:

'The production was simple and direct and wisely let the play carry itself without tricks or effects.' He praised Wickham, though commenting on the extreme youth of his appearance and that of Ophelia, who 'looked more like retiring to a nursery than to a nunnery'. Coghill himself played the Ghost—Wickham remembers him as 'perhaps the only Ghost who added a natural cough to its other ailments!' This production eventually led Wickham to write a set of notes for an actor attempting the part of Hamlet, which were published in the 1966 Festschrift for Coghill (*To Nevill Coghill from Friends*, edited by W. H. Auden and John Lawlor). He noted that the Laertes, Polonius, Horatio, Osric, and several minor characters in this 1941 *Hamlet* were all afterwards killed in the war.

Wickham directed Sheridan's *The Critic* at the Taylorian in February 1942, and Leonard Rice-Oxley wrote in the *Oxford Magazine* that 'the whole cast acted with gusto and discrimination'. Looking back, Wickham felt that the Friends' productions gave particular pleasure because it was 'a time when the cultural amenities of Oxford life were just as severely rationed as were food and clothes. Most of us felt these productions moreover to be one of the big experiences of our lives, opening our minds in a way nothing else had done to Shakespeare's skill as a dramatic artist . . . Nevill Coghill was commonly regarded as one of the most stimulating teachers we had ever met . . . All my own thinking about plays and play-production, even to the creation of a drama department in another university, has stemmed from this experience.'

In fact Oxford during the war was not quite so bare culturally as Wickham may have felt in retrospect. The theatres remained open, with the Playhouse company continuing its strenuous repertory diet of a new production each week, and the New Theatre presenting many colourful touring shows; while the University itself had other things on offer besides the Friends' productions. College productions were mounted now and then, and there was now a fairly steady stream of performances by the Experimental Theatre Club.

The ETC was founded in 1936 by Nevill Coghill, who felt it was time for the creation of a more adventurous group than the OUDS, and also for one that gave women equal opportunities. A note on its first programme said it was intended 'to give scope to all those lesser creative talents and crafts that are involved in the Art of Theatre . . . [and] to present the little-known masterpieces of the past'. At first it

had something about it of the Group Theatre and other implicitly left-wing theatrical groups then flourishing in Britain. Initially its actors performed anonymously—an idea copied from the Marlowe Society at Cambridge. The opening production was Dryden's *All for Love* at the Taylorian in May 1936. However, by 1938 the ETC was naming its cast. That year it performed a medieval morality play, *The Castle of Perseverance*, with women undergraduates in the cast. Another early production was Cocteau's *Infernal Machine*, which so impressed Daphne Levens that she wrote to Coghill asking to join at once. In 1939 the first ETC revue was staged; Coghill contributed to it himself, being an accomplished writer of light verse. By the end of the war, with such song-writing talents as Sandy Wilson and Donald Swann, the ETC's revue work could easily equal that of the Cambridge Footlights. Though its organization was formally quite separate from that of the OUDS, a representative of each club served on the other's Committee, and from the 1950s onwards OUDS and ETC casts and production teams were interchangeable. The only distinguishing marks between the two clubs by this time were the exclusion of women undergraduates from the OUDS, and its continuing commitment to classics, especially Shakespeare, while the ETC generally staged modern or unconventional work.

During the Second World War the ETC was as active as the Friends of the OUDS. In March 1942 it staged Wilde's *Salome* at the Taylorian, earning a scathing review from John Bryson in the *Oxford Magazine*: he hated the play and the production equally. The following June Coghill produced *A Midsummer Night's Dream* for the Friends of the OUDS in Magdalen Grove. 'Puck made his first entrance with an agile drop from a tree branch; we also encountered Theseus and Hippolyta on horseback.' So recalls Frank Dibb, afterwards drama critic of the *Oxford Times*, then serving in the army. To him and others surrounded by the austerity of wartime Britain, this *Dream* was a sudden, brief experience of another world. Frank Hauser, taking a short course at Oxford as an army cadet, thought it 'unforgettable', with its procession of lamp-carrying choirboys moving through the darkening Grove, 'just as we were all going off to the war to be killed'.

The programme for this 1942 *Dream* lists, in the very minor role of an 'Attendant to Theseus', a Magdalen undergraduate named Peter Brook, who twenty-eight years later created the most memorable *Dream* production of modern times. Brook was also described as

'Assistant Stage Manager and Make-up'. However, in his own recollection,

I was front of house manager, without any idea of what that entailed. All I remember is that I prevented Richard Addinsell (later to become a dear friend) from getting in, because I disapproved of his 'Warsaw Concerto' which I considered too popular, and that when a large bouquet of flowers arrived for the actress playing Helena or Hermia, I presented it to her amazement to her mother in the front row. This was because the flowers were correctly addressed to this actress as 'Mrs Brunner' and it did not seem to me possible that a young and attractive leading lady could be other than a Miss. I have no other memories, except a great suspicion of poor Nevill, who seemed at the time a great monopolist preventing would-be young directors doing anything more glorious than managing the front of house.[3]

Coghill was indeed a monopolist during these years, directing *Twelfth Night* in the summer of 1943 and *Measure for Measure* a year later. The first of these productions was observed by Anthony Besch, who was spending a year at Worcester College before army service. Forbidden 'acting leave' for this production because he had already done so much performing, Besch was delighted to discover Coghill's *Twelfth Night* being staged literally beneath his own window, in Worcester gardens. He enrolled himself as Wardrobe Master.

Malvolio leaned nightly from my window to rebuke Sir Toby . . . Simon Lee played Feste far more effectively than I could ever have done [Coghill had considered him for the part], Roy Porter was Malvolio (he later attained to a number of important ecclesiastical positions), Derek Hart [later a television personality] was Sebastian, and Olivia was Elaine Brunner, who played in four successive Friends of OUDS productions . . . Her husband was in the RAF and she was living with her small daughter in Dorchester and working as a voluntary driver for the wartime special constables . . . She had some training as a dancer, and was vivacious, witty, and abounding in fun . . . Nevill enjoyed overlapping scenes, so that while one was in progress in the focal stage area, another might be finishing visually elsewhere, and a third beginning in yet another part of the garden. He has Watteau in mind for this *Twelfth Night*, with Feste as a white-faced Pierrot.[4]

Coghill's 1944 *Measure for Measure*, in Christ Church cloisters, attracted a lot of attention. Casting was complete when he was approached by a young cadet from his own college, Exeter, who was

[3] Letter to the author.
[4] From notes for a book in preparation.

hoping for a part. The cadet's baptismal name was Richard Jenkins, and like Emlyn Williams he came from a working-class Welsh home; again like Williams, he had been taken up by a schoolteacher who perceived that he had unusual talents. The teacher was called P. H. Burton and he became the young man's guardian, arranging for him to adopt his own surname. Richard Burton had already made one professional appearance on the stage before he came to Oxford, in Emlyn Williams's *The Druid's Rest* on tour and in the West End. He now impressed another cadet who was temporarily at Oxford, Robert Hardy, with his knowingness in matters theatrical—he gave Hardy the impression that he would take over the entire ETC in a trice. Burton easily persuaded Coghill to let him understudy Angelo, the part he felt most suited to himself; and then, through what Hardy felt was a piece of Welsh wizardry all too typical of Richard Burton, the actor cast as Angelo began to fail to come to rehearsals, and finally fell ill. Burton got the part.

M. R. Ridley, writing in the *Oxford Magazine*, did not think much of him. 'Angelo has a good voice,' he wrote, 'but uses it monotonously, and has not much else.' But Coghill was deeply impressed, and afterwards claimed to have written in the Exeter College reports on cadets: 'This boy is a genius and will be a great actor. He is outstandingly handsome and robust, very masculine and with deep inward fire, and extremely reserved.'[5]

Burton certainly took his performance very seriously. His guardian came up from Wales and went through the text line by line with him while he was preparing for the part. He also somehow contrived it that Hugh ('Binkie') Beaumont, who managed the H. M. Tennent company, was in the audience and took due notice of him, with advantage for his professional career after war-service. But was it a good performance? Coghill thought it brilliant, recalling Burton's 'arms at his side, his fingers clenched, yet ever so slightly unclenching and clenching again—an almost invisible, yet overwhelming movement'. Robert Hardy was less dazzled by the Burton magic, and thought him often 'bandy', walking with a 'waddle'. Yet even he thought that 'there were moments of extraordinary power and command of the audience, a view into an unquiet soul'. Burton left Oxford a few weeks after the performance.

The OUDS was not re-formed immediately at the conclusion of the

---

[5] Quoted from Paul Ferris, *Richard Burton* (Weidenfeld and Nicolson, 1981).

war, and the first two peacetime productions were given under the auspices of the Friends. *The Taming of the Shrew*, given in June 1945 in Wadham gardens with Arthur Ashby (Exeter) directing and playing Petruchio, was a Diamond Jubilee production to celebrate the sixtieth anniversary of the first OUDS performance, and had a special prologue written by Roger Lancelyn Green (Merton), who with John Wain (St John's) played Tranio and Biondello, Lucentio's servants. *The Winter's Tale* was staged a year later in Exeter gardens, with Coghill directing; Derek Hart played Florizel, and the parts of the Gaoler and Mariner were taken by Derek Jewell, later a well-known jazz critic. Martin Starkie was assistant producer. *Isis* called the standard of acting 'far higher than in the average pre-war OUDS production, which was apt to rely on one or two precocious star-players, encouraged by a fashionable West End producer to perform tricks beyond their years'.

Peter Bayley, the Polixenes of this *Winter's Tale*, describes it as a 'justly famous' production.

Nevill's instinctive recognition of the simple fairy-tale and mythic basis of the play, his genius for showmanship and large—and often broad—effects, strongly revealed its redemptive theme, with reconciliation, reunion and harmony after sin and repentance. I think that this production influenced subsequent criticism of the play, as well as having an effect on technically better productions. To elaborate on Nevill's large and broad effects: I found Polixenes a difficult part and couldn't understand how to present a character who in simple terms was so inconsistent, a faithful friend and apparently affectionate father who suddenly turns to violent abuse of his son and even more of Perdita . . . Nevill said: 'Don't worry about it. Just hurl it out with as much voice and power as you can. Don't question Shakespeare; just follow hard in whatever direction his lines point, and you'll get it right.'

In a quiet way, Coghill had entirely changed the undergraduate attitude to acting. Those who took small parts in his productions were given the impression that they were just as important as the leading actors, and something like 'company work' began to be found in OUDS performances. But 'stars' had by no means vanished from University theatricals.

Kenneth Peacock Tynan came up to Magdalen at Michaelmas 1945, and immediately made his extraordinary mark on Oxford theatre. Daphne Levens met him during his first term, when she was taking enrolments for the ETC:

Up came this very pale, straggly-haired person, dressed in an amazing burgundy-coloured velvet suit (and this in the days of clothing coupons!)—it afterwards earned him the nickname Plum-Bum. I asked him, as was our custom, what preferences did he have in the theatre, what kind of parts did he want to play? With wild contortions, and with an *agonizing* stammer that split his face, he answered: 'N-n-n-n-neurotic y-young men.' Actually he went on to play every kind of neurotic *old* man.[6]

Tynan had already played Hamlet at King Edward's School, Birmingham, and he now produced the play at Oxford, under the auspices of the Oxford University Players, a group formed 'to present during vacations plays of unusual or historical interest'. He used the 1603 First Quarto, in which the famous soliloquy begins 'To be or not to be, aye, there's the point', and Polonius is named Corambis. Tynan interpreted the play as 'a political tragedy of assassination, espionage and fear', and dressed it in the costumes of 'a sophisticated European court in the third quarter of the eighteenth century', with an emphasis on 'lace and quizzing-glasses'; Daphne Levens remembers 'Gertrude with a riding whip and a couple of Borzois'. *Isis* called the production 'practised violence to the nerves'. It was presented at the Civic Playhouse in Cheltenham for a week in August 1948, and then was seen in London at the Rudolf Steiner Hall. The producer's name was given as 'Ken Peacock Tynan', and the cast included several people who became successful in the professional theatre. Robert Hardy (Magdalen) was the First Actor, Lindsay Anderson (Wadham) played Horatio, and Jack May (Merton) was Corambis. Tynan himself played the Ghost, and Hamlet was Peter Parker (Lincoln).

Parker, future Chairman of British Rail, had served as a Major in Intelligence during the war; while an undergraduate he played Rugby and swam for the University, was President of the Labour Club, and produced a film about Oxford for the Labour Party. He also ran the Poetry Society and easily got a First Class. 'There wasn't a darned thing he didn't excel in', says Daphne Levens. Parker himself remembers, of Tynan's *Hamlet*:

The Quarto had not been attempted since the mid-twenties, when Wolfit had done it: he came to Cheltenham and reviewed the show most generously . . . Two memories suddenly. I look at my left hand and the palm is crossed by a scar. Ken had us in eighteenth-century costume, to emphasize the court-

---

[6] Conversation with the author.

politics of the play. For the 'Frailty, thy name is woman', I was able to make a toast, taking a glass from a bureau, almost without looking: then as I muttered miserably on to the point of 'break my heart' etc., I crushed the glass. I think I had seen this in *Diable au Corps* and thought if it were done quickly—as Gérard Philipe did it—it was worth the risk. So the bowl and long stem of a wine glass was nightly swathed in scotch tape—and I had no trouble from splinters, and if the bowl didn't give way, I snapped the stem. In London, at the run-through, a new stagehand coped, and as I came to the toast I saw: no scotch tape, very short stem. Then 'but you grab a nettle don't you?', I must have thought. I did, and was rushed to hospital for stitches. They treated me as if I were an early casualty from the Chelsea Arts Ball.

At the end of the run, there was a bloody symmetry to this. My right hand was cut in the fight, and when I was 'dead', hanging over the tomb, the blood dripped steadily. I heard from the front row: 'Isn't it marvellous the way they manage the blood . . .'

The other sudden flash-back is a measure of those splendidly surprising times. During the production, Ken was writing for a short-lived élitist little mag. called *Vanguard*, rumoured to be funded by Mosley, and I was editing the Labour journal, the *Clarion*. Strange, the political swing of Ken's passions then. I always thought he was a superb actor, although he ended with little respect for actors.

Lindsay Anderson's chief memory of this *Hamlet* is that 'Ken insisted I should play Horatio with a heavy German accent (I modelled this on a combination of Anton Walbrook and Albert Basserman) and aged about seventy . . . Wolfit . . . said I was "the second best actor in the company". When the production came to London my part was taken over by John Schlesinger—I was engaged in making my first professional documentary film.'

Ken Tynan's personal flamboyance soon dominated post-war Oxford just as Harold Acton's had dominated the mid 1920s. His writing-paper was reputedly headed 'Ken Tynan, Oxford', and he conducted his productions in autocratic fashion. Among these was an ETC *Sweeney Agonistes* (June 1946); he also took a major part—Bishop Nicholas—the following February in Ibsen's *The Pretenders*, the last Friends of the OUDS production, with Glynne Wickham directing. Wickham had returned to Oxford after serving in the RAF; he recalls that Coghill 'asked me if I'd be willing to tackle an autumn or spring production. I agreed to do so . . . provided we could present it at the Playhouse. This was duly arranged and we went ahead with Ibsen's *The Pretenders* . . . It was mounted at the height of the fuel crisis, and

opened with a Gala for the Norwegian, Danish and Swedish Ambassadors. Rugs and hot-water bottles were issued in the foyer!'

Michael Croft, later founder of the National Youth Theatre, remembers this production all too well:

Oxford in Winter 1947 seemed the coldest place on earth. They said it had never been colder since the Middle Ages. With endless power cuts, draconian coal rationing, food shortages and an overall freeze-up on the river, life under Attlee's austerity government was grim all round. In this setting the OUDS choice of Ibsen's *The Pretenders* was appropriate enough—all those dread marches across the northern wastes, the frozen forests, the bleak camp sites. By any other reckoning it was a disastrous choice. In Gordon Craig's view, 'This is an extremely difficult play to make theatrically effective', and the OUDS proved him right.

Casting had begun the previous term. We were the first of the post-war generation at Oxford. Many of us had acted in the forces, some, myself included, in professional rep. We had time on our hands. We all wanted to be in OUDS and this production. As it happened I soon became impatient with the way things were going and dropped out, a decision which I later regretted, because I missed taking part in an event which is nowadays more vividly remembered by the survivors than any other single production of that time. The eventual cast seemed enormous—*everybody was in it, my dear*—and it was going to be the greatest OUDS production ever.

It was not entirely the faults within the play which caused the catastrophe. It was the inability of the director, Glynne Wickham, and his assistant Anthony Besch, to handle this awful epic, the crowds they had assembled, the settings that were designed for them, and the chorus of eighteen singers and ensemble of seven musicians whom they felt necessary to the production, coupled no doubt with lack of time and the fact that most of the cast had other interests and did not always bother to appear at rehearsals. Many were the rumours that filtered through the Playhouse coffee bar about production progress. As opening night drew near it was clear that we were either going to have a miraculous success or total disaster. Within a few minutes of the curtain going up we knew which it would be.

The play depicts the struggle for the union of Norway in ancient days, with the noble young Hakon contending for the throne against the villainous Skule and a third and evil contender, Bishop Nicholas. The directors had abandoned all existing translations and come up with their own. They maintained that the old versions were highly artificial and unsuited to the theatre (in which they were undoubtedly right), and had replaced them with what they called 'current speech coloured by knowledge of the sagas and designed to be spoken rather than read'. But even in more skilled hands the

dialogue would have seemed ridiculous, being either inappropriate to the occasion or inadequate for the sense it was trying to convey. When Sandy Wilson, playing a Birchleg, rushed into a royal banquet and declared 'The Birchlegs have won!' the line, placed in this unfortunate context, brought the house down. After ten minutes the entire audience was in hysterical uproar. I have never heard such sustained and continuous laughter in any theatre or seen so many people literally falling about as yet another bedraggled figure appeared on the grey landscape, as armies swirled this way and that, soldiers fought and chased each other, and any sense the dialogue may have had was lost in the general tumult. The moment which lives clearest in my memory came when, with Skule's defeated army scurrying to and fro, an entirely unknown soldier burst on stage, shook his spear and shrieked: 'Any man who will save his life, let him fly with me', whereupon a grizzled veteran, hidden under an enormous hood, pushed his way out of the ruck and growled: 'Which way?' (The veteran later turned out to be my friend George Scott, now head of the UK Commission for the EEC.)

Until that time, some of us had tried, out of concern for our friends in the shooting line, to frown upon the general mirth; but this was too much. One wanted the whole thing to stop for very shame and embarrassment, but there could be no escape; and there were no redeeming features. Hakon the young king was played by John Hale (later to become Professor of History at Warwick University), who had been persuaded or allowed, perhaps with the idea of suggesting the nobility of his birth, to keep his chin forever tilted in the air so that he seemed to be continually looking down his nose at anybody who appeared. By the same token Arthur Ashby, a 'mature' student if ever there was one and a marvellously rhetorical actor of the Donald Wolfit school, played Skule the Pretender, with his eyes continually raking the ground as though in search of hidden gold. The confrontations between these two were hilarious. One was reminded of the grotesque style of acting which had been sent up by Hermione Gingold and Henry Kendall in their fabulous *Sweet and Low* reviews during the war. The situation was not helped by John Hale's habit of changing suddenly from a low-pitched delivery into a high piping one which, as one critic noted, turned Hakon into 'a rather pleasant young boy playing a Prince of Elfland'. At the same time Arthur Ashby seemed oblivious to the presence of anyone else on stage, and played with a melodramatic intensity which would have made even Wolfit gasp.

The situation reached its most fatuous whenever Ken Tynan appeared, playing Bishop Nicholas. Ken must have decided that the play had some strange inner meaning of its own which it would be unwise to divulge to the audience. As a result, the lines he spoke, in so far as they were intelligible, bore no relation to the sense they seemed to contain. He further confused the issue by using speech cadences which made them sound even more nonsensical.

But his appearance alone was enough to generate further laughter. Pale of complexion at the best of times, he had chosen to make himself up (as Penny Peters, an Oxford actress of the time, declared) 'like the skeleton of the wraith of a ghoul', and he wandered over plain and through forest like some ghastly Avenging Angel—a role which may have given him thoughts for the future; for in his production of *Samson Agonistes* in St Mary's church in 1948 he chose to position himself in the nave some forty feet above the ground, and to remain there motionless throughout the entire action with arms spread wide as the Angel of God.

For poor Glynne Wickham that night there was no relief. The running time, extended by audience participation, must have been nearly five hours. I remember the curtain coming down at about half past twelve, whereupon Glynne had to go on stage to face the audience and introduce to them the ambassadors who had come up specially for the occasion.

Anthony Besch, who remembers the production with grim amusement, says that 'drastic cuts were instituted the following day. One character, played by Adam O'Riordan, who changes sides four times in the original play, had so much of his motivation cut that he decided to play the last appearance as a different character, and startled us by appearing in a very long grey beard.'

Despite the farcical side to *The Pretenders*, the production was financially successful and led to the immediate reconstitution of the OUDS, at a meeting on 11 May 1947. The Friends had succeeded in clearing the debts and had even made a profit of some £700. Coghill's 'benevolent dictatorship' had been succeeded by a committee of Senior Members under the chairmanship of John Bryson, and this now handed over the funds to a new body of undergraduate members. These consisted of those few in residence who had belonged to the OUDS before the war, together with 'all male members of the University who have assisted in any capacity in a production sponsored by the "Friends of the OUDS"'. Glynne Wickham concluded his time at Oxford by serving as the first post-war President, and he drafted a new constitution, which included the intention that OUDS should become 'a focus for dramatic activities in the University and an aid to college dramatic societies in such matters as stage equipment, and technical assistance'.

In several ways the new OUDS differed from the Society in the 1930s. The notion that it might have an advisory role to college drama groups was really the acceptance of a *fait accompli*; even before the war

Oxford drama no longer rested chiefly in the hands of the OUDS but was an activity conducted on many fronts. By 1947 college productions were proliferating; in June that year an Oxford resident or visitor could see Shaw's *Arms and the Man* performed by the St John's Mummers, the Worcester Buskins in Beaumont and Fletcher's *Philaster*, Lady Margaret Hall performing the *Hippolytus* of Euripides, and an Oriel group in a French mime, *L'Enfant Prodigue*, not to mention the ETC's production of the Aeschylus *Agamemnon* in the Louis MacNeice translation. Among all this, the OUDS no longer had an automatic prominence. Moreover the social atmosphere of OUDS was very different from that in 1939. The club-rooms were reopened in George Street during Trinity Term 1947, and Ken Tynan in *Cherwell* described an OUDS party there (at which the current joke was 'Beware the OUDS of March'): 'On the short list of notable absentees I should put Penny (Ehrlich-to-bed-and-Ehrlich-to-rise) Peters, who was ill; and Babs (Little Chum) Clegg, who was working.' Girls were in the forefront of gossip in *Cherwell* and *Isis*, and though female undergraduates were still excluded from full OUDS membership they could usually be seen in the George Street rooms. The Smoker was resuscitated, and John Schlesinger, then an undergraduate at Balliol, remembers that 'women, who were never allowed in as part of the audience, were now helping to dress us backstage'. In fact the club-rooms were nearing the end of their life; the typical post-war undergraduate had neither the money to spend on club dinners and Benedictine on the fender, nor much desire to spend his evenings in aping the life of the Garrick Club. Female companionship was, in general, much desired, while as to theatrical tittle-tattle, that was best picked up and exchanged in the bar of the Playhouse, which had largely taken over the social functions of the OUDS club-rooms. 'We gathered daily for morning coffee in the Playhouse Bar,' recalls John Schlesinger, 'to rub shoulders with the professional members of that Company, and to see which of us was more up in the latest theatrical gossip.' The OUDS club-rooms survived for a little longer, but precariously. There was now no paid Steward, and this office was held by a member of the Committee. On the other hand there were now, among the elected officers of OUDS, a Technical Director and Technical Secretary (both undergraduates), as well as the ETC Representative. (The first person to hold that office was 'Alexander Wilson, Oriel'—in those days Sandy Wilson still sometimes used his

full name.) Robert Levens of Merton, husband of Daphne, joined Coghill and Bryson as the OUDS Senior Members.

Perhaps the most important change from the pre-war OUDS was that women undergraduates were now welcomed not only into the club-rooms but the casts. Anthony Besch, who in 1947 was finishing his degree at Worcester College, says that 'sometimes one regretted that the OUDS could no longer bring in Cathleen Nesbitt, Peggy Ashcroft or Edith Evans, all towards the beginning of their careers, but it still seemed much more appropriate to audition among the many beautiful and talented girls in the University'. The first OUDS production to take advantage of this was *Love's Labour's Lost*, directed by Besch himself in Merton garden in June 1947; his cast included girls from St Hugh's, St Anne's, and Somerville, with Ken Tynan as an outstanding Holofernes—Besch remembers his performance as one of 'dazzling ingenuity'. Other undergraduate performers included Lindsay Anderson ('who even in those days looked like Berthold Brecht'); he appeared at the end to sing 'When icicles hang by the wall'. One night there was an accidental effect worthy of Coghill at the refrain 'To-whit, to-whoo, a merry note', for a large barn owl flew out of the bushes and over the audience.

Most undergraduate members of OUDS immediately after the war had done military service, and so were older and more experienced than was usual. An exception was David Raeburn, director of Dekker's *Shoemaker's Holiday* for OUDS at the Playhouse in March 1948, who to Michael Croft seemed 'an undergraduate scarcely out of school'. Nevertheless 'it was an excellent piece of theatre in which David somehow resolved the major difficulties in this particular play. He had some good actors to help him, not least Arthur Ashby who was as good as Simon Eyre as he had been dreadful as Skule. But he was challenged all the way by young Robert Hardy as Firk.'

Hardy, then a Magdalen undergraduate, was always known to friends as 'Tim', and most of his contemporaries recall him as the outstanding University actor of their day.

He left no doubt [says Michael Croft] that if he chose to act for a living, he was going to excel. At this point his forte seemed comedy. He also had the ability to play Cockney—rare in my experience among actors from the middle classes. I wrote in *Isis* of his performance in *The Shoemaker's Holiday*: 'Mr Hardy has learned his cockney from Whitechapel Road and Ronald Shiner, and not the accent only, but the assurance and the cheek. Not once did he betray himself

... He had it all at his fingertips. He was impeccably good.' In the same production I also commended a certain John Schlesinger, who showed 'sound dramatic sense and was free from the vice of perpetual motion—a property almost as important to the OUDS as it is to the ballet.'

Schlesinger shared the part of Sir Hugh Lacy with Peter Heyworth, later a well-known music critic, and among the other actors were Geoffrey Johnson Smith, future Conservative MP, and Jennifer Ramage, undergraduate daughter of Cecil Ramage and Cathleen Nesbitt, the 1921 OUDS Antony and Cleopatra.

Schlesinger, Ramage, and Hardy were in the cast again in June 1948 for Ben Jonson's *Epicoene* in Mansfield College gardens, and this time the director was Frank Hauser (Christ Church). Roger Lancelyn Green, reviewing the production in *Isis*, said it had 'hardly a fault', and was 'as perfect an evening's entertainment as Oxford amateurs have shown for many a long year'. *Epicoene* afterwards toured France under the guiding hand of Merlin Thomas, New College modern languages tutor and from this time a Senior Member of OUDS. The *Epicoene* French tour, the first of many arranged by Thomas, happened almost by accident. He and Hauser were on holiday together in Tours before the production opened in Oxford; Hauser had not yet found a suitable outdoor site for *Epicoene* in Oxford, but suddenly discovered that Tours offered a perfect one—so the tour was conceived. This was a period of tremendous Anglophilia in France, thanks to the war, and the tours were always easy to arrange. OUDS made no financial contribution and actors had to pay for themselves, though hospitality was always lavish, as Daphne Levens, who travelled with *Epicoene*, remembers:

We had *vins d'honneur* all the way through France: nothing much to eat, but masses to drink every time we got off the train. Everyone, especially the men, was drunk most of the time; I remember John Schlesinger being held under a pump to clear his head before he went on stage. John was perpetually grumbling about having constipation because the loos were so awful and he couldn't bear to use them; at last, in Avignon, he cheered up because there seemed to be a proper *Dames* and *Hommes* with separate entrances—but when both sexes rushed down the separate sets of steps they met up at the bottom! We travelled third class, sitting up all night on hard wooden seats, and one night Frank Hauser decided to go round the train telling everyone that the show was too long for French audiences, 'and Daphne, just cut your lines from 1 to 45 in Act 2 Scene 2, and John, in the next scene, drop from 100 to 225'—and so on. And after he'd gone no one could remember what he'd said,

and we all got frightfully cross when we discovered he'd cut our best lines. But of course on tour you're frightfully relaxed, you play better than at Oxford because there's no other pressure on you, and you don't have to think about anything else.

Following the re-establishment of OUDS, Nevill Coghill was making plans for the further improvement of University drama. It was a period when the official inclusion of drama in the academic curriculum seemed imminent; Bristol took this step during 1948, and other British universities considered following suit. Glynne Wickham writes:

By the outbreak of the Second World War dramatic art had at least established several bridgeheads within university life, although none of them were being exploited as yet in order to reflect or rival the full-scale Department of Drama which Yale University had daringly introduced into its degree courses in 1918. That this was likely to follow in Britain—and fairly soon—was signalled by the spread of dramatic societies into all the major provincial universities, and by the growth of Modern Language Departments, including Departments of English, many members of whose teaching staffs felt impelled to relate dramatic literature in their own courses to the practical realities of theatrical performance. Such was the case of Liverpool, Sheffield, Leeds, Birmingham and Edinburgh ... It was against this background that both Oxford and Cambridge found themselves faced with having to decide whether or not to attempt to regulate the wide and varied interests in dramatic art, theatrical and practical, which they had allowed to proliferate ... Both had this confrontation wished upon them by external benefactors.[7]

At Cambridge the benefactor was Judith E. Wilson, who gave a large endowment towards the teaching of drama. At Oxford the money came from the film producer Alexander Korda, who handed over five thousand pounds for this purpose at the end of the war, and promised that more money could become available from American film assets frozen in Britain. Oxford used some of the money to send a team of dons to America to 'investigate the study of the drama' in universities there, and to recommend how Oxford ought to proceed.

The members of this 'Drama Commission' were Coghill, Maurice Platnauer of Brasenose, A. H. Smith the Warden of New College, and T. C. Keeley of Wadham. They left in the spring of 1945, and had planned to spend five weeks in America; but 'we were late in starting, the passage across the Atlantic took three weeks, and we had to spend a

7 'A Revolution in attitudes to the dramatic arts in British universities, 1880–1980', *Oxford Review of Education*, III, 2 (1977), pp. 116–17.

considerable time in making arrangements for our return'. They abandoned plans to visit Hollywood to study the use of films for educational purposes (which hardly sounds relevant) and were only able to visit three campuses where drama was taught, Yale, Western Reserve at Cleveland, and Iowa University. At Yale they met Allardyce Nicoll, the Professor of Drama there, and also talked to Harley Granville-Barker who was teaching at Yale and Harvard. These two doyens of dramatic studies told a somewhat astonished delegation that they 'deprecated undergraduate acting, not merely as a waste of time, but also as uneducative; for "a student who is required to act a part in a play immediately becomes interested in his part, and ceases to let his mind turn on the significance of the play as a whole" '.

This sank into the Commission's collective mind, and on their return to Oxford they concluded that there should be no School or Faculty of Drama established there, nor even a post-graduate course. Yet they felt that Oxford would be well served by the construction of 'a University theatre in which plays of various dates, languages and styles can be produced by a professional company, perhaps an inter-University Repertory, under conditions something like those of their original production'. So wrote Coghill in the *Oxford Magazine* in June 1945. He informed readers that the Commission was 'preparing plans for a building which will contain, besides a stage adaptable alike to Elizabethan, Restoration, and modern presentations, a cyclorama, accommodation for an orchestra (for opera), and rooms in which the OUDS or other dramatic societies can hold rehearsals'. The only strictly academic proposal was that 'there should be a Reader in Drama, whom we envisage as both a dramatist and a producer: Mr Barker, perhaps, or Mr Bernard Shaw'. This final suggestion seems a little eccentric; Shaw was then eighty-nine and Granville-Barker nearly seventy.

The Drama Commission made these recommendations in full in a report published during 1945; it was reissued three years later with a set of plans by the architect Frederick Gibberd for a University Theatre. These plans were on a grand, even grandiose, scale; though the building would seat no more than 700, its stage was extremely versatile, having removable proscenium arches and machinery to construct forestages and alter the character of the stage in other respects, so as to adapt it for productions in every style from Elizabethan to Edwardian. At the rear was an arena for open-air

productions. No site was specified, but the architect's drawings show the building as having a river frontage with punts moored alongside. The estimated cost was £187,000.

Coghill and his associates were besieged on one side with demands from undergraduates that the University Theatre be built forthwith (why a three-year delay before the plans had been drawn up, they asked), and on the other by outraged cries from senior members of the University who thought the project ridiculous and a terrible waste of money. To the latter group Coghill replied that it was proposed to get a government grant 'to pay for the entire scheme in perpetuity'. At the time the Board of Trade, with Harold Wilson at its head, was giving generous hand-outs for University expansion, and bestowed at least an informal blessing on the Oxford University Theatre project. Yet even at its inception, in a period of post-war optimism, there was something slightly unreal about the plan; Glynne Wickham calls it 'so staggeringly expensive as automatically to forbid fulfilment', and suggests that this was really Oxford's way of disposing of the whole idea of drama teaching. At all events the publication of the plan was followed by a long official silence on the subject.

Coghill meanwhile continued to be an inspired producer in his own eccentric way. In May 1948 Princess Elizabeth made an official visit to Oxford, and it was decided that the occasion should be marked by a special OUDS performance. He himself wrote *The Masque of Hope*, described by *Isis* as 'a pleasant and unusual pastiche of Spenser and Louis MacNeice'—though Merlin Thomas remembers it as 'a terrible text'—and organized its performance in the open air at University College. John Schlesinger, writing in *To Nevill Coghill from Friends* (1966), recalls that Coghill

was nothing if not ambitious in his demands. Trumpeters were to be placed in niches on the top of University College tower. Flags were to unfurl at a given cue; the character of Rumour (played by Robert Hardy) was literally to explode out of his cavern; and the masque was to culminate with a flight of doves released from the College archway . . . simultaneously with the pealing of all the bells in Oxford. I remember the final dress rehearsal, rather formally presented before the Senior Members of the University, with a don's wife standing in for HRH. Rumour's explosion from his cavern was thought to be too traumatic in its effect for a pregnant Princess, and was cut . . . The doves . . . had fed too well. All that could be seen was a distracted dove-keeper kicking their baskets, and audibly exhorting them to 'Get on, you little buggers.'

But Coghill's most memorable *coup de théâtre* came just over a year later, when he and Graham Binns (a Corpus Christi undergraduate) produced *The Tempest* in Worcester College gardens. The part of Prospero was given to a University College undergraduate named David Williams, who later became a professional actor and director as 'David William'; he had already made a success as Richard II at the Playhouse in March 1949. As Prospero in June that year he was joined by Jack May as Antonio, Nigel Davenport (Trinity) as Gonzalo, William Gaskill (Hertford) as Adrian, and John Schlesinger as Trinculo. Caliban was an American undergraduate from Wadham named A. W. J. Becker, and Ariel was played by Charles Hodgson (Lincoln).

Hodgson recalls that when Coghill offered him the part he suggested 'that I should avoid any tricksiness but also that I should perfect my cartwheels, I always had a passion for the ballet and believed I could look as though I could dance . . . In that spring vac. I did a great deal of work in the garden at home, trying to look at ease when cartwheeling.' Then rehearsals began. 'It was one Sunday morning that I clearly remember feeling that the production was going well. We had just finished playing Ariel's first entrance when David William looked down to where I crouched at his feet eagerly awaiting Prospero's orders. "Well done, brave spirit", he said, Nevill nodded, and I was totally happy.' In fact the acting was overall not particularly good (Frank Hauser, perhaps with a little exaggeration, remembers it as 'awful'); but the production was unforgettable for Coghill's visual effects. Hodgson describes them:

To finish *The Tempest*, Nevill wanted the repaired ship to dock at the water's edge—in this case the shore of Worcester lake nearest the audience—and for Prospero, having said farewell to his island, Caliban, and Ariel, to embark with the court and, as he sailed away, really to drown his book, full fathom five. Ariel would trip across the water in five balletic leaps, on a board which had been constructed to reach out about twenty yards into the middle of the lake. This line of duckboards was built two inches under the water level, and made it look as if I was walking on the water itself.

As Prospero reminded us that his 'ending was despair | Unless it be relieved by prayer', the huge vessel (a series of punts lashed together and surmounted by the replica of a Venetian sailing ship) was punted into position by the sailors, Prospero set Ariel free, and bade farewell to Caliban who dropped back into the water whence he had originally crawled. Here, at the lake's edge, close to the bank, a galvanized iron tub had been placed into which Caliban

could fall, and hide himself from the audience, who believed him to have gone into the water. (During rehearsals, children being shown round the garden used to come over to him for a chat.)

As the boat sailed away into the darkness, lit by a single spot, I was to leap out across the lake, stop and blow kisses to Prospero and his friends in the boat, then turn and run back over the submerged boards until I reached the shore again; then towards the trees at the back of the lake, still waving to the boat. In those trees Nevill had built a ramp which enabled me to run right up until I seemed to be standing above the highest branches. Once steadied at the top, I was to turn and spread my arms, as though appealing to the heavens, and there beneath me a flare exploded, and every light in the auditorium and across the lake went out, as though dowsed by the magic of Ariel himself. It was superb, a set-piece which has been etched into the memory of our Oxford generation.

The duckboards beneath the lake surface were not easy to construct —it was rumoured that the Worcester College rugger 'hearties' had threatened to loosen them before each performance—and the ramp into the trees was just as shaky, but there were no accidents. Nor were these Coghill's only visual effects in this extraordinary production. Peter Bayley remembers that 'the table for the banquet scene *ran* on to the acting-area through the trees, the four men who carried and propelled it being hidden by the long table-cloth. A typical piece of glorious vulgarity was the large pumpkin in the middle of the banquet-table, the top of which suddenly, when the table came to rest, flipped open and a tiny blackamoor child stepped out and ran away. At the end of the play Nevill's love of show again had a vulgar (but perhaps only an irreverent) streak, for the galleon which came across the water to take the Neapolitans and Milanese back to Italy—a brilliant idea and picture—had a real and richly-endowed girl as a figurehead, and for a moment one thought of the Chelsea Arts Ball.'

Not surprisingly, *The Times* reported on the production at some length.

The gardens of Worcester invite amphibious spectacle. Dull of soul would be a producer responsible for *The Tempest* who did nothing in particular with the curving lake which almost of its own accord appears in the fading light of a still June evening as the tree-fringed lagoon of an enchanted island.

Mr Nevill Coghill and Mr Graham Binns, wisely, do not rush at opportunity. While the day holds the water's edge is a mere shore from which Miranda watches the storm with pity and terror, along which the shipwrecked courtiers pick their way from a far point and on to which the slimy Caliban clambers.

But as darkness falls and the coloured beams play upon the water, turning the indifferent swans to silver and gold, and making magical sport with the water-lilies, lake is no longer and lagoon and stage are one.

Juno and her attendant goddesses are ferried across its lamp-burnished surface in a gondola, a barge, or whatever it pleases you to call a punt when it carries spirits called from their confines by a wizard's wand. On the shore, trees walking as men and transforming themselves into whips to the discomfiture of Caliban and his confederates should prepare us for further wonders, but the lighted galleon emerges with startling suddenness from behind a mass of overhanging bushes and bears the company back to Milan, leaving Caliban in bewildered possession of his own island, while Ariel, happy in his release from the service of man, speeds along the far curves of the lagoon to vanish in a shower of sparks.

The *Times* critic particularly commended A. W. J. Becker's Caliban, Charles Hodgson's Ariel, and John Schlesinger's Trinculo, which he said showed 'a clear comic idea and a good attempt to express it'. Schlesinger himself has recalled the impact of the production: 'Nightly, as we tripped over the undergrowth round the side of the lake, on our way to the dressing tents, to be welcomed by friends and rather tearful relatives, and a delighted Nevill Coghill, beaming like some enormous shaggy schoolboy, we all knew that we were part of something unique.'

8

Towards a University Theatre

THE OUDS club-rooms finally closed in 1950. The previous summer
an All Star Matinée was held at the New Theatre to help their ailing
finances (the performers included Emlyn Williams, Robert Speaight,
and John Gielgud), but it was finally decided to shut them 'to prevent
further losses'. In the years that followed various OUDS Committees
made moves towards re-establishing club premises, but there was no
real demand. The only serious cause for regret was that closure led to
the dispersal and loss of many of the Society's records. Today such
items as survive are stored in the Bodleian Library.

The OUDS was a little in danger of losing its identity at this period.
In February 1950 there was a proposal to amalgamate it with the
Experimental Theatre Club (ETC). Among the opposers was Tony
Richardson, who thought it essential that the ETC retain its
independence. 'The OUDS', he declared, 'is damned by respect-
ability, whilst the ETC is saved by the virtues of insecurity and
insincerity.' John Schlesinger, also opposing, called the OUDS 'a
gentleman's club ... beyond the means of many' (this was shortly
before the club-rooms closed), while he described the ETC as 'the
wandering Ishmael of the University' which gave an opportunity to
people who might not otherwise be able to participate in drama. The
amalgamation was rejected. A woman undergraduate who was present
at the debate observed that women were fortunate in that they could
reap the benefits of the OUDS without paying for membership. Sex
discrimination continued to be practised in the OUDS throughout the
1950s. 'Ladies are not allowed to become members,' states a notice
issued in Michaelmas Term 1954, 'but are most welcome to take part
in the Society's activities and have all the privileges of full membership
except those of attending General Meetings and paying a subscription.'

Tony Richardson was described by *Isis* as 'the *enfant terrible* of
Oxford theatre'. He came up to Oxford from Bradford in 1948, having

already formed his own local amateur company 'in the grime of the mill areas'. He produced *King John* at his college, Wadham ('the entire technical staff walked out half an hour before the curtain was due up', said *Isis*), and became a trenchant university theatre critic. For ETC he directed *Peer Gynt* with Hugh Dickson as Peer; Anthony Curtis remembers it as 'the most exciting undergraduate production of the time, staged against a background of hanging ropes'. Richardson became President of the OUDS, and directed *The Duchess of Malfi* for the Society in 1951 with Nigel Davenport playing the Cardinal. Peter Bayley in the *Oxford Magazine* called the production scenically magnificent, but complained that Richardson 'is one of those who cannot leave a play alone', and criticized him for too much 'hurly burly' and for encouraging mannered acting.

Another prominent OUDS figure during these years was the future impresario Michael Codron, who wrote a number of OUDS Smokers and pantomimes. For a time a pantomime became an extra annual feature; that of Christmas 1949, devised by Codron, had Schlesinger, Nigel Davenport, and Robert Robinson (Exeter) in the cast. The 1951 *Cinderella* (again directed by Codron) cast the future ballet critic Clement Crisp and Harvey McGregor (now the Warden-elect of New College) as the Ugly Sisters, and in the 1952 *Dick Whittington* Ned Sherrin was the Fairy and Nigel Lawson, future Chancellor of the Exchequer, was one of the chorus boys ('Les Boys'). Codron had come up to Oxford from St Paul's School where he produced revues; he became President of ETC, and Daphne Levens remembers him as a 'frightfully bossy' director who once gave her a severe lecture for talking in rehearsals. Robert Robinson's main interest was journalism and he became editor of *Isis*, but he found himself drawn again and again into theatricals.

The occasional OUDS evenings of One-Act Plays and Original Plays continued after the war. At a One-Act Plays session in May 1950 the medieval *Castle of Perseverance* was performed under the direction of William Gaskill, with a cast including Robert Robinson, John Schlesinger, David William, Clement Crisp, and Shirley Catlin; *Isis* called Gaskill, who later directed at the Royal Court alongside Tony Richardson, 'one of our few sensitive and successful producers'. Shirley Catlin, daughter of Vera Brittain, is now the politician Shirley Williams. She was reading PPE at Somerville, where she presided over the college dramatic society. 'She writes and acts,' says a programme

note of 1950, 'but her main ambition is politics. A keen Labour supporter, she is next term's President of the OU Labour Club—the first time the post has been held by a woman.'

A feature of OUDS life introduced in about 1950 at the suggestion of Merlin Thomas was 'Drama Cuppers', an inter-collegiate competition to discover acting talent among freshmen, held in the middle of the Michaelmas Term. The aim was to discover talent among undergraduates as soon as they arrived at Oxford, in which Cuppers has always proved very successful. The standard of performances, however, is usually highly variable. For example at a 1958 Cuppers the cast of Charles Williams's nativity play *Seed of Adam* walked off the stage before the end 'because of the unrestrained mirth of the audience' (*Oxford Mail*). The curtain line of the first scene was 'Nuts, nuts, nuts, nuts', and Peter Bayley of University College, the Senior Member who was adjudicating, called the play 'rubbish'. Michael Billington, now drama critic of the *Guardian*, was among the freshman cast and remembers it vividly.

I don't know if you've ever tried to play religious verse drama to a slightly boozy Saturday night Oxford audience, but I don't recommend it. The play was greeted with mounting hilarity, and when the heroine cried 'Parturition is upon me' (a line I shall never forget) the audience went wild with laughter. The director was in the play and on stage, and at that point hissed to the rest of us 'Get off'. So we obediently trooped off after him, leaving an empty stage and a frustrated audience baying for more. Could Oxford theatre really be like this?

Yet at the same Cuppers, according to the *Oxford Mail*, 'Miss Caryl Churchill of Lady Margaret Hall, the authoress of *Downstairs*, the Oriel College production which gained third place, was honoured by the adjudicator by being called up on to the stage.'

The number of productions staged by OUDS was now steadily increasing; by the mid 1950s the Proctors were allowing up to four 'private productions' per annum (for members and guests) as well as the two major shows. Church halls and other large rooms were pressed into service as theatres. Meanwhile the University Theatre project launched by Nevill Coghill in the mid 1940s languished; new scientific laboratories sprang up in the 'Keble Road triangle' in North Oxford, but no foundation stone was laid for any temple of the arts. The theatre plans had been launched on the tide of post-war optimism, but in the more sluggish waters of the 1950s they seemed unlikely to reach port.

An *Isis* leader of February 1950 called them 'too ambitious and too expensive to be, in these inclement times, anything more than a long-term dream. And meanwhile the immediate need for a University Theatre increases; this term, for example, over a dozen University and College productions are taking place; five of them will be coming off in one week ... More than one producer must view with dismay the smallness of his stage and hall.' The writer pleaded for a simple, cheap University Theatre, perhaps adapted from an existing building. Simultaneously the Playhouse was once again going through hard times. In January 1950 its financial position was said to be 'grave and disturbing' and Frank Shelley, the overworked director of the resident repertory company, had to resort to an endless round of thrillers and warmed-up West End leftovers in order to fill even half his seats each week.

With so many University theatrical activities, the OUDS major productions might almost have disappeared in the general mêlée. In fact during the early 1950s there was a series of memorable shows, though the quality was by no means even. In February 1950 the then President, Alan Cooke (later a television producer), directed an *Othello* with John Godwin and Guy Brenton as Othello and Iago, Peter Dews as Brabantio, and Robert Robinson as Cassio. David William gave it a savage review in *Isis*; of Peter Dews he observed: 'There is no reason why he should have been wearing gym-shoes. Mr Robert Robinson ... gets drunk too quickly, and generally underplayed the pathos of the situation.' Robinson eventually married the Desdemona of this production, Josée Richard. Anthony Besch, who since leaving Oxford had been working for John Counsell (ex-OUDS member and nephew of Doggins) at the Windsor Rep, came back to produce *A Midsummer Night's Dream* in New College garden in the summer of 1950. The production earned praise: Peter Dews as Quince 'was the parent of all kindly harassment and ill-digested learning', and 'Mr Nigel Davenport as Bottom seemed happiest in tragical vein' (*Isis*). Peter Dews remembers struggling against the 'summer' weather: 'An early blocking rehearsal *in situ* got snowed off, I recall ... At one of the later rehearsals I remember Anthony saying to me "No, don't stand there! Over there! No, there! By that daisy!" You know how many daisies there are in a college lawn.'

This production toured Germany during the long vacation, in tandem with *The Knight of the Burning Pestle* directed by William

Gaskill. Simultaneously 'The Oxford University Players', a group set up for the occasion, set off for an American tour, organized by Robert Levens. They were to perform *King Lear* with Peter Parker in the title role, Shirley Williams (then Catlin) as Cordelia, Peter Dews as Gloucester, Jack May as Kent, John Schlesinger as Oswald, and Ronald Eyre as the Fool. The company was also to perform Ben Jonson's *The Alchemist*, with Schlesinger in the role of Subtle.

Ronald Eyre records that *Lear* 'was to have been a production by Tony Richardson; and I remember with an outsider's interest (for at that stage I wasn't definitely one of the company) that he wanted his Lear to wear a yellow duffle coat against a purple cyclorama. I remember, too, visiting Tony in his rooms during the spring of 1950, when the strain of wondering whether I was to be on the tour or not became too much, and being made to admire a tank of terrapins while he told me he thought I had talent as an earthy comedian (Alan Cooke already wanted me to play Abel Drugger in *The Alchemist*) but none of the spiritual qualities needed for Lear's Fool. In the upshot he bowed, or was pushed, out as director and with him went Hugh Dickson, a notable ETC Peer Gynt, who was to have been the Fool.'

David William replaced Richardson as director, and Roger Lancelyn Green in *Isis* described a rehearsal in Oxford before the company set off: 'Lear (Peter Parker) was towering majesty from the moment he came on the stage: every inch a king—but such a king of violent passions as would indeed disinherit a daughter in an access of temper: particularly the only Cordelia (Shirley Catlin) I have ever seen who was every inch King Lear's daughter—attractive, sympathetic, but possessed with the family temper.' Parker had played Lear before, but in the Nahum Tate late Restoration version of the play, performed by OUDS and ETC members at the Fortune Theatre in London the previous year. Parker recalls that Tate 'had introduced an Edgar–Cordelia romance, smoothed speeches ("Blow, winds, and burst your cheeks"), and had Lear and Cordelia win the battle at the end . . . It was fascinating, but excruciatingly frustrating. Next year . . . I tried again, this time with the real thing. We began with Tony Richardson as producer, then, after some blow-up, David William took over. That was when Shirley Williams was a lustrous Cordelia (eyes and voice made everything out of "Nothing"). Ron Eyre was a remarkable Fool, solid and dreamy, there and gone. Peter Dews, Gloucester, accurate and moving.' Also in the company was Norman Painting, a

Birmingham University graduate who had studied for a B.Litt. at Oxford and was now working for the BBC—he created the part of Phil Archer in *The Archers*. On the tour he played Albany in *Lear* and Dapper in *The Alchemist*.

For Ronald Eyre, rehearsing for the Fool was 'little fun', because he had been instructed to play the part as ageless and sexless. ' "Sexless" wasn't much of a problem as I'd come hot from a Methodist childhood in South Yorkshire and two years keeping my lid on as a Wireless Mechanic in the RAF (it's odd how many of those lids stuck). "Ageless" did not seem insuperable either. I had been described in my first term and my twentieth year as "a squat little man of thirty-five", and my first piece of Oxford acting had been an ancient cuckold in *The Old Bachelor* for Univ. Players; so I was clearly on some kind of sliding scale. Acting, as I then understood it and would probably understand it still if I tried it again, was an exercise in being beside oneself, and raised alarming possibilities and questions. Hiding in public. Backing into the limelight. Directing seemed, for me, less dangerous.'

The *Lear* company had to pay thirty pounds each towards the cost of the tour. 'So I found myself,' writes Eyre, 'at the end of my first year, standing on a bleak airstrip (Luton, was it?) and watching the arrival of this tin drum that was to shake us up all the way to Gander, then to New York and the Mid-West. Our fellow passengers, on shoe-strings too, were mostly unshaven Neapolitan monks on their way to family reunions (which I saw and still remember) on the tarmac at Idlewild Airport.' The flight took twenty-eight hours and the plane arrived at its destination in darkness. 'By night, then, we came to Hygienic Barbary,' wrote Robert Robinson in *Isis*, 'bewildered among the metal forests, the slot-machine reserves, wide-eyed along the untrodden ways dedicated to the auto.' Shirley Williams, too, wrote in *Isis* about what she saw, describing 'the breathless, dark moment before the curtain went up in a new town, for nearly every night was a first night; the muddled, miserable heat in the station wagon, jolting over hundreds of miles of dusty cornfields'.

They visited a Lutheran college in Indiana, the University of Michigan at Ann Arbor, Chicago, Boston, New York—in all nine states and at least fifteen stops. 'Our nearly uncut *King Lear* became a test of the staying-power of the audience, who, fortunately, stayed', wrote Shirley Williams. Norman Painting noticed how American audiences 'seemed much more earthy, more concerned with basics

than a contemporary Oxford audience. In a way they seemed as one might imagine an audience of Shakespeare's own time to be. They responded noisily to the slapstick humour of *The Alchemist* . . . [and] received *King Lear* not as one of the highest peaks in dramatic tragedy, but largely as a play of sexual intrigue . . . There was . . . an enormous diversity in the places where we played: vast auditoriums seating thousands some nights; small, inadequate halls seating only as many hundreds the next.' Shirley Williams recalled one stage 'so big that trucks were among the props and the few steps of a stage run became a sprint . . . The plays became living things, changing their expression to suit their audiences.'

The tour was a gastronomic jolt for a company used to post-war English food rationing. Peter Dews 'posted my ration book to my parents before we caught the plane so that they could benefit from my absence'. Ronald Eyre was amazed by 'the biggest breakfast of our lives, taken at Shannon Airport'. Dews had never eaten a steak until he got to America.

In rehearsals Shirley Williams had been recurrently told by the director to comb her hair. 'She had a great way of involuntarily shaking her mane like a mop between the wings and centre stage,' says Eyre, 'and invoking a turbulent view of Cordelia that he did not want. *His* favourite, of the three sisters, was certainly Regan (Josée Richard), in canary satin that trailed behind her.' On tour, Eyre shared a room in a small Mid-West university town with Robert Robinson. 'He wanted reassurance about his chances with Josée Richard. How should I know? But I said yes, and they went off together to (could it be?) the source of the Mississippi. She has now been Mrs Robinson for a long time.'

Norman Painting thought that on the tour itself Shirley Williams was outstanding: 'Like Peter [Parker], she was sturdily built—anything but a will o' the wisp—although her youth gave her a kind of ungainly beauty. They were quite credibly a father and daughter, once Peter had his make-up on: Shirley's Cordelia, in its strength and stubbornness, was clearly a chip off the old block. But this was not the only quality which made her performance so believable. As a person she was—and is—forthrightly honest, with a directness that brooks no argument. Shirley invested her Cordelia with that same uncompromising firmness. Goneril and Regan flattered Lear and gained more than their share: Cordelia, like Shirley, refused to say anything that she didn't

mean. She said nothing; she got nothing. So her performance, and the resulting relationship between her and Lear, was a most compelling and effective piece of theatre, even though neither Shirley nor Peter had the sort of natural, or acquired, stage technique which gave such finesse to other performances in the production.'

Painting also observed the relationship between Lear and Cordelia off stage: 'As we rehearsed for the American tour, the truth was clear for us all to see: on Shirley's part, at least, this was a love affair, and an idealized undergraduate one at that. What became equally clear, during those gruelling weeks of travelling and performing in the heat of the American summer, was that Shirley was not to be the future Mrs Peter Parker ... At this time, Shirley was not yet 20; Peter 26. Both were brilliant intellectually, full of the drive and beauty of youth, both outstanding in their generation. In theory, they could have made a dazzling couple; in fact ... the basic chemistry was wrong ... I remember one very hot American night, somewhere in the middle west. Everyone else had gone to bed, and Shirley and I sat in the quadrangle of the college where we were staying, and talked most of the hot night away, telling each other our secret feelings and merely by doing so, contriving to relieve them. Only a few days before, I had received a letter telling me of the end of a relationship which at the time meant a great deal to me; and I believe it was on that very evening Shirley had realized that, in spite of great affection and mutual respect between her and Peter, a more enduring and close relationship was not to be.'[1]

Robert Robinson's description of America as 'Hygienic Barbary' was written for *Isis* shortly after his return to Oxford—and to his surprise it produced cries of outrage.

When the article came out I was stopped in the street by a don I knew. 'You shouldn't have done it. Some of us are hoping to spend sabbaticals over there and this sort of thing just doesn't help.' I moved on, startled. All I'd done was be a bit lofty. I'd made jokes about coke machines and launderettes (creatures from outer space, they were, in 1950), larded the piece with stuff about the Americans not being very good at thinking, pulled their legs about universities where you could get degrees in creative angling, and said the national drink was pink ice-cream in ginger-beer. To my further amazement, the following Wednesday there was a page of letters [in *Isis*] complaining about the thing ... The phone rang while I was in the *Isis* office receiving the congratulations of

---

[1] Norman Painting, *Reluctant Archer* (Granta Books, 1982).

less fortunate scribes. It was *Time* magazine—could they print a picture of me? . . . Which they got. I came out looking like a dwarf caught in the middle of a fire-eating act . . . They'd reprinted the article and this time the letters rolled in from all over the world . . . I was coming to recognize the sort of insult you only got when you'd really drawn blood, and I glowed when I read them. There was only one that slipped under my complacency—'If he wears the crown of wit, let him watch it doesn't slide down over his ears'—because while we'd being doing these two plays in America that's exactly what a crown had done. I was sustaining the not absolutely central role of the Duke of Burgundy in *King Lear*, and the crown I was given wasn't a very good one. In fact, one night before we went on, it came apart, and I stuck it together with elastoplast . . . I tell you, I used to wake up in the night thinking about that, and it lent the words of my hostile correspondent a surreal menace.[2]

A year after the *Lear* tour came the Festival of Britain, and that summer OUDS was involved with no fewer than four outdoor shows as part of it: Dryden's *Marriage à la Mode* in Magdalen Grove, Milton's *Comus* in the Maison Française garden, and two plays in All Souls Great Quadrangle: Nevill Coghill's production of *Samson Agonistes* and John Hale's of *Cymbeline*. The following spring Coghill directed the fourth OUDS *Hamlet* in the Playhouse, with David William in the title-role. Derwent May in *Isis* called it 'a cool performance' by William, which 'underlined with a new force [Hamlet's] rejection of life'. Ronald Eyre remembers William playing the part 'heroically, suggesting that there was no one around at the time bold enough to tell him that he was born to play it dreamy'. John Wood played Osric; he appeared as Malvolio in the June 1952 *Twelfth Night*, and the following spring, while President of OUDS, he took the title-role of *Richard III* which he co-directed with David Thompson. Ned Sherrin in *Isis* had 'no reservations' about this production and Wood's performance, which, after the usual villainous start, 'discards a measure of the malignancy in emphasizing the charm and grim humour that make Richard credible'. John Wood went straight down from Oxford to the Old Vic company. The part of Buckingham in his *Richard III* was played by P. J. Kavanagh (Merton), now a well-known poet and writer. For a time Kavanagh was attracted by the theatre; he recalls that 'OUDS helped me towards the solution of a dilemma. I wanted to be a writer but was a better actor. The praise (and girls) I got as an actor I knew to be bad for what I wanted to do and be. Quandary. How else

---

[2] Robert Robinson, *The Dog Chairman* (Allen Lane, 1982), pp. 43–4.

could a solution be attempted but by having the opportunity to try out two selves. Bless OUDS, therefore.' In fact he was to spend almost a decade as a professional actor before settling to literature.

Kavanagh was Pandarus in the June 1953 *Troilus and Cressida*, directed for OUDS by Merlin Thomas. In this first OUDS production of the play Alasdair Milne, future Director-General of the BBC, was Troilus and Sheila Graucob was the undergraduate playing Cressida. Michael Elliott (Keble), later a distinguished professional director, was Achilles. The *Isis* critic reported that both Milne and Graucob lacked 'the necessary vocal intensity', and the *Oxford Magazine* was equally unenthusiastic about their delivery; both reviewers gave more praise to Kavanagh. In fact this Troilus was afterwards to marry his Cressida; moreover in the same cast Paris married Helen and Ulysses married Cassandra. *Troilus* went on the fifth OUDS French tour, and was the opening production in the new Jardin Shakespeare in the Bois de Boulogne.

The same summer an Oxford Theatre Group was formed for the first Oxford contribution to the Fringe at the Edinburgh Festival; the company presented Strindberg's *Miss Julie*, Molière's *Tricks of Scapin*, and a revue, getting full houses and enthusiastic reviews. Thus another Oxford theatrical tradition was established; from now on, indeed, the Oxford Theatre Group, with its independent financing and board of directors and no Senior Member, began to play almost as influential a part in University theatre as OUDS and ETC, though it existed only for the production of plays at Edinburgh. Its second season at Edinburgh in 1954 saw no fewer than seventy-seven company members living in 'the club premises of the City Lighting and Cleansing Department in Advocate's Close', with the girls segregated in a house in Canongate. Two young professional directors, Alistair McIntosh and Casper Wrede, staged *Ralph Roister Doister* and Marlowe's *Edward II* with a cast that included Ronald Eyre and Patrick Kavanagh. A programme note reported that, off stage, 'domestic chores in dining hall and dormitory are done by members of the Company in turn. The pleasanter sides of army life are tolerable for six weeks.' Tolerable perhaps, but only just. In later years, when OTG had made its home in a masonic lodge near Edinburgh Castle, the barrack-like conditions drove at least one company member (the present writer) to seek other accommodation for the duration of the Festival.

Though women undergraduates were given plenty of chances to

perform at Edinburgh, during term-time OUDS still seemed half inclined to relegate them to a back seat, and during the mid 1950s professional actresses began to appear again with the Society. Only one out of the six women in a production of *King John* (by Michael Elliott and John Powell) in March 1954 was an undergraduate, and when three months later Jack Good directed *The Taming of the Shrew* in Commedia dell'Arte slapstick style in the garden of Black Hall, St Giles, a professional, Dilys Hamlett, played Katharina. Jack Good, who afterwards became an influential television producer of 'pop' programmes (he created the BBC's *Six-Five Special*), wrote enthusiastically in *Isis* that he was reviving 'the pre-war OUDS practice of employing professional actresses', and another correspondent in the magazine declared that to use professionals was 'constitutional and, in view of both the attitude of most tutors and the general level of acting, wholly unexceptionable'.

Dilys Hamlett appeared again in Oxford a few weeks later as the Queen of Hearts in a memorable OUDS production of *Alice in Wonderland* in the Priory House gardens, Christ Church—memorable not only for performances by Jack Good as the Duchess and Ned Sherrin as Tweedledum, but also because a convenient underground air-raid shelter provided concealed entrances and exits which were used to great effect; moreover by good luck or good planning Great Tom struck six just as the Hatter and Hare complained 'It's always six o'clock!'

Throughout this period the Playhouse remained in an insecure financial position. In October 1954 it was announced that Frank Shelley's resident company 'may have to close down in January, if not before', chiefly because of poor audiences. Nevill Coghill was now chairman of the company; a *Manchester Guardian* correspondent, reporting the theatre's troubles, shrewdly observed: 'I should think its chances of becoming a permanent university theatre would be very much alive, for the great £500,000 scheme put forward almost six years ago . . . is moribund.' But as yet nothing was done to convert the University Theatre scheme into a plan to acquire the Playhouse. A Gala to raise money for Shelley's company, the Oxford Repertory Players, was held in December 1954; and a season by the Elizabethan Theatre Company (directed by Peter Wood and John Barton) followed by a successful première of a children's musical play, *Listen to the Wind* (directed by the young Peter Hall), led to better box-office receipts, if only temporarily.

In February 1955 OUDS mounted their one hundredth major production, the *Hippolytus* of Euripides, in a new translation by Kenneth Cavender, the current Ireland Scholar at Balliol. The choice of play did not go unopposed; Nevill Coghill told the OUDS Committee that it 'was high time that OUDS did a Greek Play', but *Isis* grumbled about it. Dilys Hamlett was cast as Phaedra, three of the other four women's parts were taken by professionals, and Jack Good and Jeffrey Wickham played Theseus and Hippolytus. Casper Wrede was brought in to direct, assisted by Michael Elliott (thirty years later, Wrede and Elliott worked together at the Royal Exchange Theatre, Manchester. The *Isis* correspondent who had grumbled about the choice of play eventually conceded it to be justified, and praised the production, but the national press generally thought it disastrous. The performances were staged in the Divinity School, which was extremely cold, while Wrede's decision that most of the actors should speak through masks made the whole thing seem like a parody (according to the *Times* critic). The one hundredth production was also marked by the publication of a short history of the OUDS by Michael Pimbury, the previous year's President, and by an exhibition at the Ashmolean entitled 'Seventy Years of OUDS' (*Isis* observed that 'Ken Tynan's boots were not on show'). The *Oxford Mail* discovered that the only survivor of the first production, the 1885 *Henry IV*, was an 86-year-old retired printer, Mr E. F. Alexander, who as an Oxford schoolboy had appeared in it as a page.

In June 1955 Nevill Coghill directed an *As You Like It* in Worcester College gardens which made no particular impact, while the production of *Volpone* in Hilary Term 1956 was so poorly received that Merlin Thomas abandoned plans for a French tour, telling the Committee that 'adverse criticism in the national press would make it difficult to ask for a grant from the French Embassy'. However, an OUDS production of *The Merchant of Venice* by Daphne Levens in Mansfield gardens in summer 1956 did get to France. Mrs Levens recalls that 'it rained cats and dogs' in Oxford, so that 'Portia's remarks about "It droppeth as the gentle rain from heaven" seemed ironic'; moreover the rain continued in France.

We were rained off at the Sorbonne, and I persuaded them to let us use the Salle Richelieu, where the stage was a narrow ribbon entirely dominated by a grand piano. The concierge said he couldn't possibly move it—it would cost him his job—and a senior official said the same. So I mustered half a dozen

men from the cast, got a blanket and some ropes, and they had it off the stage in a moment. Afterwards I was congratulated by a top person at the Sorbonne: '*Madame*, no one has dared to move that piano since Napoleon's time, and now you have achieved it!' Another difficulty was that there were no stage lights in the hall, and when I asked if some could be found and plugged in, the concierge expressed deep horror. But, he said, *he could provide some light himself.* He would give no explanation; I must just leave it all to him, and tell him precisely *when* I wanted it. So I waited until the performance was well under way and it had started to get dark, so that the chandeliers couldn't really provide enough light, and then I said: 'Monsieur, there is a big *tirade* coming up, may we have some light?' And the concierge disappeared, and a moment later there was a strange noise, *vroom, vroom, vroom*, as if someone were winding the handle of some kind of machine. And then suddenly, *poufff!* a magnesium flare burst into light over the stage. The actor delivering the soliloquy was nearly knocked off his feet! He took a visible start backwards, and when I went backstage at the interval and told them that this was what they must expect during big speeches, Jeffrey Wickham who was playing Shylock was outraged. 'The best part of my life, and this!' I said, 'Don't be alarmed, it's obviously what they expect. And you know, they might ask for an encore.' Well, in the trial scene, up came Jeffrey's big speech as Shylock, 'Hath not a Jew eyes? Hath not a Jew hands?', and sure enough *vroom, vroom, vroom—poufff!* But Jeffrey was prepared, and he really gave it to them—and sure enough at the end they got up and shouted '*Bis, bis!*' And do you know, he actually gave them the whole speech all over again, gave them a real encore!

In April 1956 the Oxford Playhouse shut its doors. Frank Shelley's company had not been able to continue in business for long after the 1954 crisis, and no other producer or impresario had made a continuing commercial success of the theatre in the months that followed. Closure and reopening had become a monotonous routine during this period, attracting little attention outside Oxford, and it was only by chance that an old OUDS member, Frank Hauser, now a professional director, heard of the latest shut-down. He decided to go to Oxford and have a look. The Playhouse, he discovered, 'was like a sick aunt; people visited it out of kindness rather than because they wanted to'. On the way back to London he thought of 'the only good idea I've ever had: I wouldn't present a series of old or well-known plays as all the other Playhouse companies had done, I'd do new ones'.

Hauser started to look for financial backing, 'and here OUDS helped me in two ways.' First, the Society had raised five hundred

The OUDS Diamond Jubilee production, 1945: *The Taming of the Shrew* in Wadham College, (*above*) with Arthur Ashby as Petruchio and Elaine Brunner as Katharine; (*left*) Roger Lancelyn Green as Biondello.

(*Top left*) Ken Tynan (centre) as Holofernes in Anthony Besch's 1947 production of *Love's Labour's Lost*; (*below left*) Peter Parker as King Lear in 1950; (*below right*) Nevill Coghill directing in Worcester College garden.

Patrick Garland (left foreground) as Coriolanus in 1959.

(*Above*) Nevill Coghill in rehearsal with Richard Burton for *Dr. Faustus*, Caroline Bennitt behind; (*right*) 'Do you know, darling, I'm beginning to think I've just about had the face that launched a thousand ships.' An Osbert Lancaster Pocket Cartoon at the time of the 1966 *Dr. Faustus*.

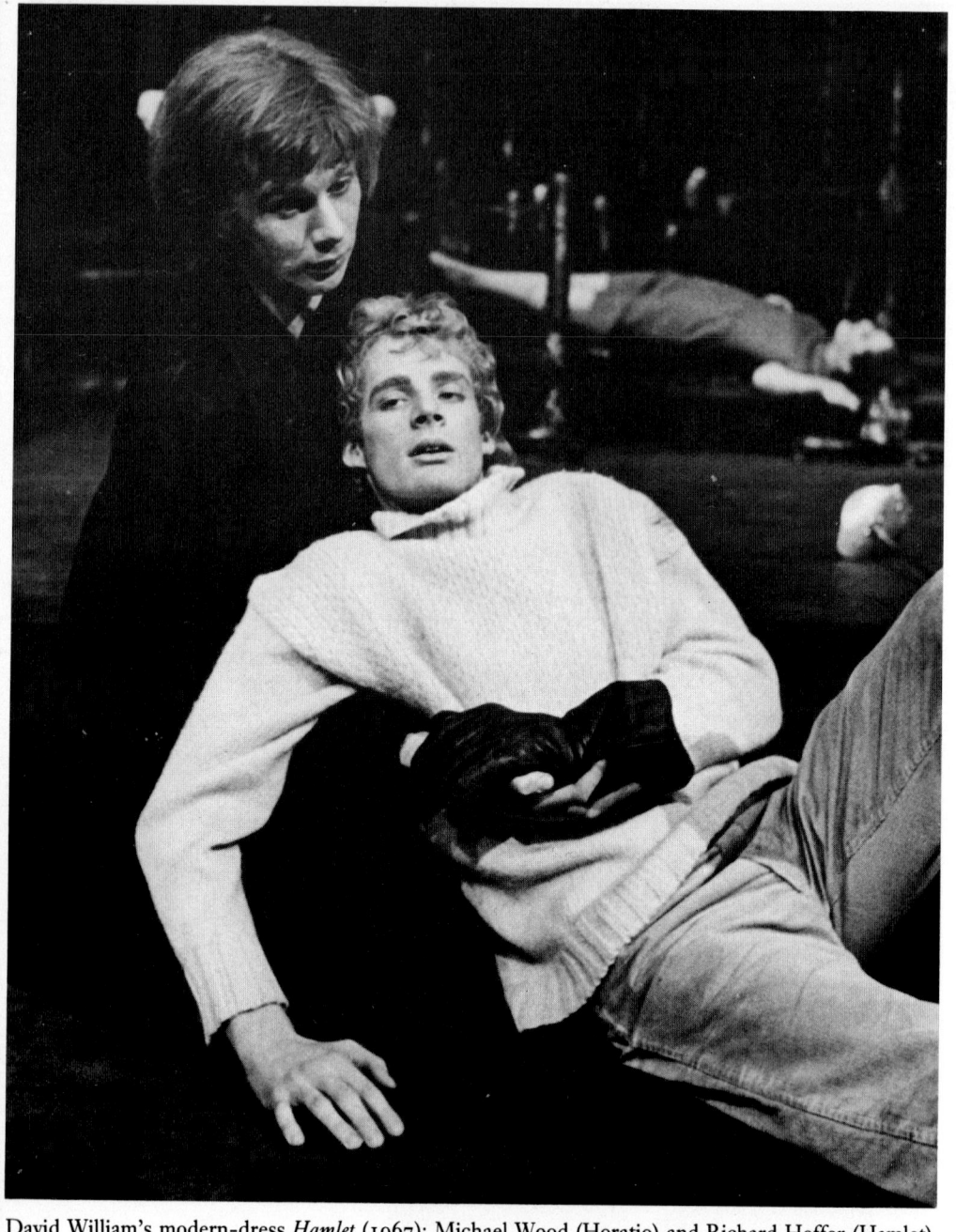

David William's modern-dress *Hamlet* (1967): Michael Wood (Horatio) and Richard Heffer (Hamlet).

Diana Quick takes over the Presidency (Hilary term 1968) from David Marks (left); on the right are Simon Welfare (Secretary) and Jonathan Davies (Junior Treasurer).

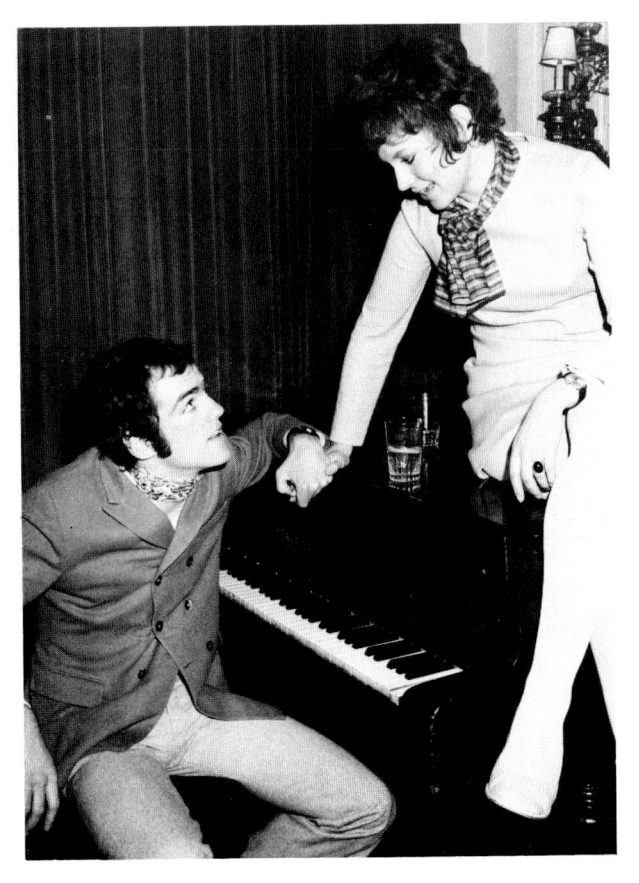

Michael Gwilym as Romeo, and Rona Bower as Juliet in 1969.

Imogen Stubbs, Yvonne Coen, and Jenny Waldman in Stephen Pickles's 1980 production of *The Three Sisters.*

Patrick Harbinson's 1982 production of *Cyrano de Bergerac.*

David Abraham as Moon in Lorca's *Blood Wedding*, a 1983 OUDS production by Lucinda Coxon.

pounds to help save the Playhouse, and this was handed over to Meadow Players, the name Hauser chose for his new team. Second, Hauser went to see Richard Burton ('who was what he was partly because of OUDS') who was playing Othello at the Old Vic, and asked him if he would come and act for Meadow Players. Burton said he couldn't because he had a film coming up, but immediately gave Hauser a cheque for £2,000 as a loan towards founding the company. Hauser recalls that Burton, a man surrounded by high-powered financial advisers, 'used to say in years to come that this two thousand pounds was the only investment he'd ever made which hadn't folded up on him'.

The total capital for Meadow Players was only £4,500, and clearly the company would have to be deftly managed. Here too OUDS played a part. One day in Oxford Frank Hauser ran across one of his old OUDS contemporaries, Peter Parker, who was running a Duke of Edinburgh's Conference on Human Relations in Industry. Hearing that Hauser was taking over the Playhouse, Parker strongly recommended the Conference's social secretary as manager for the new company. Her name was Elizabeth Sweeting. She had lectured in English at University College, London, and then, wanting practical experience of drama, had gone to work for H. M. Tennent's, who put her in charge of the Lyric, Hammersmith. From there she was sent to Glyndebourne, where she met Benjamin Britten and was drawn into his English Opera Group as its General Manager—whereupon she found herself helping to found and run the Aldeburgh Festival. After a decade of Aldeburgh she decided to make a break and learn personnel management, so she enrolled as a trainee at Marks & Spencer and was put behind a till; but from there she was quickly snatched up to the Duke of Edinburgh's Conference, and in Oxford she found herself being pestered almost daily by Frank Hauser, who had decided that she was indeed the person he needed to run the Playhouse. 'Eventually, just to get him to go away, I said yes!'

The beginnings of Meadow Players were very shaky; the staging of some half-dozen unknown plays in the first three months drove away many of the theatre's old faithful audience who came for the West End hack pieces, and the company had not yet built up its own following. Vernon Dobtcheff in *Isis* in February 1957 reported that audiences were still 'wantonly thin'. But Hauser quickly began to find outstanding actors and actresses who would come to Oxford to work for him. Some,

like Leo McKern, Sean Connery, Edward Woodward, Nyree Dawn
Porter, and Joss Ackland were at the beginning of their careers; others,
among them Rachel Roberts, Catherine Lacey, Joan Greenwood, and
Dirk Bogarde, were already well known. Hauser could only offer them
a fraction of what they would earn in the West End ('I paid them
twenty-five pounds a week and it was costing them forty'), but he liked
to stretch them rather than to type-cast: 'Casting was the secret.
Everyone gave Joan Greenwood comedy parts, but no one but me ever
asked her to play Hedda Gabler.' Nevertheless at the end of the first
season Meadow Players were virtually insolvent: 'We'd spent our first
year's budget *and* our second.' They were saved by the advice of their
chairman, Alan Bullock (now Lord Bullock), Master of St Catherine's.
'He told me to take what little cash we'd got out of the bank, put it in the
safe, and just carry on. Then I found an Anouilh play called *Dinner with
the Family* and we were saved.' This was the company's first of many
West End transfers.

So began the golden age of professional theatre at the Oxford
Playhouse, a period of seventeen years during which undergraduates
and Oxford residents could see an outstanding series of plays and
productions. Chekhov and Shaw were much in evidence as well as
lesser-known playwrights, but Hauser's greatest gift was for the
discovery of classics of European theatre which had been overlooked
by English producers—combined with inspired casting. Elisabeth
Bergner as Giraudoux's *The Madwoman of Chaillot*, Edward Woodward in Molnar's *The Wolf*, and Alan Badel in Sartre's *Kean* were three
such *tours de force*, while such performers as Judi Dench, Barbara
Jefford, and Leo McKern showed their affection and admiration for
Hauser by frequent return visits to the Playhouse stage.

It might have been expected that the presence of such fine actors
would have had a beneficial effect on University performers. Certainly
those undergraduates who, having worked as stage-hands on OUDS
and ETC shows at the Playhouse, were able to get casual work shifting
scenery with Meadow Players, learnt a great deal from observing
Hauser's company and its productions. But Hauser says that most of
the time he had little contact with undergraduate theatre; it seemed to
him that OUDS and ETC 'were always starting from scratch, and
never managed to learn from old mistakes'. Moreover his job was made
more difficult by having to share a theatre with amateurs. 'People
would come up to me in the street and congratulate me on a production

which had in fact been an OUDS show, while because of the undergraduates the Dorrill family who owned the New Theatre liked to make out that Meadow Players and the Playhouse was simply a nursery for would-be professionals.'

During 1957 Nevill Coghill revived his University Theatre plans. On 12 March Congregation (the University's 'parliament') debated a proposal for an all-purpose auditorium for concerts, lectures, and plays, to seat between four and five hundred people, and to be built either on the Keble Triangle or Holywell Great Meadow sites. The resolution was passed to press ahead. In consequence fresh plans were commissioned, and an architect produced rough drawings for a building of much less ambitious design than the original University Theatre project. However, it would still cost about £60,000, and it was announced that this money would have to be raised voluntarily—or the project would have to compete 'with a long list of established priorities in the University building programme'. Moreover no specific site was suggested for the theatre. 'It was at this time', reported the *Oxford Magazine* four years later, 'that an alternative proposal, that had been first mooted (but unsuccessfully) during the Vice-Chancellorship of A. H. Smith, was brought up once more, namely that the University should seek to acquire the Playhouse.'

The Congregation debate came in the middle of the run of the 1957 OUDS *Dr Faustus* at the Playhouse, with Coghill himself directing. Vernon Dobtcheff was Faustus, Jeffrey Wickham played Mephistopheles, and the future playwright Dennis Potter (New College) appeared as the Clown. Adrian Mitchell, reviewing the production for the *Oxford Mail*, called it 'safely above the OUDS standard'. As usual Coghill had dreamt up a spectacular visual effect—the concealing of the trapdoor, through which Faustus would make his final exit to hell, with a large book which would carry him down with it as it descended. John Cox (writing in *To Nevill Coghill from Friends*) recalls that 'on the first night, sparks from a smoke-puff set fire to the book and the audience enjoyed the unforeseen excitement of watching Faustus descend willy-nilly into real flames. The suspense was quickly broken as militant stage hands, uttering very corrupt text, shot fire extinguishers up through the gaping mouth of hell all over the bemused front-row audience.'

The following summer Peter Dews, then a television drama producer with the BBC Midland Region, returned to Oxford to direct an

open-air *Henry V* for OUDS. The title role was taken by Patrick Garland, who was in his first year at St Edmund Hall.

Garland, like most of his contemporaries, came up to Oxford after two years National Service. Already an accomplished amateur actor (and also a poet whose work had been read on the Third Programme), he quickly made a mark on Oxford theatre as Oswald in his college's production of *Ghosts*—Frank Dibb reviewing it in the *Oxford Times* spoke of his 'stage presence of notable quality'. It was previously unknown for a freshman to take the lead in an OUDS major, but nobody seemed surprised at Peter Dews's choice of Garland for the summer production, in Magdalen Grove. The results were excellent.

'The OUDS at long last seems renascent', wrote Ken Tynan in the *Observer*. 'Mincing and fluting, those trademarks of recent OUDS productions, have been rigorously banished: instead, we get the sort of honest, sense-before-sound sturdiness that has lately been the prerogative of the Cambridge Marlovians . . . With the thickening dusk, warmed by Mr Dews's liberal use of torches and braziers, the great war-poem came across in full and glowing comradeship . . . Harry himself, Patrick Garland, conquered lack of inches and facial unimpressiveness by sheer driving intelligence: high promise here.' Garland himself, recalling the production nearly thirty years later, thinks he really was 'pretty good', despite his youth and inexperience: 'When these things work—and one notes it's often an outdoor production —it's really nothing to do with stage technique. Elizabeth Sweeting put it superbly after one marvellous open-air Shakespeare at Oxford. She said: "The real point is that the undergraduates *wrote the play*. They *made it up*." And that's really the way it seems at its best. You get a kind of divine spark when that youth force is unleashed.'

Dews managed a stage effect that J. B. Fagan had tried to bring off with his *Dream* in Magdalen Grove many years before. Tynan wrote: 'I am ready to believe that Mr Dews actually rehearsed the jingoistic stag who, the night I was there, prematurely charged the French camp all by himself.' Dews says this was indeed a put-up job: 'The night Tynan was in, we got one of the deer in the Park across the stage. It upstaged the cast and pinched Kenneth's notice. We had a wonderful press and made a record profit. People kindly said it was the best OUDS Major since Nevill's *Tempest*.' Later that year Dews directed *Henry V* for BBC television, and he engaged Garland to play a herald and understudy

John Neville, who had been cast as the King. 'Mr Garland has been boldly acclaimed the best Oxford actor since goodness knows when', wrote Vernon Dobtcheff in *Isis*. Garland was soon elected President of OUDS.

The next OUDS major, *King Lear* at the Playhouse in February 1958, was directed by a Harvard graduate, Stephen Aaron, and gave a chance of greatness to Vernon Dobtcheff as the King. Patrick Garland describes Dobtcheff as 'the Harold Acton of our Oxford years', a connoisseur of theatre whose *bon mots* were treasured by his contemporaries. Garland himself played Edmund and the future film and television director Ken Loach (St Peter's) was Kent. Dobtcheff's Lear proved vigorous, even noisy—Adrian Mitchell in the *Oxford Mail* wrote that he had 'a voice like a limited church organ' and the *News Chronicle* called him 'the loudest Lear ever'. Mitchell thought that Loach 'makes a sturdy Kent, with not too much of the gentleman about him', while Garland was praised by the *Times Educational Supplement* for making Edmund 'a fascinatingly pliant portrayal of villainy'.

Ken Loach remembers that the director chose to present the play uncut on a bare stage. The resulting four and a half hours 'punished the audience into submission'. He also recalls that Stephen Aaron used improvisation in rehearsals, 'which we hated, but I found it very valuable in the end. I suppose I can trace something of my own methods as a director back to that.'

Garland continued to be very busy as an actor during his OUDS presidency ('that was why I got a Third'). He appeared in an OUDS production of *A Man has Two Fathers*, a new play by John McGrath, then an undergraduate at St John's (Tynan called it 'an undergraduate play of extraordinary quality'); as Bamforth in Willis Hall's *The Disciples of War*, directed by Peter Dews for the Oxford Theatre Group at Edinburgh; as the Cardinal in *The Prisoner* by Bridget Boland, performed by an OUDS cast as part of the Devon Festival at Barnstaple; as Creon in *Oedipus at Colonus*, an OUDS production at the Playhouse in November 1958; and, as a swan song, as Coriolanus for the OUDS major in March 1959.

This *Coriolanus* was directed by Anthony Page from the Royal Court, and had a professional Volumnia, Susan Engel. Page imported the up-and-coming designer Sean Kenny, and commissioned a score from Dudley Moore, who had just taken his degree in music at Magdalen. ('Dudley Moore's music arrives in gradual packets from

various Connecticut dance halls', reported *Isis*.) Besides Garland the cast included, among the walk-ons, Richard Ingrams (University College), Jonathan Cecil (New College), and Michael Billington (St Catherine's).

It was reviewed in the *Observer* by Michael Croft, who said that the production 'suffered from an excess of good breeding', but spoke of 'a Coriolanus of remarkable force and clarity by Patrick Garland. Mr Garland has obvious limitations—a lack of vocal as well as physical weight, and an overlong harping on one impassioned note, but he played with a driving intensity and a true sympathy with the verse which compelled attention throughout.' Garland himself recalls his Coriolanus as much less successful than his Henry V, and T. C. Worsley, writing in the *Financial Times*, dismissed the production as 'a thin year for talent . . . very dull'. Certainly Richard Ingrams, writing pseudonymously (as 'Hugo Prayermat') in the Oxford satirical magazine *Parson's Pleasure*, accused the director of being humourless: 'No amount of method and sincerity of performance can stop an audience from laughing when a Volscian soldier waits for Coriolanus to turn round before fighting him.' But, waspishly, he called Garland 'magnificent [when] the talent-scouts were in the audience'; while Daphne Levens in the *Oxford Magazine* spoke of Garland as giving an 'unexpectedly moving' performance. Garland joined the Bristol Old Vic as an actor the following September, and was seen on BBC television in the series *The Age of Kings*. Not for some years did he turn to directing—'something I had never done at Oxford'.

During the summer of 1959 a public appeal was launched for funds for a University Theatre. Printed letters were sent to all resident members of the University, and OUDS and ETC contributed one hundred pounds each. Merlin Thomas told *The Times*: 'A secretary of the fund has been appointed in every college to sell "brick" tokens of 2s. 6d. each.' He explained that the University Theatre Fund Committee was definitely 'thinking of a complete theatre on a site of its own'. Richard Burton was approached, sent a cheque for a hundred pounds, and came down to attend an undergraduate performance. But no statement was made as to where the theatre would be sited, or what form it would actually take.

John McGrath, having established his reputation at Oxford as a playwright, turned to direction, and the summer of 1959 saw his memorable production of Aristophanes' *The Birds* in a garden in Christ

Church. Sean Kenny again designed, and the music was once more provided by Dudley Moore. Jonathan Cecil played Euripides, Giles Havergal (Christ Church) was Epops, Michael Gearin-Tosh (Corpus Christi) was the Choragos, Michael Billington played a Priest, Ken Loach was the Inspector, David Rudkin (St Catherine's) was Second Messenger, and the future ITN newscaster Peter Snow (Balliol) played the Triballian God—'he did it as de Gaulle,' recalls Ken Loach; 'other characters were done as take-offs of Macmillan and Eisenhower'.

Michael Billington remembers this *Birds* as 'a dazzling, modern-dress production; an astonishing cast . . . A recollection of abundant gaiety.' Billington also recalls Dudley Moore making a stage appearance in an open-air production of *Bartholomew Fair* that summer: 'We toured to Leicester and to an open-air festival in Stratford. David Webster and Ken Loach directed . . . My main memory . . . is of Dudley Moore who played a walk-on role as a pear-seller. Night after night on tour Dud would sit at a piano in Leicester and perform cabaret routines till the early hours. A group of us got fed up with this and asked to be moved to another dorm. A few years later Dud was performing these same routines to huge acclaim on TV.'

Ken Loach directed again, this time in tandem with Merlin Thomas, when OUDS presented *Measure for Measure* in the Playhouse in February 1960. Loach also played Angelo—'quite disgraceful to direct *and* play the lead!' he says—and Thomas remembers his Angelo as being far too subdued: 'He had been ticked off for ranting in another University show, so he went too far the other way.' Loach, like Garland, became a professional actor after leaving Oxford, and it was not for some years that he discovered his particular directorial talent, which led him to make such realistic documentaries and films as *Cathy Come Home* and *Kes*. 'I took a long time to shake off the influence of Oxford theatre. In fact everything I've done since is really a reaction to the self-indulgence and vanity of it.'

Michael Billington, by this time drama critic and arts editor of *Cherwell*, wrote a hostile review of the Loach *Measure for Measure*; Loach replied in print, 'attacking me personally and accusing me of sour grapes since I had auditioned for the production and failed to get a part. That was the first attack (of many in later years!) on my critical honesty, and I remember being much miffed.' Billington got his own chance to direct, for a Sunday night ETC production at the Playhouse

in Hilary Term 1960, and it 'earned me a brief notoriety'. The play was Nigel Dennis's *The Making of Moo*. Billington

chose the play because I liked it and because Ken Tynan said it was the only atheist play in English drama. It involves three characters inventing their own religion in some native country. They substitute 'Toast and Tomato Juice' for the Communion and their ersatz faith leads inevitably to blood and cruelty. In those days one had to get Acting Leave from one's tutor to do a play. And my Anglo-Saxon tutor, Dennis Horgan, who was also the Junior Dean at St Catherine's, refused me permission to direct the play on the grounds (he was a sincere Catholic) that he disapproved of it. With the natural arrogance of youth, I protested at this. It seemed to me an improper use of the Acting Leave weapon, which was designed to ensure that people's academic work did not suffer. And I then nurtured vague hopes of becoming a director. Eventually, I took my case to the Master of the college, Alan Bullock. *Cherwell* ran a front-page story on it, and had to be persuaded from using a cartoon of my body being crucified on the Martyrs' Memorial. But what blew the whole thing up was when Bullock reluctantly overruled Horgan and gave me Acting Leave, at which point Horgan resigned as Junior Dean. The day this happened, Fleet Street descended. I did my best to hide from the newshounds, and I recall Daphne Levens, wife of Robert Levens, the don assigned to the production, giving me sanctuary. I was unhappy at having made the college the centre of a scandal at a time when Bullock was going round the world raising funds for the new St Catherine's buildings. Equally I felt outraged at Horgan's attempts at moral censorship. I remember a particularly odd tutorial when he was taking me through *Beowulf* and neither of us said a word about the incident: Grendel's mother ruled. Anyway, I went ahead with the production. But I think it turned out to be a slightly damp squib after all the publicity: I remember a bad review in *Cherwell* from my current editor on the *Guardian*, Peter Preston.

In OUDS during the 1950s it was still 'against the Society's traditions to do modern plays'—words used by Michael Pimbury in his 1955 history of the Society. In consequence undergraduate playwrights like Michael Billington's contemporary at St Catherine's, David Rudkin, had to turn to the ETC or college societies if they wanted their plays performed. Billington recalls the Apollo Society at St Catherine's giving a reading of Rudkin's play *Afore Night Come*, which not many months later was performed by the Royal Shakespeare Company. 'Rudkin was obviously a huge talent,' Billington recalls, 'a Midlands Irishman with a preacher-father, a Joycean gift for language and an omnivorous passion for the cinema. We read a number of his

plays at the Apollo: one, I recall, showed a group of characters conversing in guttural noises and only gradually discovering languages as we went on. The college didn't know what to make of Rudkin. He did a strange full-scale production of *The Dance of Death* in which I played a sentry marching up and down a tilted plank and visible only from the waist down. David also wanted to stage *The Trial* with me playing virtually everyone except K., and an adaptation of a Plautus comedy. Alas, the plans came to nothing, largely I suspect because of undergraduate suspicion of Rudkin.'

In the summer of 1960 John Duncan directed, as the open-air OUDS major, his own adaptation of Marlowe's *Tamburlaine*. This is universally remembered as one of the great Oxford productions. Peter Holmes was Tamburlaine, and the cast also included Gordon Honeycombe (another future ITN newscaster) as the King of Soria and Richard Ingrams as Mycetes. Ingrams recalls that the play was 'played in a huge space in St John's garden with the cast sprinting into position. Tamburlaine was Peter Holmes who was then working as a navvy on the motorway.' Ken Tynan reviewed the production enthusiastically in the *Observer*: 'The lawn is alive with swirling soldiers, who stop dead in their tracks the instant anybody speaks; when the speech ends, they zoom about again, coming to rest in starkly stylized postures as soon as the next syllable has been uttered.'

John Duncan staged a production of Mystery Plays this same year (1960) in University College chapel, and for Michael Croft this 'far outshone any other university production I have seen anywhere at any time. John, who was a keen cricketer and a good drinking man, managed to involve most of his college in the production. He rounded up the cricketers and footballers—even some of the rowing types—and, using the bar of the Eastgate as his headquarters, drew from his whole team a performance that was profoundly moving and continually exciting. Because few, if any, of the performers thought of themselves as actors the text came through, in all its simplicity, with an extraordinary impact . . . It was regrettable that John's considerable talent should have been lost to the theatre. After leaving Oxford he became a television director, then drifted into the post of Head of Light Entertainment for Yorkshire Television and finally gave up the profession altogether. He now runs a bookshop in York. One day I hope they will ask him to do the *Mystery Plays* there.'

John Duncan's work provided a flourishing finish to the 1950s,

which had been a vigorous decade in Oxford theatre. Yet Michael Billington observes that Oxford 'didn't make the same impact on the world at large as Cambridge theatre of the same period, which produced Trevor Nunn, Ian McKellen and many more. Why? Cambridge theatre, I feel in retrospect, reflected the textual rigour and moral force of the Leavisite approach to literature, Oxford the more traditional and quietly appreciative attitude—what Jonathan Miller once unfairly called the "Yum Yum" view of it. Of course one didn't feel this at the time. And of course Oxford has produced outstanding individual writers, performers and directors. But it hasn't affected post-war English theatre as powerfully as Cambridge, and this may be a direct reflection on the different approaches of the two universities to teaching and to life in general.'

During the spring of 1960 the rumours became current again—this time in *Isis*—that the University might buy the Playhouse, and that the project of building an independent University Theatre had been deflected to this end. The first published undergraduate comment (anonymously in *Isis*) was, to say the least, cautious.

One hopes that this scheme has not already gathered so much momentum that it is impossible to stop it . . . What we need is . . . a well equipped building, where undergraduates will have time to prepare for performances properly, instead of setting the scenery and arranging the lighting in the twenty-four hours before the curtain goes up. We need above all a place to rehearse, to make scenery and to experiment with lighting. Will we get them if the University buys the Playhouse? Probably not . . . We would have limited time in, and access to, a building which isn't even the sort we want. We don't just want a stage and auditorium. Above all we don't want a proscenium arch. We want to be able to act on an apron, or in the round as well . . . In short, then: either the Meadow Players have the Playhouse, or we do. There is no room for both. We don't want to lose Frank Hauser, and we don't really want his building anyway.

A week after *Isis* had published the rumours about the University's intentions, Robert Levens made a statement in the *Oxford Magazine* (19 May 1960), calling the Playhouse plan 'a hitherto well-kept secret', and continuing:

Since it became apparent that Oxford will not support a permanent repertory company, Meadow Players have been using it as a base for a limited number of high-quality productions and sub-letting it at other times, thus shouldering a much heavier burden than is justified by their own requirements . . . If . . . the

University is able to acquire the leasehold . . . development plans . . . could be carried out many years before an entirely new theatre would have been likely to get beyond the blue-print stage.

There were in other words two factors behind the University's plans: the desire to preserve the Playhouse from possible closure, in the light of the financial strain imposed on the resident professional company (the then owners of the lease) who had to maintain the building even when they were not using it; and, quite independently, the University's desire to acquire a ready-made theatre rather than wait until a purpose-built University Theatre could be funded and constructed.

In retrospect, the second seems to have been far the more powerful motive. Meadow Players were not in financial trouble; their reputation was now well established, and Hauser's policy of presenting productions for a short run in Oxford and then taking them on tour (while sub-leasing the Playhouse to other companies) was proving satisfactory. Indeed Hauser believes in retrospect that Meadow Players would have done better not to sell the lease of the Playhouse, and to have gone on being solely responsible for its policy and upkeep. On the other hand, at the time the University's offer of relieving them of the responsibility of maintaining the actual structure of the theatre was very tempting; the day-to-day running of the Playhouse itself was certainly an additional strain on their finances. So they responded in friendly fashion to the University's overtures.

Those negotiations had of course been conducted chiefly by Nevill Coghill, who wrote in the *Oxford Magazine* on 26 May 1960 that they 'seem now well on the way to a successful conclusion'. The tone of his remarks was breezy, though he admitted: 'To acquire the Playhouse rather than to have planned a new building may at first seem a grave recession from the high hopes once held of incorporating an entirely new "contemporary" auditorium.' But he concluded with a flourish: '*Habemus Theatrum.*'

Why had Coghill pushed the Playhouse proposal through in camera, and apparently without consulting OUDS, ETC, and other under-graduate theatrical bodies? Probably embarrassment at the continuing non-appearance of a University Theatre was a large factor—it was now fifteen years since the project had first been mooted, and three since Congregation had given its support. In truth the University Theatre notion had never been embraced more than half-heartedly by Senior Members, while Coghill, the only person who was really prepared to

devote much time or energy to the project, probably preferred to acquire a conventional theatre with all its stage machinery and other facilities than to construct a slightly avant-garde auditorium designed with theatrical experiment in mind.

At the time, Coghill was criticized by his fellow dons as well as by undergraduates; an editorial in the *Oxford Magazine* at the end of the 1960 summer term called the Playhouse announcement 'sadly mistimed', and objected to the lack of consultation. It concluded: 'By now most people seem to have accepted . . . that the transfer of the lease to the University will do more good than harm if this acquisition is put to the best use; but what the best use is remains to be worked out.' The transfer of the Playhouse lease[3] went ahead; Meadow Players disposed of it for only £20,000, the cost of the original building, so that the University acquired its theatre for only a fraction of what a new building would have cost. Meadow Players would continue to use the Playhouse for many weeks of the year, but now became the University's tenants. Oxford was the first university to acquire a theatre in full running order; Elizabeth Sweeting, who left Meadow Players to become Administrator and Licensee of the theatre itself, wrote at the time that it was 'a logic, of a wild kind perhaps, to involve the University with show business'. Some amusement was caused by the fact that, on 1 January 1961, the day that the Playhouse officially became University property, the show running there was *Charley's Aunt*.

[3] It runs until 2037, the centenary of the theatre's construction. The ground landlords are St John's College.

9

Habemus Theatrum

UNDER the new arrangement Meadow Players were to have the use of the Oxford Playhouse for 'at least twenty weeks a year, and a few more, if they so desire, by agreement'. The OUDS, the ETC, and other undergraduate societies would usually have the theatre for four weeks every term between them, and the remaining time would be shared mostly between visiting companies and local amateurs. The overall government of the theatre rested with the Curators of the University Theatre (a committee of dons) but the day-to-day running was placed in the hands of a Joint Management Committee, consisting of three Curators, the Administrator, and six undergraduates 'nominated from within the student body representative of the major societies and other dramatic activities'.

It appeared, then, that undergraduates would have a considerable part in formulating the policy of what was supposed to be largely their own theatre. In practice they soon found that their plans and needs must often take second place to the requirements of the resident professional company, and to the consideration of filling as many seats as possible and thereby making the theatre commercially viable. Inevitably the OUDS and ETC often felt they were being made to stand aside for the benefit of the professionals, who in their turn got an equally unsatisfactory deal, having to tussle with undergraduates for the use of the theatre in the 'best' weeks of the year (the middle of each University term).

Unfortunately some undergraduate shows staged at the Playhouse scarcely deserved to be seen on the boards of a professional theatre. 'People are bound to ask who, having read the script, passed it for Playhouse production', commented the *Oxford Magazine* of a Christ Church Dramatic Society performance in 1961, soon after the University's takeover. And a 1965 *Isis* review of a fairly typical term's undergraduate shows observed: 'Technical proficiency was the highest

189

common factor—all too often it seemed the only factor.' Certainly while undergraduate stage managers and lighting operators, drawn from a small pool of enthusiasts, usually worked on many productions and so learnt their jobs very thoroughly, many student actors appeared on the Playhouse stage with little or no previous experience. Moreover the quality of OUDS and ETC shows was considerably diluted by most undergraduates preferring to take large parts in college productions rather than smaller roles in those mounted by the University societies. Patrick Garland had grumbled about this during his OUDS presidency, and the same complaint would often be heard again. On the other hand the standard of OUDS shows in the early 1960s was higher than the average because of the continuing use of professional directors.

In the Hilary Term of 1961 Michael Croft, who had founded the National Youth Theatre, staged *Richard II* for OUDS, with the King played by an undergraduate and former Youth Theatre member, Richard Hampton. Daphne Levens in the *Oxford Magazine* described Hampton's as 'a very remarkable performance'. Croft remembers the production

for two distinctive performances by two extraordinarily tall actors, both about six feet five. Peter Snow played Northumberland and Gordon Honeycombe the Bishop of Carlisle. Peter was master of the theatrical send-up. He found it almost impossible to treat any line or situation seriously. He wore forever the bemused air of a man who has not the slightest interest in the proceedings taking place before him. Even in the poignant moment when Richard is dragged away to Pomfret Castle, Peter could not resist looking quizzically down at the Queen's sorrow-stricken ladies-in-waiting as though he would like to date them. But he reserved his major send-up for the Bishop of Carlisle. Something about the Bishop, or about Gordon's performance or his melancholy appearance, fascinated Peter so that, even during the *longeurs* of Flint Castle and Westminster Hall, his gaze continually turned upon Gordon as though he had, as it were, failed to do up his ecclesiastical flies. Northumberland's comment outside Flint Castle on hearing that there is a holy man inside with the King—'Oh, belike it is the Bishop of Carlisle'—caused Peter endless amusement. He spoke it differently at each performance, changing the emphasis from syllable to syllable and generally conveying the impression that the Bishop was probably involved in some unusual sexual activity, possibly with Bushy, Bagot and Green had they been there. Those three characters, in fact, became the subject of a brilliant calypso devised by Ian McCulloch, who played Percy, which had the refrain:

Habemus Theatrum

Now who was the Queen—
Was it Bushy, Bagot, Green—
Or was it one of the Pages?

Michael Croft's *Richard II* was followed a year later by Peter Dews's production of *Henry IV, Parts 1 and 2*, the two plays being performed in sequence on some days and separately on others. Dews had just directed the complete cycle of Shakespeare's history plays for BBC television; he recalls that for his OUDS *Henry IV* 'there was a cast of about 50. I know the Playhouse backstage was crammed.' David Senton, the then OUDS President, played the King; Nigel Frith was Hal, Oliver Ford Davies was Falstaff, and John of Lancaster was played by Michael Johnson (University College)—the future film actor Michael York. John Carey in the *Oxford Magazine* thought that Dews had 'sacrificed depth to surface' in his glittering production, and found Hal 'babyish' and Falstaff 'a funny old simpering grandpa'. But for Dews's stage manager, Sheridan Morley, then a Merton undergraduate, the production was an enriching experience.

I think I learnt more about the theatre in those two months than I ever had before and perhaps since. Peter Dews called the company up to Oxford immediately after Christmas, so that we had about a month of rehearsal before term started and then another month before we opened ... Dews was a tremendous father figure, a fund of marvellous theatre stories, and achieved a quite remarkable level of production by the simple device of ignoring the University altogether once he had drawn his students from it ... He expected a totally professional level of involvement which he in fact got from everybody, even those who had Finals coming up. It was a unique and extraordinary thing to be involved with.

Sheridan Morley appeared as one of the mechanicals in the next OUDS major, Nevill Coghill's June 1962 production of *A Midsummer Night's Dream* in Worcester gardens. Nigel Frith played what the *Oxford Magazine* called a 'convulsively comic' Bottom, and Starveling was Adrian Benjamin, a heavily bearded Wadham undergraduate who during the next five years created a series of eccentric and energetic Oxford productions, ranging from *Alice* to *Tristram Shandy*; he then went into the Church. Sheridan Morley recalls that in this *Dream* 'Nevill had the bright idea of rehearsing us totally separately so that when we came to do the play in Act V the "court" had genuinely, until the dress rehearsal, never seen it ... It was rather a nostalgic affair,

with audiences remembering all the other Nevill triumphs, when he'd had Puck walking away over the water, and in the war when he'd used the whole of the deer park in Magdalen.' For this production Titania's bower was a floating raft to which Oberon ran across the water in order to administer the magic potion. To Peter Bayley, who remembered the 1949 *Tempest*, these effects now 'seemed contrived and unjustified; his real inspiration couldn't sustain repeating'.

The 1963 Hilary Term OUDS major was *Othello* with a strong cast—Oliver Ford Davies (Othello), Giles Block (Iago), Michael Johnson (Roderigo), and Annabel Leventon (Desdemona), who were all to become successful professionals—but the results were disappointing. While it was touring France in the Easter vacation, the Playhouse closed for nearly a year for alterations. Immediately after acquiring the theatre, the Curators had announced a major plan for improvements: the enlargement of the orchestra pit so as to make opera possible, and the construction of a lift which would convert the pit into an apron stage; the remodelling of the proscenium to make it less of a 'picture frame', creating 'assembly' entrances on to the apron stage; increased lighting and flying capacities and general improvement of backstage facilities; the provision of a modern lighting and sound control box at the back of the auditorium; and the removal of the theatre's wardrobe accommodation from the front of house to an extension backstage. The budget for this was some £50,000, and an appeal was launched to raise the money. Nearly £25,000 was contributed in the first year, including donations from the Wolfson Foundation and Associated Television.

OUDS productions continued while the Playhouse was out of use; most notable among them were John Duncan's versions of Aeschylus' *Prometheus Bound* and Skelton's *Magnyfycence* in New College in June 1963. Designed by Barry Fantoni, *Magnyfycence* was done as a grotesque cartoon in the *Beano* or *Dandy* style; the cast included Michael Johnson, Nick Arnold, Michael Emrys Jones, and Doug Fisher. When the Playhouse reopened in January 1964 all these performers were in the cast of Michael Rudman's OUDS production of *Twelfth Night*, the first University show to be presented in the reconstructed theatre. Johnson was Orsino, Emrys Jones was Aguecheek, Fisher played Feste, Arnold was a Priest, and Annabel Leventon was Viola. Michael Rudman, American-born and educated, and studying for a second degree at St Edmund Hall, took a little time

to find his feet as an undergraduate director; Daphne Levens in the *Oxford Magazine* called the production 'cheerful, and patchily enjoyable, but lack[ing] distinction'. Rudman became President of OUDS.

His chief rival as a director in student theatre at Oxford in the mid 1960s was Braham Murray. In February 1964 the ETC (at the Playhouse) presented Murray's *tour de force*, a revue-style production on the theme of capital punishment entitled *Hang Down Your Head and Die*. The show, scripted by David Wright, was in a similar style to Joan Littlewood's *Oh! What a Lovely War*, and was painstakingly assembled and rehearsed for many months. The cast included Michael Emrys Jones, Adele Weston, Robert Scott, David Wood, and two future members of *Monty Python's Flying Circus*, Michael Palin and Terry Jones. Of all these, David Wood (now a well-known children's playwright) earned the greatest praise; Edward Mortimer in *Isis* wrote that he 'bids fair to be the clown of the century . . . not only a virtuoso at singing and playing the fool, but also [he] wrote some of the best songs himself'. *Hang Down Your Head and Die*, perhaps the most remarkable achievement of post-war Oxford student theatre, quickly ran into trouble with the Lord Chamberlain's office, which at that time still censored plays. The company was told to omit a scene depicting the execution of the Rosenbergs, and was also forbidden to perform a hanging scene which was to provide the climax. However, various influential people were persuaded to intercede with the censor, among them former OUDS President Gerald Gardiner, who was at that time the Lord Chancellor and was to play a prominent part in the abolition of theatre censorship a few years later. In consequence *Hang Down Your Head and Die* was able to point its moral fairly pungently (the hanging scene was restored); after a very successful run in Oxford it played for a time in the West End, and was then seen in New York. Daphne Levens, reviewing it, said that the 'enterprise and imagination' of the show gave 'not only proof of the vitality of University drama, but a fair argument for its validity'. Capital punishment was abolished in Britain the following year.

David Wood played Algernon in *The Importance of Being Earnest* directed by Nuala O'Faolain as an OUDS minor in May 1964, and in this production the part of Gwendolen was taken by Maria Aitken (St Anne's). The following November she took the part of Babette Biedermann in Max Frisch's *The Fire Raisers*, another OUDS minor. Offstage, Maria Aitken was among those now campaigning for the

admission of women to full membership of OUDS. In 1958 the OUDS Committee had observed that a decrease in the Society's membership in favour of the ETC was partly the result of the ETC's admission of women, but a motion to let them into the Society just failed to gain the two-thirds majority necessary for any constitutional change. In April 1964 the matter was raised again by Doug Fisher and David Aukin, and a General Meeting was held in the summer term to vote on the issue, but there was no quorum. Another General Meeting was convened on 11 October when, according to the minutes, 'the discussion became rowdy and prolonged, resolving into a division between the antianachronists, who recognized the important part played by women in the university theatrical scene, and the chivalrous traditionalists, who pointed out that in any event there seemed to be no raging passion to become members emergent from the women themselves'. There were 54 in favour of the admission of women, 25 against, and 3 abstentions—so that the two-thirds majority was again not achieved. Following this, a petition for the admission of women was signed by about twenty OUDS members, and at the next General Meeting on 29 November 'the proposed amendment to the Constitution . . . was finally passed . . . with a large majority'. The vote this time was 47 for, 3 against, and 3 abstentions. Maria Aitken jokingly said some years later that she had 'had to chain myself to the Playhouse railings' to achieve this.

During the summer vacation of 1965 OUDS presented *A Midsummer Night's Dream* in the garden of Alveston Manor Hotel in Stratford-upon-Avon. A plan which sounded idyllic went badly wrong, owing to poor relations with the Forte company who owned the hotel: they banned the student performers from the hotel itself, objected to them singing 'Jerusalem' loudly at midnight from the tented camp beneath its windows, provided inadequate sanitation (one bathroom for twenty-five men), and were not mollified by being told by one OUDS member: 'My father could buy this hotel several times over.' The following February *King Lear* was the OUDS major at the Playhouse; a promising cast—Clive Mitchell as Lear, Sheila Dawson as Cordelia, David Wood as the Fool, and Simon Brett as Edgar—was taken over at the last minute by Peter Bayley, as 'an emergency stand-in for a professional director who had an untimely nervous breakdown'. He had to rehearse the play in only four weeks, and noticed that 'lighting and design people were beginning to dominate—unhealthily, I

thought—and I had to fight to make the lighting man give up the 130 changes he proposed (I felt we needed about 30 at most); and the costumes, excellent in design, were never all finished'. Daphne Levens, reviewing, thought that the play scarcely came across at times—'Words lay on the air unpropelled by thought or genuine feeling.' But she praised David Wood's 'wild fool with a sudden poignancy in movement', and Bayley himself, though admitting the limitations of the performance, recalls that he was 'several times in tears' at certain moments, particularly Lear cradling Cordelia in his arms at the end, with 'a hint of reverse *Pietà* . . . Dame Helen Gardner approved of the latter, and spoke in a famous lecture a year later of how Shakespeare ends his greatest play with "this secular *Pietà*". She also wrote to me about it, and said, too, that she had never seen a Cordelia weep so much—"but that is right of course".' Sheila Dawson who played Cordelia afterwards became a professional actress, as 'Sheila Ruskin' (at Oxford she studied at the Ruskin School of Drawing), and was for a time married to David Wood, who wrote his first children's play, *The Owl and the Pussycat Went to See*, in collaboration with her.

David Winter wrote in *Isis* in June 1965: 'Outside Oxford something called the "dramatic revival" is supposed to have taken place . . . It attacked and almost demolished the idea that all the theatre need do is "put on" plays . . . But the committees of the University clubs seem to lack, at this moment, people committed to the theatre as art.' Certainly Christopher Hampton, who came up to New College in 1964, found it no easier to get his work performed than David Rudkin had done a few years earlier. 'I had very little to do with OUDS,' he writes, adding, 'this was not for want of trying; I attended a number of auditions to no avail.' OUDS did perform his first play, *When Did You Last See My Mother?*, but this was almost by accident.

I'd written the play before coming up to Oxford and, since I had very little idea of what to do with it, I hadn't even bothered to type it out. Then, at the beginning of my second year, i.e. at the end of the Michaelmas Term, 1965, OUDS announced it was going to produce a season of undergraduates' plays. I typed my play out and submitted it. There was a meeting at the beginning of the Hilary Term, at which it was announced that the season would consist of a musical by Michael Sadler and a play by an Algerian student. My play had not been chosen. However, a couple of weeks later, David Jessel, who was then the Secretary of OUDS, came to see me and confessed that Sadler's musical was too expensive and that my play, which had the merit of being exceptionally

cheap, had been chosen to replace it. Could I get the play on in three weeks?

I cast the play quickly, deciding, after a becoming hesitation of about five minutes, to play the leading part myself (reasoning that no one else would have time to learn the lines) and asked an indigent friend of mine, Charles O'Hagan, who at that point was dividing his time between the House of Lords and a sofa in my sitting-room and who had (and still has, as far as I know) virtually no interest in the theatre, to direct the play. He agreed. As the time for the opening approached, the leading man in the Algerian student's play went down with chicken-pox (or something equally unlikely) and before we knew where we were, the OUDS festival of plays written by undergraduates consisted entirely of *When Did You Last See My Mother?* We opened in February 1966 in a tiny theatre in a prep school in Headington (Josca's Little Theatre it was called) and were lucky enough to get a very good review in the *Guardian*. This led rapidly to the play being published by Faber's, my finding an agent, and the acceptance of the play by the Royal Court Theatre, where it opened in June. I had no further dealings with OUDS.[1]

Far more appealing to the majority of undergraduate actors than any search for writing talent among their own number was the announcement late in 1965 that the following spring *Dr Faustus*, to be directed at the Playhouse by Nevill Coghill, would star Richard Burton and Elizabeth Taylor as Faustus and Helen of Troy. Burton had agreed that he and his wife would give their services to mark Coghill's retirement from the Merton Professorship of English Literature, and to help raise money for further improvements to the Playhouse. It was also a chance for Burton to turn his back on Hollywood for a few weeks and return experimentally to the English stage. He told a reporter during 1965, 'I get terrible bouts of homesickness', and before the production opened he said: 'I've been wanting to play Faustus for more than twenty years.' Asked if there was a parallel between Faustus selling his soul to the devil and himself giving up the stage for Hollywood, he remarked cryptically: 'Everybody is offered a choice.'

The Burton–Taylor–Coghill *Faustus* was not without its organizational difficulties. On the very day that booking was to open at the Playhouse, Elizabeth Sweeting heard that the Burtons had postponed their visit by a week; arrangements at the theatre were hastily changed, and the dates on all tickets were altered by hand ('I said, "Go out and buy some felt pens!" '). Ken Bonfield, the theatre's technical director, constructed a special trapdoor and lift to raise Helen of Troy from the

---

[1] Letter to the author.

depths for her first entrance, but Elizabeth Taylor proved to be less sylph-like than had been supposed and the equipment was inadequate to support her; instead, she entered from the wings in a cloud of dry ice. But rehearsals (with an undergraduate, Nick Young, doing most of the detailed direction) proceeded smoothly, and were held in the gymnasium of Oxford Police Station to screen the Burtons from reporters and autograph hunters. A special rear exit from the Randolph Hotel was built to allow the stars to get to their dressing-rooms without going through the street, and the production opened on the night of Monday 14 February 1966, presented by 'OUDS in association with the University Theatre' and designed by a professional, Hutchinson Scott.

Burton's performance was competent and never embarrassing, but far too low-key for the play and the nature of the occasion. Michael Pye in *Isis* judged that on the first night 'he seemed at half-pressure, only a giant and not yet a Titan', and Daphne Levens felt that his 'brooding, distanced manner' suggested that Faustus got no pleasure out of the tricks and shows that Mephistopheles provided for him, 'and the part is deprived of contrast'. The national press was of much the same opinion. *The Times* wrote that Burton 'starts promisingly . . . but . . . develops no further'; Bernard Levin in the *Daily Mail* called his performance 'shallow'; and Milton Shulman in the *Evening Standard* said that Burton 'only explodes into true tragic and spiritual dimensions in Faustus's final speech'. Most critics made kindly remarks about Coghill's production, but *The Times* was more forthright, calling the performance

a sad example of university drama at its worst. The evening begins with a growling organ period of interminable length leading to the anti-climax of a chatty Chorus—an opening that typifies the rest of the production. It makes a great show of solemnity which is continually punctured by the quality of the acting. The cast themselves—notably below the OUDS standard of previous years—are largely to blame. But their inadequacy is needlessly exposed by Nevill Coghill's direction which aims at stateliness and achieves only lethargy. Mr Burton seems to be walking through the part and his contribution to the stiff high-jinks in the Vatican are almost as embarrassing as those of the undergraduate actors. Those who visit the production to see Miss Taylor as the speechless apparition of Helen of Troy will not be out of the theatre before 10.45.

Understandably, few London critics were prepared to pay much

attention to individual undergraduates, though a benevolent Harold Hobson in the *Sunday Times* commended Andreas Teuber (Mephistopheles), Robert Scott (the Chorus), Nicholas Loukes (the Cardinal), and David Jessel (a knight). And though the cast of *Faustus* may have benefited little from the production in terms of theatrical experience, they certainly had their share of star-gazing, for the Burtons proved hospitable and welcoming to everyone, and on the last night threw an extravagant party for the company in the Randolph.

During the summer of 1966 the *Faustus* production was filmed in Rome, with the OUDS cast again supporting Burton and Taylor; Burton himself directed. The result was even less satisfactory than the stage version; Ray Miles wrote in *Isis* when the film was released rather over a year later:

On the Oxford Playhouse stage Richard Burton underplayed the central role; on film his performance has an unbearable staginess which rings false. On stage Elizabeth Taylor made two stunning appearances as Helen of Troy and provided a justifiable climax to the play; on film, she appears about 15 times in different guises ... When Faustus cries: "See, see where Christ's blood streams in the firmament" it is something of an anti-climax to have some red smoke drifting against a backcloth straight from the London Palladium ... *Dr Faustus* is an insult to an intelligent audience, saved only by Andreas Teuber's sensitive Mephistopheles; although Burton, as director of the film, keeps the camera on himself most of the time.

It was hoped that the film would provide further funds for new works at the Playhouse, but the total received by the University Theatre from the entire *Faustus* project came to no more than £5,000. However, the Burtons themselves generously agreed to finance a new building to contain a studio theatre, workshops and offices, and a club-room for OUDS, and plans were soon drawn up.

Inevitably *Faustus* overshadowed all other undergraduate theatre during the early part of 1966—an OUDS *Winter's Tale* in May with Simon Brett and Alison Skilbeck as Leontes and Hermione went almost unnoticed—and it was responsible for an almost complete lack of interest in auditions for the Oxford Theatre Group's play at the forthcoming Edinburgh Festival. At Edinburgh, the play in any case now attracted far less attention than the revue. Recent revue stars such as Michael Palin, Terry Jones, and Robert Hewison had been getting a lot of favourable notice in the national newspapers, and this year a cast which included Diana Quick (Lady Margaret Hall) and Nigel Rees

(New College) hoped for as much success. The play was regarded as little more than something to fill out the evening before the late-night revue. In consequence no particular attention was paid to the Oxford Theatre Group's announcement that it would stage *Rosencrantz and Guildenstern Are Dead*, a new play by an almost unknown writer called Tom Stoppard.

The play had originally been written as a one-acter, in which form the Questors Theatre at Ealing had performed it. Stoppard then began to expand it to full length, and at this stage the Royal Shakespeare Company took an option on it, intending to present it in tandem with David Warner's Hamlet. But they were dissatisfied with its conclusion (as was Stoppard), and eventually suggested that Stoppard should look elsewhere for a production. After a while he tried Frank Hauser, who passed the script to the Oxford Theatre Group.

Among those who auditioned for it was David Marks (Magdalen), a versatile undergraduate character actor who went on to become President of OUDS. Marks remembers that at the beginning *Rosencrantz* seemed 'a very dubious enterprise'; not enough people auditioned to fill the cast, and the Oxford Theatre Group had to borrow actors from London drama schools before the play went into rehearsal. From Oxford, Marks himself was cast as Rosencrantz, Janet Watts as Ophelia, and Jules Roach as the Player King; Clive Cable (Guildenstern) and Frances Morrow (Gertrude) were both drama students. The original director resigned before the production began rehearsals, and the Oxford Theatre Group could find no one to take over the production other than their technical director, Brian Daubeny, who had no experience of producing actors. According to Marks, Daubeny 'gave us some elementary blocking' when they arrived in Edinburgh, 'but then used to escape from it all and go for long walks up Arthur's Seat'. Stoppard himself put in several appearances at rehearsals—Marks recalls him getting off the overnight sleeper from London, 'wearing what was then I suppose a pre-Chairman Mao type suit, smoking Guards cigarettes and chewing Spearmint gum incessantly'—and was soon visibly appalled at the inadequacies of the production. Towards the end of the two-week rehearsal period, says Marks, 'he and I and Clive and Jules spent two sleepless nights going through the text, word by word. Tom made some amendments, and tried to inculcate in us the exact way he wanted it spoken. His delivery at that time was very Czech, very conscious of the words being rolled

around in the mouth—he said you had to *savour* the words, and you did so more in his case because of the way he spoke. To hear him speak the lines, you realized what the cadences were: you could hear the poetry and the jokes. I think I picked up something of it, and Clive and I would go out to some godforsaken pub on the coast near Edinburgh, so we could learn the lines properly. But it didn't stop Clive from drying once the run started! He and I would sometimes find ourselves caught in a maelstrom of repeating the same pages over and over again.'

Rosencrantz and Guildenstern Are Dead opened at the Cranston Street Hall on 24 August, and next morning the reviewers declared themselves puzzled. 'What's it all about, Tom?' asked the headline in the *Daily Express*, while the *Glasgow Herald* dismissed the play as 'as offputting a piece of non-theatre as has been presented at the Festival for many a year'. But the following Sunday Ronald Bryden had this to say in his *Observer* theatre column:

The best thing at Edinburgh so far is the new play by Tom Stoppard . . . an existentialist fable unabashedly indebted to *Waiting for Godot*, but as witty and vaulting as Beckett's original is despairing . . . Behind the fantastic comedy, you feel allegoric purposes move: is this our relation to our century, to the idea of death, to war? But while the tragedy unfurls in this comic looking-glass, you're too busy with its stream of ironic invention, metaphysical jokes and linguistic acrobatics to pursue them. Like *Love's Labour's Lost*, this is erudite comedy, punning, far-fetched, leaping from depth to dizziness. It's the most brilliant debut by a young playwright since John Arden's.

'It was that last phrase', says David Marks, 'that made everybody sit up. After that, the houses started to improve, and we heard rumours about people from London slipping in at the back to see it.' Eight months later, in April 1967, the play opened at the Old Vic in a National Theatre production, with Edward Petherbridge and John Stride in the title roles; and Stoppard's name was made. The Oxford Theatre Group's contract with Stoppard had, by good management on its part, included a clause which ensured that it received a percentage of his royalties from the play for several years to come.

Oxford was not able to profit from the brief presence, during 1965–6, of someone else who became a household name in theatre. Andrew Lloyd Webber arrived as a freshman at Magdalen at Michaelmas 1965, to read Modern History. David Marks, who was at the same college, soon got to know him well. 'I remember in his rooms in New Buildings he had the biggest collection of rock and roll records

I'd ever seen. He'd sit doodling at the piano.' Lloyd Webber had already met his lyricist Tim Rice, and had worked with him on *Joseph and his Amazing Technicolour Dreamcoat*. Now he and Rice were planning a musical about Dr Barnardo, to be called *The Likes of Us*, and for a time David Marks was co-opted as author of the 'book'. 'We made a demo disc during 1966,' says Marks,

with various session singers and me doing some narration. The vague idea was to have it done in Oxford—we thought we could do better than the resident princes of the ETC musicals, David Wood and John Gould. And I must say I really had a strong sense that Andrew *was* going to make it in a big way. He and I used to go to West End shows, and have almost fictional-type conversations in which Andrew would say 'One day all this will be mine,' or something like that. He certainly had his eye set for it. Anyway, I've got one of the three extant copies of the record of *The Likes of Us*, but it'll never be performed, because some of the songs were eventually cannibalised for a musical called *Jeeves!* (with a book by Ayckbourn), which flopped. And Andrew left Oxford during his second term; he hadn't done any work, and he was nominally going to study harmony at the Guildhall. And of course we all know the rest.

In the Hilary Term of 1967 Frank Hauser, for the only time during his years at the Playhouse, directed for OUDS. The result was a *Love's Labour's Lost* in a glittering eighteenth-century setting (designed by Kathy Henderson). Irving Wardle in *The Times* wrote that the visual impact of the production and the music by Paul Drayton gave the play 'an exquisite spring-time atmosphere'. The casting made use of most of the best undergraduate talent of the time: Nigel Ramage was Berowne, Bruce Alexander (now with the Royal Shakespeare Company) was Dumaine, David Marks played Don Armado, Petronella Pulsford (who now acts professionally as Petronella Ford) was the Princess, Nicholas Arnold and Simon Brett were Holofernes and Costard, and Ivor Roberts was a fine sinister Mercade. Yet this company, though certainly not lacking in youth and beauty, did not quite carry off the play. Don Chapman wrote in the *Oxford Mail*: 'All too often one is aware of Mr Hauser's clever strokes of production being acted on rather than acted out, of seeing an effect tossed away that would bring the house down in professional hands.'

David Marks showed how much could be done by a theatrically minded undergraduate at Oxford in the 1960s—at least by one with tolerant tutors. During the same term as *Love's Labour's Lost* he appeared as Becket in *Murder in the Cathedral* for the ETC; immedi-

ately afterwards he toured France and Italy with *Love's Labour's Lost*, then on his return to Oxford played the leading part of Bill Maitland, the disintegrating solicitor, in John Osborne's *Inadmissible Evidence*, an OUDS minor directed at the Playhouse by Michael Rosen, with Richard Heffer, Caroline Bennitt, and Hermione Lee (now a television book critic) among the cast. About ten days later he was back on stage in an ETC musical, *And Was Jerusalem* (book by Michael Sadler, lyrics and music by David Wood and John Gould), and next month headed the cast of a sprightly *Toad of Toad Hall* in his own college, Magdalen. His contemporaries had by now decided that such a tireless actor must have something of Mr Toad in his personality, but Marks gave up the stage when he left Oxford and became a barrister. In the Magdalen *Toad* the part of the Chief Weasel was played by Michael Rosen, now well known as a children's poet and in those days a leading undergraduate radical, active in the Oxford version of the 1968 student unrest. Rosen's own play *Backbone*, directed for the ETC by Chris Honer, found its way to the Royal Court soon after its Oxford première.

Just at the time that many student actors were pledging themselves to left-wing militancy, it was an embarrassment to OUDS that the cast of Ray Miles's production of Aeschylus' *Agamemnon*, newly translated by Anthony Holden, should find themselves the guests of the Colonels' right-wing government when they performed in Greece during 1967. This provoked attacks on the OUDS Committee, who pleaded ignorance, though some members of the company still remember the incident with embarrassment. Something of politics hung a little in the air, too, over the OUDS *Hamlet* in February 1968, for like the recent David Warner *Hamlet* at Stratford this was a modern-dress production which portrayed the prince as a restless student. The director was David William, by then well established in the professional theatre; he was called in late in the day after the original director had left the production, and he made some sardonic remarks to the *Guardian* about the state of affairs in Oxford theatre: 'In the time available I just hope we manage to get the text acted. It is pretentious to try to put on a play in the time they allow themselves—just four days rehearsal in a theatre. The drama has no status in this university—all you get is "I've got a tutorial, I've got a tutorial." *Hamlet* is a tutorial . . . Abolish OUDS, abolish the Experimental Theatre Club, abolish the lot and set up a drama department—there is, after all, a department of music.' In fact

his *Hamlet* earned good reviews. Richard Heffer in the title role was widely praised for his energy—Anthony Holden in *Isis* called him 'a cocky, quick-witted Hamlet'—while Diana Quick's Ophelia was generally regarded as outstanding. Sean Day-Lewis in the *Daily Telegraph* called her 'consistently moving, a performance of wronged innocence that will long be remembered', while Michael Billington in *The Times* said she was 'touching and credible'. Michael Wood, now well known for his television history programmes, played Horatio.

Diana Quick had appeared with the National Youth Theatre before coming to Oxford to read English at Lady Margaret Hall. In Hilary Term 1968 she was elected unopposed to be the first woman President of OUDS, and also the first woman Committee member. By this time she had taken her degree and moved on to a B.Litt. In an interview with the *Oxford Mail* after her election she said of her forthcoming presidency: 'The main thing I would like to see happen is for people to be able to learn from the mistakes of others. I would like to arrange technical classes in movement and voice production, and get really good teachers to come to Oxford. But money is the problem.' In fact neither during her presidency nor afterwards did OUDS manage to establish any regular system of professional drama tuition for its actors.

At Christmas 1968 Diana Quick was Hermia in a much-praised *Midsummer Night's Dream* presented by the newly formed Oxford & Cambridge Shakespeare Company, a group whose chief function was to tour American universities. Richard Cottrell directed, Michael Rosen played Starveling, and Bottom was another Oxford undergraduate, Jeremy Treglown, now editor of the *Times Literary Supplement*. The Oxford & Cambridge company was in action again a year later, with Jonathan Miller directing a much praised *Twelfth Night*. The Oxford contingent this time included Mary Jane Mowat (Olivia), Hilary Henson (Viola), Hugh Thomas (Malvolio), and Michael Wood (Orsino), while Cambridge supplied, among others, Mark Wing-Davey (Aguecheek) and Jonathan James-Moore (Belch). The music was by Stephen Oliver. In 1970, again with Miller directing, Hugh Thomas played the title role in *Hamlet*. The company was a great success artistically but unfortunately had to be wound up because the tours were prohibitively costly.

Jeremy Treglown was Mercutio in an OUDS *Romeo and Juliet* in February 1969, with Richard Stroud directing, and the title roles taken by Mike Gwilym and Rona Bower. Andrew Samuels wrote in *Isis* of

Rona Bower's performance: 'Looking quite stunning . . . she adhered to the principles of classical acting—clarity of diction, economy of gesture, confidence of movement. Her pleasantly relaxed Juliet emerges with a lot of credit.' Daphne Levens in the *Oxford Magazine* observed that 'Jeremy Treglown whips Mercutio's wit into a harsh frenzy, but understands his style . . . Romeo, on Mike Gwilym's terms, is out on a limb of his own: dressed like a serving-man, sunk in hang-dog adolescence, a self-deprecating lover, of all things, and much embarrassed by the silver-sweet stuff and nonsense.' She and other critics judged that the production ultimately failed because of 'a fatal reluctance to express the play's passion by giving way to its poetry'.

An old OUDS tradition was revived at Christmas 1968 when Gyles Brandreth, then a New College undergraduate, produced H. J. Byron's *Cinderella* with Caroline Bennitt in the title role, choreography by Michael Coveney (now drama critic of the *Financial Times*), and music by Nigel Osborne. Tim Maby appeared as the Rat Coachman. 'Brightly inventive but lacked shape and direction,' judged Daphne Levens rather severely in the *Oxford Magazine*, though she added: 'Michael Coveney's splendid toe-in-cheek choreography was a triumph.'

'OUDS has been very much a part of my life since I was a little boy,' says Gyles Brandreth.

My father Charles Brandreth was up at the University in the 1920s; OUDS had an enormous impact on him, and I was brought up to believe that first of all you automatically went to Oxford, and then when you got there you had to become President of the Union, Editor of *Isis*, and put on a play for the OUDS. In fact I *think* the reason I'm called Gyles spelt with a 'y' is that I'm named after Gyles Isham, the golden boy of OUDS in the 1920s—my father maintained that the spelling was some old Brandreth family tradition, but I suspect the truth is that he worshipped Isham (as so many did). When I actually arrived at Oxford in 1967 the first thing that surprised me was that the cross-fertilisation between the different enthusiasms at the University wasn't quite what my father had led me to believe. There wasn't the universality of interests that he certainly maintained there had been in the twenties, when someone like Gerald Gardiner could become involved in a wide range of activities. In the rather intense atmosphere of the late sixties I think you made your particular bed and you lay on it. You were either (for instance) an OUDS person *or* an ETC person; you certainly were looked on with a bit of suspicion if you tried to ride all the horses that the University had to offer.

Anyway, I became President of the Union and Editor of *Isis*, but I found that

getting involved with OUDS was a trickier proposition than my father had led me to believe. However, I was very determined, and that was really the reason that I went for a pantomime. At the time I had no particular interest in pantomime at all, but it occurred to me that the right tactic as an outsider, to get myself an OUDS production at the Playhouse (because that seemed to me the only thing worth doing), was to go for something surprising and totally different. So I wrote a note to Diana Quick introducing myself, and she and I met *for a drink*, which in those days seemed to me really rather a 'fast' thing to do! Also she was dressed in black leather—or it *seemed* to be leather; I suspect now it was probably plastic! *I* felt that it was really my right, a kind of paternal gift, to direct an OUDS production, but she explained to me that I would have to 'audition'. So I went before the serried ranks of OUDS officers and hangers-on (of whom there seemed to be an awful lot), and held forth, explaining why it was *essential* that at a time of student rioting all over the world—I myself had indeed just returned from Paris where the students were in the streets—the OUDS should do a *pantomime*. My thesis was (and I've been using it ever since): 'When we get up tomorrow morning, we may well be able to do without our tragic awareness for an hour or two, but we shall desperately need our sense of the comic.'

Now, as well as explaining your reasons (as a potential director), you had to do a bit of actual directing—you had to be seen in rehearsal. I got Diana to do a love scene; it was a thing that they set, a bit of Shakespeare, I think. And I always feel that the clincher, the *moment critique* that actually won it for me, was when I told her that what I wanted her to do to express the anguish of love was *place her top teeth over her bottom lip*. Undoubtedly it was at that instant that the OUDS Committee thought 'Yes, this is our man.'

Brandreth's choice of Byron's *Cinderella* subsequently led him to become an enthusiast for, and expert on, the Victorian and Edwardian pantomime, and as well as writing several books on the subject he founded the British Pantomime Association, which he says 'has had a real impact on restoring traditional values to pantomime'. It was also during *Cinderella* that Brandreth met his future wife, Michelle Brown, who was among the girls who auditioned for the title role.

Brandreth was in the cast of a June 1969 OUDS production of Molière's *Le Misanthrope*, performed in French at the Playhouse in conjunction with the University French Club. Merlin Thomas directed this, the first of several such joint productions, in which a high standard was achieved largely because of the presence in two of them of David Marks. His Alceste in *Le Misanthrope* was widely praised, while Hermione Lee wrote (in *Isis*) of his Orestes in the 1970 production of

Racine's *Andromaque*: 'David Marks's superb performance showed up the lack of technical assurance in the other actors. His reaction to Pyrrhus' announcement that he has decided to marry Hermione, a slow faltering movement across the stage and a quiet "Ah dieu!", and his formal disintegration into lunacy, were magnificent moments which no one else in the production could emulate.'

Diana Quick's ambition for good professional tuition for OUDS actors was achieved for a few weeks when Clifford Williams from the Royal Shakespeare Company directed Thomas Middleton's *A Chaste Maid in Cheapside* in February 1970. Jeremy Treglown wrote in *Isis*: 'Clifford Williams certainly fulfilled his intention of teaching the craft to OUDS actors. *A Chaste Maid in Cheapside* was such a technical achievement that it is difficult not to sound like a pleased adjudicator at some eisteddfod . . . The best performances, like that of Hugh Thomas, were usually generous and self-effacing.' Don Chapman wrote in similar terms in the *Oxford Mail*: 'Clifford Williams has done more than I would have thought possible . . . Cunningly confined within the limits of a ramped stage like the one he employed for his celebrated [Stratford] production of *A Comedy of Errors*, [his actors] have to react to one another. They have to watch how they move. They have to take the action at a cracking pace. And this compression results in a much greater interplay of characters than is usual in undergraduate productions and a much greater attention to detail in the smaller parts.' Besides Hugh Thomas as Yellowhammer, the cast included Charles Sturridge, Sheila McIlwraith, Frances Hazelton, Ian Small, Caroline Bennitt, and Mary Jane Mowat.

Hugh Thomas, who had played the head prefect in Lindsay Anderson's film *If . . .* (1968) while still a schoolboy, played Goldberg in an OUDS minor production of Pinter's *The Birthday Party* in May 1970, became President of OUDS, and, before turning professional actor, made a stage adaptation of Dickens's *Hard Times* which Charles Sturridge directed for the ETC in 1971. John Ryle in *Isis* described this as 'a brilliant production in the tradition of *Oh! What a Lovely War* . . . The music by Stephen Oliver [is] atmospheric enough to give an overall melancholic aura to the whole play.' Oliver, then a music graduate at Worcester College, turned *The Duchess of Malfi* into an opera (it was performed in Michaelmas Term 1971) and provided music for other OUDS productions in following years—among them Nicholas Kent's *Pericles* (1975) and Keith Hack's *Troilus and Cressida*

(1977)—while beginning to make his name as a composer in the professional theatre.

For the second time in their history, OUDS presented *Coriolanus* in March 1971. This time the director was Stephen Wall, English tutor at Keble College, and Coriolanus was played by Charles Sturridge (who ten years later directed the memorable Granada Television adaptation of Waugh's *Brideshead Revisited* in which Diana Quick played Julia). Michael Billington wrote of his Coriolanus that it was 'a swift-moving, well-spoken, solidly traditional version . . . At first Charles Sturridge simply reminds one of the gentleman in *The Young Visiters* who was "very sneery"; but in the crucial scenes with Volumnia and the Tribunes he brings out the boyish petulance and emotional immaturity.' Stephen Wall chose to direct the play because of Sturridge's abilities—'he was a real actor, physically in command of the space, and he proved to be wonderfully exciting to work with'. Sturridge played Macbeth for OUDS a year later, with Joanna Jane Powell as Lady Macbeth. In February 1973 she appeared as Hermione in an OUDS *Winter's Tale*, directed by Andrew Brown; the Bear was played by the poet Andrew Motion, whom she afterwards married. She was the second woman President of OUDS, serving during 1972–3.

Patrick Garland, the first OUDS Coriolanus, returned to Oxford in June 1973 to direct an open-air *Twelfth Night* in Worcester College gardens, during a period of flawless summer weather. Charles Brett in *Isis* described it as 'a splendid, colourful, and wholly enjoyable production'. There were touches of Coghill, too: 'The illumination of the departure of the lovers on the lake with fireworks was particularly splendid and impressive.'

Among undergraduate directors for OUDS at this period the strongest impression was made by Mel Smith, afterwards well known in *Not the Nine O'Clock News*. His production of *Rosencrantz and Guildenstern Are Dead* in March 1972 was praised for being 'inventive and amusing' (*Isis*), and his version of *The Tempest* two years later was equally popular and inventive—Stephen Wall recalls 'a white box set (after Peter Brook), multi-channel sound, two Ariels (one of them female), etc'. 'Mel Smith skimmed the surface pretty triumphantly,' wrote David Snodin in *Isis*. 'There is something of the brash confidence and innocent abandon of a novice about his initial approach to every text he handles, which, in the case of this production at least,

brought one nearer to the human heart of the play, the thing itself, than many a more self-consciously academic interpretation.' Smith became President of OUDS; a contemporary, Alan Halliday, remembers that as an actor 'he had a phenomenal memory: he could learn the most enormous parts, moves and all, in just a few hours if he had to stand in for someone at short notice'.

By 1973 preparations had at last begun for the extension to the Playhouse, planned ever since Richard Burton and Elizabeth Taylor had promised to finance it after their 1966 *Dr Faustus*. The delay was largely because of the time required to purchase extra land and buildings adjacent to the theatre, but also because, despite their generosity, the Burtons found it no easy matter to transmit actual cash into the hands of the University Theatre. Elizabeth Sweeting dined with them in London, along with Nevill Coghill, and 'told Burton: "We need money now, because there are builders literally standing there waiting for pound notes"; and Burton ran his hands through his hair and groaned, and said, "Oh dear, it's all in blue chips."' The Taylor–Burton Building, as the extension was officially named, was opened during 1976. The Burtons visited it a year later in the company of Francis Warner, English tutor at St Peter's College, admirer of Samuel Beckett, and himself an avant-garde playwright. It was alleged at the time that Burton 'will play Timon of Athens and King Lear in Oxford productions before long', but nothing ever came of it. (Similarly Warner's projected Samuel Beckett Theatre beneath the quadrangle of St Peter's has so far remained unbuilt.)

The 'Burton Rooms', as they became generally known, eased pressure on the cramped backstage facilities at the Playhouse, and provided space for studio performances and such events as the OUDS Drama Cuppers. But it seemed to Elizabeth Sweeting, then nearing the end of her time at the Playhouse (she was succeeded by Barry Sheppard), that the Rooms did not create quite the social centre for Oxford theatre that had been hoped for, nor greatly change the character of the Playhouse. A coffee machine was installed in the so-called OUDS club-room on the first floor of the building, but outside rehearsal or Committee-meeting hours the place was usually silent.

At about the same time that the Rooms were being built, the fortunes of the Playhouse underwent another change. On 21 October 1973 a Gala performance in the theatre celebrated the jubilee of J. B. Fagan's

original Playhouse (the Gala, organized by Gyles Brandreth,[2] included appearances by Michael Denison, Valentine Dyall, John Gielgud, and Richard Goolden); but only a few months later the Arts Council of Great Britain reduced its grant to Meadow Players, and Frank Hauser, who had endured more than one financial crisis since his company's formation in 1956, decided to call it a day. Meadow Players were disbanded, and the Curators of the Playhouse, after considering a number of applications, invited a young director named Gordon McDougall to form a new company, Anvil Productions, which began work at the Playhouse during 1974 with McDougall and (a little later) Nicholas Kent directing many of the productions. Anvil enjoyed several London transfers during the following ten years—their 1975 production of the Brecht–Weill *Happy End* was the first—and they staged new plays by C. P. Taylor, Howard Barker, Nigel Williams, and Doug Lucie, the last two of whom had been undergraduate actors at Oxford. However, their espousal of radical theatre and their sometimes unconventional approach to the classics did not always appeal to the kind of Playhouse audience that Hauser had built up, and to many people the decade 1974–1984 seemed a less happy and successful one at the Playhouse than the Hauser years.[3]

Nicholas Kent directed *Pericles* for OUDS in 1975 (before he joined the staff of Anvil Productions) with a remarkable performance as Pericles by Paul Whitworth. Alan Halliday describes Whitworth as 'a matinée idol with a considerable female following at every perform-ance! He left Oxford shortly afterwards (in the middle of his post-graduate degree) to join the RSC, and was immediately singled out for several paragraphs of praise by Harold Hobson in a six-line part—Romeo's page! Then he played Lysander in John Barton's

---

[2] Brandreth says he was asked to organize the Gala by Elizabeth Sweeting because he was someone likely to be able to bring together undergraduate and professional actors harmoniously; in fact he was struck by the discord between these two elements—'There was no real involvement between the OUDS and the professional company'—and he found just the same thing when he organized another Gala at the Playhouse ten years later.

[3] Stephen Wall, the present chairman of Anvil Productions, dissents strongly from this view. He writes that the audience figures for Meadow Players and Anvil 'show a pretty consistent average over both companies' lives'; that Anvil 'has continued to get a lot of attention from the national press, even though their coverage of Oxford has declined'; moreover, he says, the company's standards 'are implicitly endorsed by the continuation of Arts Council funding (no cut in the new [1984] Arts Council of Great Britain strategy)'; and 'as one who regularly reviewed Frank Hauser's shows for the *Guardian* . . . I would say that though Frank got some bigger lead actors the present company has a consistently better *ensemble* . . . Anvil has failed to *improve* on Meadow Players' audience, but the competition is now much greater from television, the Royal Shakespeare Company, and the National Theatre.'

Dream.' Also in the cast of *Pericles* was Halliday himself, who the previous summer had earned high praise from Harold Hobson for his performance as Father Ignatius in a play of that name by the present writer staged at Edinburgh by the Oxford Theatre Group; Hobson wrote of Halliday: 'I have never seen an amateur performance which, for sustained authority and passion, is in the same league.' In *Pericles* Halliday doubled as Cerimon and (in a filmy costume devised by designer Bruno Santini) the Bawd in the brothel scene:

We were all blacked up [Halliday recalls] to look like a troupe of arab entertainers in the desert and several tons of sand were tipped on the Playhouse stage. This production was such a success that Sam Wanamaker invited us to play for a limited season at his newly constructed Bankside Globe Theatre (the previous one, a tent, had blown away in a storm). The sand came with us too, and the polythene bubble in which the play was performed during the summer months ensured that we had desert conditions. One night I remember, during the reconciliation scene, beautifully played by Paul Whitworth and Muriel Odunton (the black undergraduate actress who was Marina—she subsequently had her own TV 'sitcom', *Mixed Blessings*, about a mixed marriage), a launch went past on the river below with voices singing 'Viva España'.

Pericles was at first directed by James Roose-Evans, who left the production after a disagreement; Stephen Wall generously acted as caretaker director for a fortnight until Nicholas Kent could be brought in. This led OUDS to invite Wall to direct *Othello* for them a year later. A black undergraduate actor, Hugh Quarshie (now a professional with the RSC), gave a striking performance in the title-role; Wall says he 'took away all the element of impersonation', while Alan Halliday was a 'marvellous' Iago. Shortly afterwards Wall resigned from his Senior Membership of OUDS under pressure from the President, Simon Bell, and his Committee. The row arose because Wall had become chairman of Anvil Productions, the professional company at the Playhouse, and had negotiated two extra weeks for them to perform at the theatre during the Michaelmas Term—weeks that were taken away from OUDS and other undergraduate groups, though they were given others in compensation, in other terms. The OUDS Committee saw this as a betrayal of undergraduate theatre. Wall on the other hand says he was fighting for the chance for the professionals to build up a loyal and regular audience by playing for as many continuous weeks as possible in the theatre, uninterrupted by amateur shows; he argued

that without this there might no longer be a Playhouse for OUDS to act in.

From the late 1970s onwards there is regrettably little objective record of OUDS productions, for by this time national newspapers and journals were making it their policy not to review amateur shows. Moreover the *Oxford Magazine,* usually an impartial judge, had ceased publication, while *Isis* and *Cherwell* would only occasionally review productions. But two things stand out in this recent period.

The first is the considerably increased number of OUDS productions. In 1980 there were five, in 1981 nine, and today about ten a year. Of these, classics still predominate, but there are plenty of modern works (Stoppard, Orton, Brecht, Alan Bennett, and Ionesco during the early 1980s, for instance). In 1979 OUDS also departed from tradition in presenting its first publicly staged revue, *Inferiors,* with a cast including Rowan Atkinson. This large number of productions chiefly results from the fact that OUDS, with its major Shakespearian and other classic productions, generally gets good box-office receipts (better on average than the ETC), especially from low-cost open-air shows, and so is able to finance a large number of smaller-scale shows. Indeed an outsider coming to a present-day OUDS Committee meeting might think himself at a session of the Arts Council, so much are the proceedings taken up with listening to proposals by, and handing out money to, prospective directors. Present-day Committee membership is likely to provide sound training for anyone considering a career in theatrical administration—and indeed has done so in a number of cases.

The second characteristic of the most recent years is surprising in view of the depressed economic condition of professional theatre: the large number of young ex-OUDS actors who have become successful in the entertainment business in recent years. No list can be comprehensive, but here are some of the success stories.

Philip Franks, the 1977–8 OUDS President, joined the Royal Shakespeare Company and played Bertram in a celebrated *All's Well* that went to Broadway; at the time of writing he is to star in a forthcoming television serialization of *Bleak House.* Peter Wilson, who performed in Mel Smith's *Tempest* and the 1975 *Pericles,* left Oxford to direct at the Lyric, Hammersmith, and the Bush Theatre; his productions have included the 1983 West End *Charley's Aunt* which starred Griff Rhys-Jones (and briefly Mel Smith when Rhys-Jones was ill).

Geoffrey Perkins, writer of revues while at Oxford, has produced *The Hitch-hiker's Guide to the Galaxy* and *Radio Active* for Radio 4; and Richard Curtis, who similarly contributed to OUDS Smokers and revues, has written for *Not the Nine O'Clock News* and other TV shows. Christopher Wenner, Roderigo in the 1976 *Othello*, became a household name as a *Blue Peter* presenter for several years before filming with the BBC in El Salvador. Adam Norton, who appeared in many OUDS productions in the late 1970s, can now be seen at the National Theatre and on television; Alan Halliday describes him as 'a wonderful raconteur and inventor of long ballads for OUDS Smokers, e.g. *Under Milk Wood* rewritten as *The Magic Roundabout*; star of the Mermaid Society, an offshoot of OUDS for leading OUDS stars of the day—they met in Balliol to drink vast quantities of claret, read all the parts in a play in turn (usually Oscar Wilde or Sheridan), and with an elaborate loving-cup procedure at the end, quoting from Keats'.

Jon Plowman, who directed *Charley's Aunt* as an Oxford summer show and appeared in Kyd's *Spanish Tragedy* ('when he met his end,' recalls Halliday, 'he was left swinging on a noose like a pendulum from one side of the stage to the other for a whole scene'), now produces the Russell Harty Show—in itself an OUDS connection, for Ronald Eyre taught Harty at a school in Yorkshire after leaving Oxford. Monica Kendall (Desdemona in 1976), Tim MacInnerny (Richard II in the OUDS major in Hilary Term 1978), and Nigel Levaillant (Bolingbroke in the same production), are all professional actors. Matthew Francis, a leading OUDS director and actor of the mid 1970s (then under his real name, Francis Matthews), now directs at the National Theatre and with Patrick Garland at Chichester. And Stephen Pickles, *enfant terrible* of undergraduate directors in the late 1970s, is now a screenplay writer, critic, and opera director. Halliday writes of him: 'Before an OUDS directors' audition he would proclaim: "I am going to freak—them—out!" To Committee members who had voted against him he would simply say, as they rode past on their cycles, "Fall off!" At last in 1980 the Committee backed him and gave him a Michaelmas Major production of *The Three Sisters* which many people in the audience thought was the most moving they had seen. It was designed by him too, very much in the style of his own room in Holywell Street, hung with velvet and exotica in the high Wagnerian manner.'

Imogen Stubbs, Irina in this production and Cressida in Keith Hack's 1981 *Troilus*, went to RADA after Oxford, while Jenny Wald-

man, Masha in *The Three Sisters*, became administrator of the Foco Novo Touring Company. Jon Cullen, Hector in a 1981 *Troilus*, left New College for the Guildhall School; Mark Payton, Menelaus in the same production and Candide in a 1981 staging of Voltaire's play, went straight into the West End. Recent years have been 'a very exciting period with some notable performers and performances, *most* of whom are now part of the British theatre'—so remarks Alan Halliday, who himself has achieved distinction not in the theatre, but as a painter.[4]

But it would be wrong to mark the hundredth year of the OUDS with complacency; nor does anyone at present associated with Oxford theatre seem inclined to do so. The dominant note is self-criticism. 'We do too much Shakespeare at school play level,' declares Tessa Ross, OUDS President during 1983–4; 'we're too arrogant, we're too spoiled.' Frank Hauser, now a freelance director and drama teacher, looking back to his many years' experience of OUDS, feels the same: 'At a place like Oxford, theatre really ought to be better. They're a slovenly, lazy, self-satisfied crew who think it quite funny to have a failure on their hands.' So what might be done to achieve a consistently higher standard of production and performance?

It is noticeable that the first 'golden age' of the OUDS, the mid 1920s, was the first period in which outstanding professional directors were invited to take on undergraduate casts. The other period of particularly high standards was just after the Second World War, when Oxford theatre was largely dominated by Ken Tynan and Tony Richardson, but—perhaps more significantly—this was also a time when the average age of undergraduates was much higher, most men having served in the armed forces before coming up. It seems that mature experience of some kind, whether among the undergraduates themselves or imported in the form of a professional director, is almost inseparable from higher standards. Probably it is not fair to expect students to achieve very much on their own. As Frank Hauser puts it, 'It's like two virgins going to bed together and expecting they'll know what to do.'

Professional directors are still used by OUDS, but at present not

---

[4] Stephen Wall adds: 'Some mention should also be made of backstage and front of house alumni, e.g. John Matthews (now with the Arts Council), Scirard Lancelyn Green (who now runs a lighting hire company), Andrew Ptaszynski (in management), and Heather Maitland (the present assistant in publicity at the Playhouse).' The Oxford Playhouse Company (Anvil Productions), Wall points out, has employed a number of graduates straight from the University, and has helped many to get Equity cards.

very often. Keith Hack directed *Troilus and Cressida* in 1977 and Matthew Francis returned to OUDS in 1983 to stage *As You Like It*, but on the whole undergraduate directors have been given all the chances in recent years. Hack's production was perhaps too radical for popular taste; certainly it alarmed some of his cast. Alan Halliday was invited to join the company (which included Doug Lucie as Menelaus), 'but when I discovered that Hack was going to have Helen of Troy swinging about on a trapeze the whole time and interrupting the proceedings with obscene expletives whenever she felt like it, I pulled out'. Matthew Francis had a talented cast for his *As You Like It* which included Jason Morrell (a notable undergraduate actor of the present generation), but there is now a body of opinion which holds that if professionals are to be used they should be older and highly experienced—a J. B. Fagan, a Peter Dews, or a Patrick Garland rather than somebody still learning his trade in the professional theatre.

Even the most competent professional can do only limited things in the few weeks allotted for rehearsal, and the question always hovers on the edge of any discussion of University drama at Oxford: ought there to be formal drama teaching as part of the academic curriculum? Frank Hauser is among those who feel that there should. 'A Drama Faculty is essential if Oxford theatre is ever to come into any order', he wrote in *Cherwell* in 1967. 'The need for professional coaches, particularly in movement and voice, is indisputable. The arrangement of a coherent series of productions, related to each other, would make a better programme than the choice of a dozen committees. All these are things which even the most modest Faculty could begin to organize. Without it, Oxford theatre will continue to blossom and wither in the old crazy way.' Hauser feels the same today, having recently taught drama in American campuses. Nor does he accept that a Drama Department would exclude many of the people who have over the years enriched student theatre without intending to become professional actors or directors—the scientists, for example, who have acted in plays or worked backstage. As he says, 'Drama departments usually exclude the merely stage struck, which is a good thing.'

Merlin Thomas, who has had a long experience of OUDS (he is still a Senior Member of the Society), feels much the same; he would like to see a Drama School in the University, offering joint degrees with the English, Modern Languages, and perhaps also 'Lit. Hum.' (Classics) Schools, much on the model of Bristol University. He does concede,

however, that this might keep out some enthusiasts; in his experience drama departments tend to look down on student shows that have nothing to do with them.

Most others who have close experience of OUDS and other student drama bodies are less inclined to favour the establishment of a full Drama Department than to plead for some kind of drama teaching on the fringes of the English Literature syllabus, which would be available to all undergraduates, and could somehow be tied in to their productions. Elizabeth Sweeting and Tessa Ross, for example, both favour the establishment of a visiting Professorship of Drama, much on the lines on the University's Chair of Poetry, which would be held for a few years on a part-time basis by an outstanding professional actor or director, who would give classes and lectures. Meanwhile Stephen Wall has done something to introduce practical drama into the English syllabus: during the past eight years or so he has held classes jointly with Gordon McDougall, artistic director of the Playhouse company—two-hour rehearsal seminars with professional or student actors and an under-graduate audience, in which the practical problems of staging a text have been examined, and the relationship between the academic study of a play and theatrical practice has been discussed.

However, there is a more pressing problem than the desirability or otherwise of teaching theatrical technique to undergraduates: the uncertain future of the Playhouse. During 1981, when Oxford University was facing severe national cutbacks in government finance to higher education, it came to the notice of the Hebdomadal Council (the University's 'Cabinet') that the Playhouse was being subsidized by the University to the extent of approximately £100,000 per annum. The Council abruptly issued an ultimatum that the theatre would have to close if this loss could not be substantially reduced. At the suggestion of Stephen Wall, a Curators' Appeal Committee was set up under the chairmanship of Christopher Ball, Warden of Keble, and this set out to raise £50,000 per annum during the following five years, on the understanding that the Hebdomadal Council would continue to sub-sidize the theatre if the deficit could be reduced by half. Denis Arnold, the Professor of Music and Chairman of the Playhouse Curators, explained that the Appeal was 'to buy time to put the Playhouse on a sound footing'. Ball proved an expert fund-raiser, but nearly gave up the job in despair a year later when the Hebdomadal Council suddenly changed its mind and demanded that the full five years' support

sum—£250,000—be found within the next twelve months or it would close the theatre. However, he went ahead, and a year later the Appeal reached its target. There were major donations from trusts, but a considerable sum (about £20,000) was raised by undergraduates, the OUDS Presidents during these years taking a very active part in the Appeal. The English Faculty Board gave £5,000 (it was the only Faculty to support the Appeal) and money was also raised by another Gala at the Playhouse, once again organized by Gyles Brandreth, with Peggy Ashcroft, Michael Denison, Robert Hardy, Ned Sherrin, and Emlyn Williams among the performers who gave their services. A joint OUDS and Combined College Societies production of *Rosencrantz and Guildenstern Are Dead*, directed at the Playhouse by Jeremy Smith in May 1983, contributed its takings to the Appeal.

'Next year the OUDS reaches its centenary,' wrote OUDS President Adam Swift in the programme at the Gala; 'it would be a real tragedy were we to celebrate this date with the closure of our theatre.' Thanks to the success of the Appeal, this threat has been removed, and OUDS will give their centenary production on the stage of the Playhouse during Hilary Term 1985. But the long-term future of the theatre is far from secure. During 1984 Gordon McDougall resigned as artistic director of the resident professional company, and there is no doubt that his successor Richard Williams will have a challenging task. Williams, who has been running the Contact Theatre Company in Manchester, has also been closely connected with Manchester University, certainly a qualification for somebody who will have to cope with the dual role of the theatre. Yet the Playhouse, since its foundation in 1923, has never had a secure financial footing, and it would be absurd to suppose that it can suddenly become stable. Moreover in the present economic climate one may wonder for how long and to what extent a hard-pressed University can be expected to subsidize it. There are of course other subsidies, at least for professional companies appearing at the theatre, who get much of their support from the Arts Council, and the local authority makes a small contribution—derisorily small in comparison with many other councils. But the University is the chief source of non-box-office income.

The future of the Playhouse as the University Theatre must seem all the more uncertain in view of the fact that many people feel it has not been able to carry out its dual role satisfactorily. Perhaps during the 1950s Nevill Coghill would have been wiser to press ahead with the

funding and construction of a modest-sized purpose-designed auditorium solely for the use of students. Certainly Merlin Thomas, Elizabeth Sweeting, and Frank Hauser all believe that a small studio theatre would have been the answer, and perhaps still is. And, given that to mount a production of even a modest kind at the Playhouse now costs a student body at least £2,000, there are undoubtedly many among present-day undergraduates who would be glad to see the creation of such a studio theatre. Quite apart from financial considerations, many student productions would seem less pretentious and more attractive in more intimate surroundings. However, Christopher Ball points out that it would now cost the University far more to dispose of the Playhouse, pay off its staff (who are employed on incremental salary scales as University technicians, which makes the terms of their employment better than those of stage staff almost anywhere else in Britain), and then buy or build a studio theatre, than it would to retain it. He feels that, instead, the Hebdomadal Council should formulate a precise policy towards the theatre, which it has never yet done; that the Curators must become more businesslike, and their membership be more widely representative of the theatre's various users; and that the roles of the theatre's Administrator and the director of the resident company need to be examined to see if the Playhouse cannot contribute more vigorously to the University's artistic life. In fact a working party to consider these and other issues was set up during 1984 by the Curators under the chairmanship of Christopher Butler, English tutor at Christ Church and a former Senior Proctor.

One might hope that the OUDS Centenary in 1985, with David Lubin (Queen's) as President, will be marked by a wide-scale debate about the future of Oxford theatre. But Oxford does not usually go about things in that way. Muddling on in a cheerful and sometimes amateurish fashion has been typical of Oxford drama for the first century of OUDS, and it seems a little improbable that this will change radically. Things, one suspects, will be much the same; the same accusations of cliqueishness, exclusiveness, and self-worship will surely be directed against the OUDS Committee in a hundred years from now, should it still exist. As Frank Hauser puts it, the vices of which OUDS is often accused, 'amateurishness, sycophancy, over-confidence', are not peculiar to Oxford theatre; 'they are in fact typical of Oxford'.

And ought it to be otherwise? Those who have gone on from OUDS

to become successful professional actors are acutely conscious of the deficiencies of technique in student theatre, but also grateful for the irregularity of the whole thing, the chance to make mistakes without any loss of face. Maria Aitken observes: 'Undergraduate theatre is very unreal, you play enormous parts which are totally unsuitable rather badly.' Michael York suggests that the sheer quantity of parts many undergraduates undertake, and the business of appearing repeatedly in front of audiences, is invaluable: 'One hears of drama school students, full of theory but without experience, who petrify in front of an audience.' Giles Havergal, now directing at the Citizens' Theatre, Glasgow, looks back on his Oxford days and is convinced that, for all the shortcomings of undergraduate theatre, there is a degree of enthusiasm and commitment in it often lacking in the profession: 'There have been times when I've said, "My God, I wish I could have the commitment of a bunch of students."' Patrick Garland feels exactly the same: 'You rarely get that divine spark in the professional theatre. The actors don't really *care* about it in the same way. Our major professional actors are steely—and neurotic. The result may be light years better, but it's met with by a series of lucky accidents rather than by real commitment.' Garland opposes any formal drama teaching at Oxford: 'Drama schools are utterly different. At their worst they're like *Fame*. The theatre is a profession of neurosis, misery, and unemployment, and it seems all too often to produce life's losers, who can't do anything else. You shouldn't go to Oxford for that. You should profit from everything else, and do acting as a sideline. God knows the University has already produced far too many actors (I won't name names) who were made to think they were marvellous at Oxford, but who've just flopped in the profession afterwards. I don't want to see anything that would add to their number.'

Ronald Eyre feels that, even if Oxford is treated simply as a training ground for the professional theatre, there is much to be said for it: 'I am pretty sure that, if any training had been more rigorous and selective, I'd have been squeezed out. If it had been more systematic and solemn, I'd have rejected it. There is some middle way possible in theatre, I hope—serious in the sense that theatre is worthless without seriousness, playful in the sense that it's only a play. I can't say that Oxford taught me to find it. But it didn't obstruct.'

Index

Index

Index

Index

Index

Index

225

Index